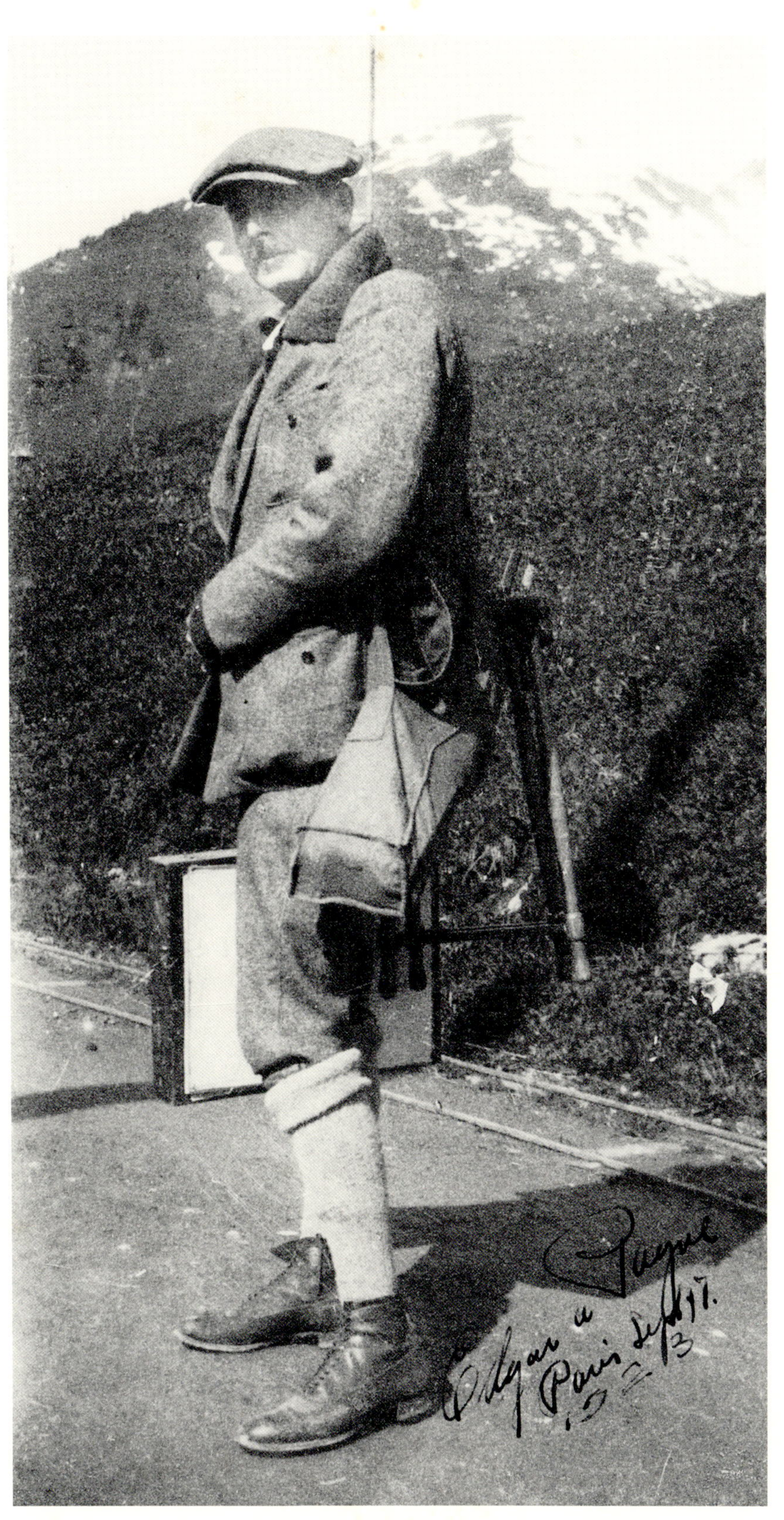
Edgar A Payne
Paris Sept 17.
1923

Frontispiece
Edgar Payne in the Alps with the sketching gear he carried into the field. He signed it the following winter in Paris.

THE DRAWINGS OF EDGAR PAYNE 1883-1947

Introduction
by
Jean Stern

notes by
Evelyn Payne Hatcher

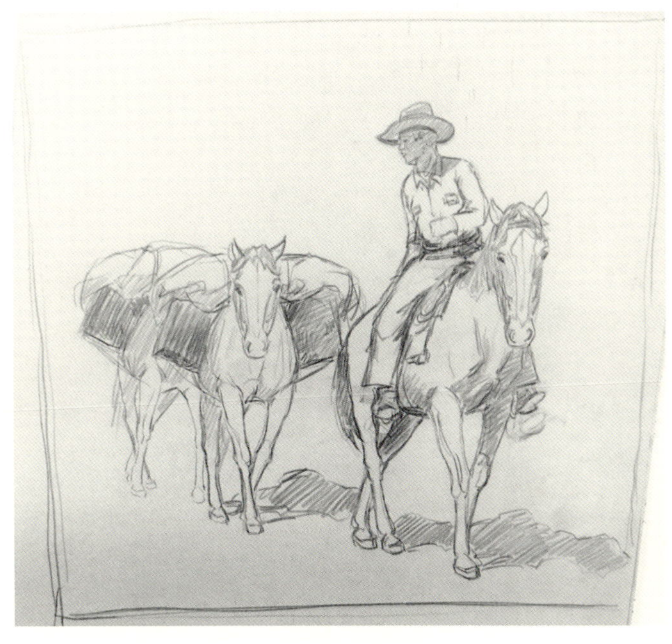

Payne Studios
3104 Silver Lake Road Minneapolis, MN 55418

DISTRIBUTED BY

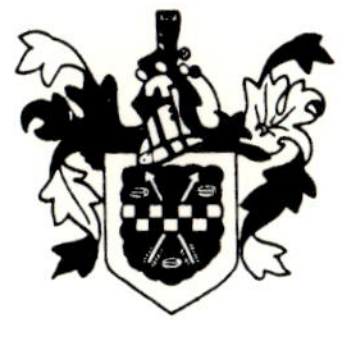

DeRu's Fine Arts
949-376-3785
1590 S. Coast Hwy.
Laguna Beach, CA 92651

First Edition

ISBN 0-944699-04-9

To
Dewitt C. McCall III
Who had the idea for this book

Table of Contents

Introduction

All visual art is based on drawing. Before artists can understand color and space, they must be skilled at drawing. In a traditional art school of the past century, students began their studies by taking a series of classes in black and white drawing for the first two or three years. The process would begin with drawing simple geometric shapes in various lighting situations. In this manner, the student would master modeling, that is to say, the proper rendition of volume and shape in a three-dimensional space.

Thereafter, the student spent months drawing plaster casts of illustrious Greek and Roman statuary. Then, they would turn to drawing the human figure from life, usually from a nude model but not always the ideal perfection of vigorous and youthful men and women, but often of ordinary, aging or even disfigured people. These classes were typically held in crowded teaching studios. Finally, they would learn to draw the human face, in a hundred different expressions and attitudes, and these would be as portraits or combined to the figure.

Having become a master draftsman, the student would thereafter embark on another grueling two or three years to learn the secrets and divine manifestations of color.

Edgar Payne was one of the most prominent and influential artists of the first half of the twentieth century. Curiously, this great painter's entire course of art education amounted to an inconsequential two-week stay at the Art Institute of Chicago. He enrolled in a portraiture class but felt hampered and quickly lost interest. He was, therefore, a self-taught artist.

Had Payne followed the regular academic course of art instruction described above, he too would have started with drawing. Nevertheless, he understood the importance of drawing and he relied on it all his life to define, interpret, refine and resolve the creative process of painting. Payne could not have been a great painter had he not been a master at drawing.

Edgar Payne drew constantly. In the ancient tradition of artists, he rarely went anywhere without a sketchbook and pencil, and drew just about anything he encountered. Such innocuous little details — the way a tablecloth falls off the edge or how a person leans against a doorway in a café, indeed, anything at all — ends up in an artist's sketchbook, usually crammed chaotically on any part or corner of the page.

Many of the drawings in this book, however, are fully rendered study drawings that relate directly to finished paintings. Some are part of a series of drawings that relate to one specific painting. They show the work as it was originally conceived and how it evolved over time to a finished oil painting.

Many, however, do not relate to any finished work. They represent experiments that went nowhere, ideas that had no evolutionary promise and were set aside to permit the start of other, more productive work. But like all experiments, whether successes or failures, they taught the artist an important lesson which would forever be retained in his internal data bank of artistic inspiration.

Unfortunately, it is a common oversight to dismiss drawings as insignificant by-products of the artistic process. Quite to the contrary, they offer a rare and deep glimpse into the very root of the creative process, they are the records of thoughts, emotions and aspirations, closely held and otherwise rarely revealed or expressed to the majority of us who are not artists.

Edgar Payne's drawings are wonderfully expressive. They are indeed the material evidence of that unique magic that found comfort in his life's work and now lives on after him.

Jean Stern
Executive Director
The Irvine Museum, Irvine, CA

Preface

My father, Edgar Alwin Payne (1883–1947), was a man who loved the outdoors, and spent most of his life painting, or thinking about painting, landscapes. His drawings were a record of his thoughts, his notes to himself. They tell us a good deal about the processes that went into his art, but now we see that many of them are works of art in themselves.

The drawings in this volume are not selected from Payne's work for any analytical reason — they are simply what the years have left me and what I tell about them are what the years have left me as memories. I seldom watched him sketch out in the field, and some things I have to infer from what I do remember.

It would have been interesting to start with the simplest notebook drawings, and work through to finished paintings, but that turned out to be impractical with the material at hand. Thus the subjects influenced the arrangement, but as subjects matter they are not a complete sample of the kinds of subjects he drew or painted.

As the drawings were for his own use, he did not title them, so I have added titles. The alpha-numeric figures before the titles were done by my late husband, Jack Hatcher, when he catalogued all the works we had, and those Mother brought with her when in her last years she came to live with us.

When my father went out sketching it usually meant painting using the sketch box that also held paints, brushes, palette and canvas boards. But he also made many pencil sketches in notebooks. He always carried pencils and art gum in his pocket, and often a small notebook. I do remember that he used 6B Venus pencils which he cut into halves and thirds, and except when putting in some details, held with the blunt end toward the palm of his hand, like charcoal. He sharpened his pencils with the pocket knife he always carried — quickly, with long elegant strokes.

Sometimes the drawings were little composition studies, so the only way we know that they were done outdoors is because they were in the notebooks. These field notes might be made at any time that he was out sketching, perhaps while he was looking for the right spot to set up his sketch box. But sometimes he concentrated on drawing, to record the anatomy of the horses around the trading post, or the details of rigging of boats in the harbor. The details he studied so carefully are rarely found worked out in finished oil paintings, but he knew what he was simplifying. I was always taught that whatever was simplified, changed or distorted for esthetic effect, had to rest on a knowledge of the actual structure, which is best learned by drawing.

My artist friend, Jerry Ingeman, made many helpful suggestions, and as the works are in a great variety of sizes, shapes and mediums, took photographs of all of them for reproduction.

My thanks also to to Mr. Jean Stern, Executive Director of The Irvine Museum in Irvine, California, for taking time out of his busy schedule to write an introduction.

EPH

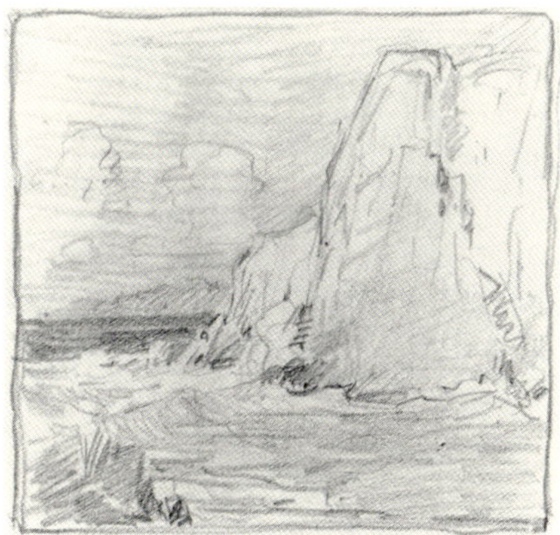

Chapter I

Studies of California Landscapes and Trees

It is my guess that these drawings were done very early, before we went to Europe, maybe even before we lived in Laguna Beach, because of the resemblance to paintings done at this time. The drawing of Devil's Gate Dam tells that it was drawn early in the 20th century, as anyone who knows where the Rose Bowl is will recognize. It is hard to tell the composition drawings he made at home from drawings of a similar size that were made outdoors, so it is also a guess that they were drawn in the field, but I have no recollection of his doing them, as I do the European sketches. If my placing them in time is correct, I was about 4 years old.

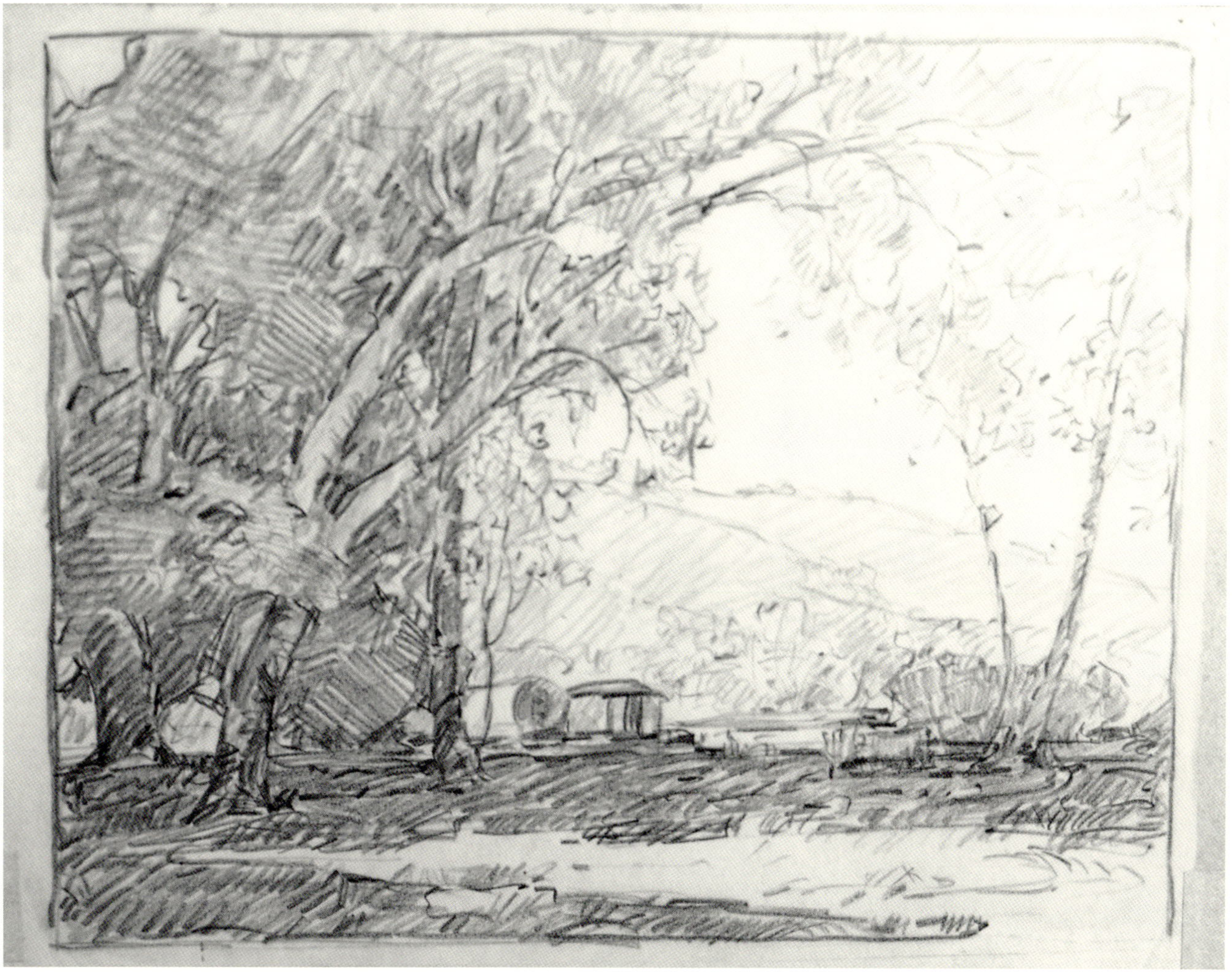

(S-11) Sycamores 8" × 10"

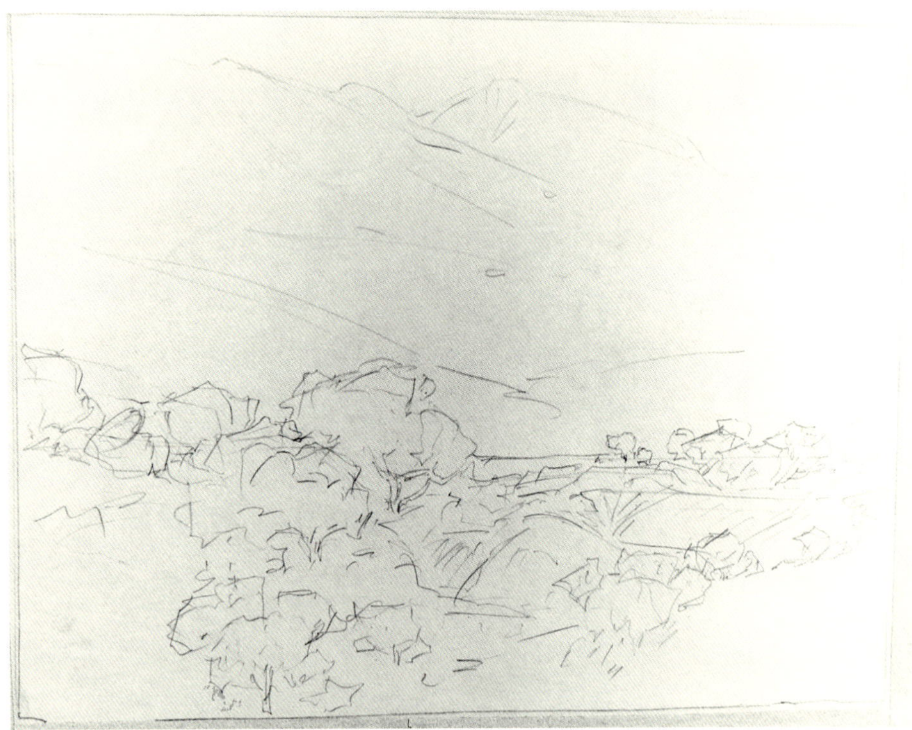

(X-120-5) Devil's Gate Dam, Pasadena 8" × 10¼"

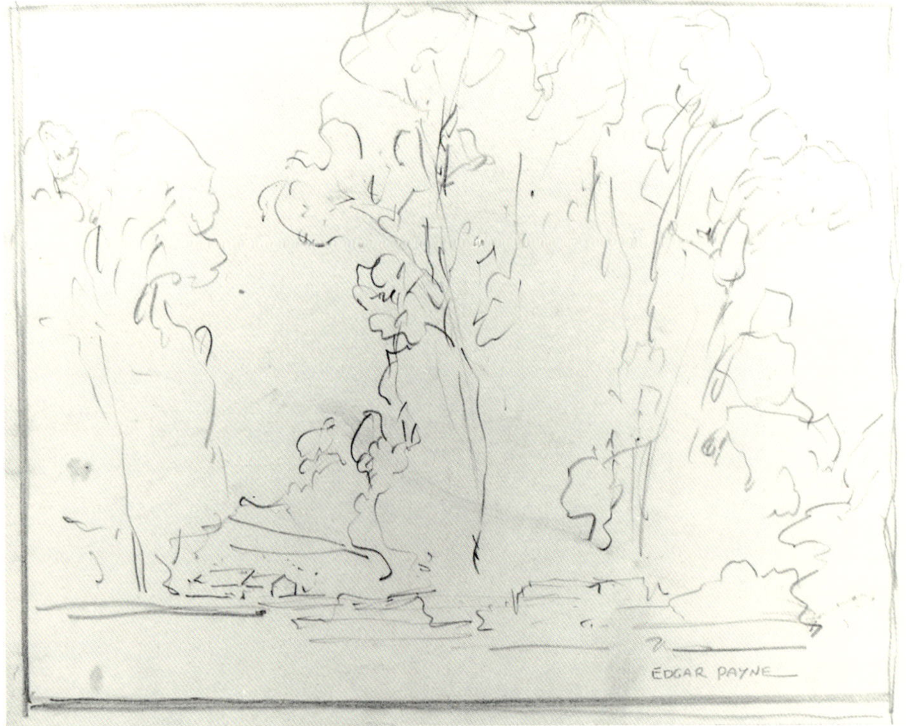

(M-13) California Tree Study 8" × 10"

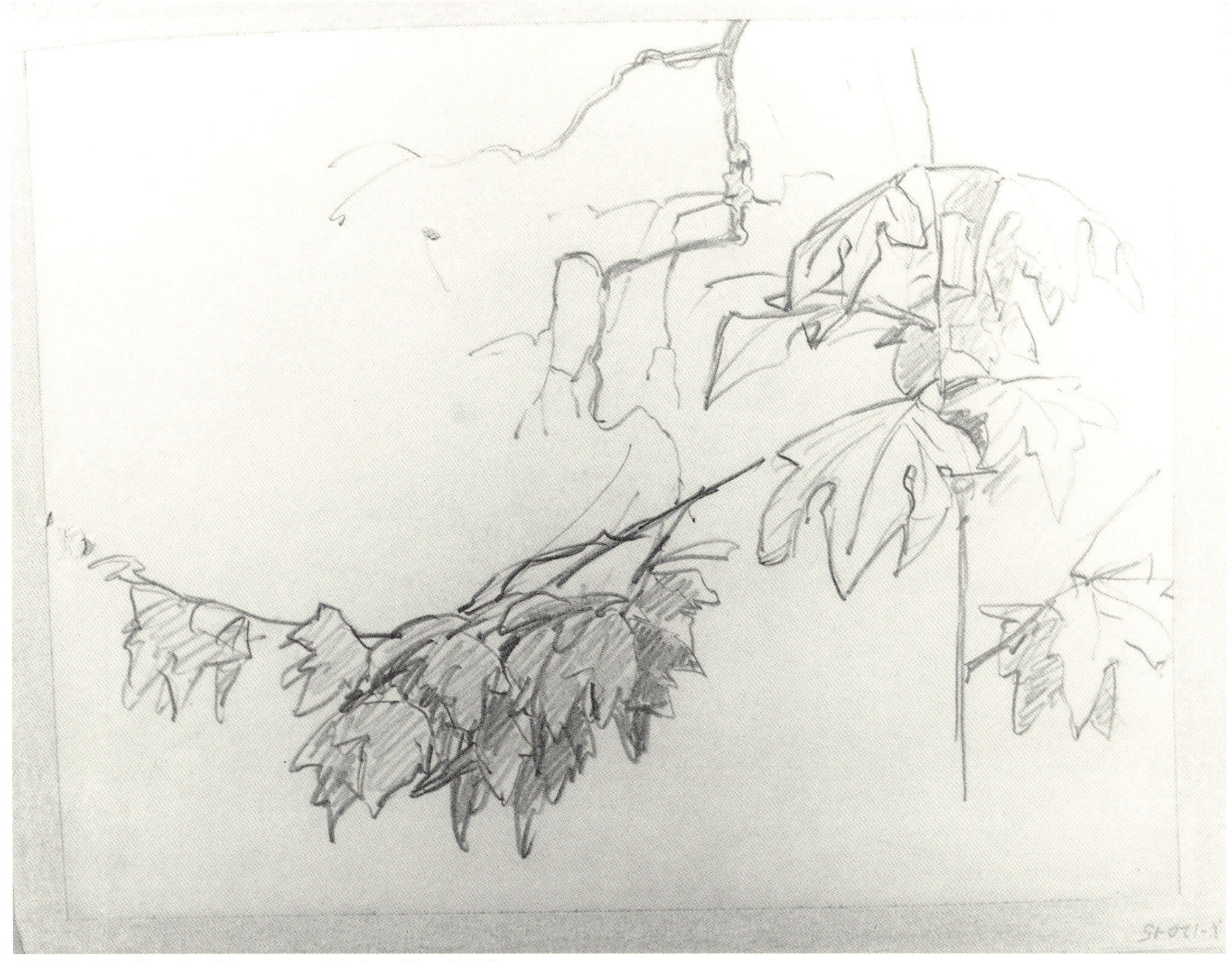

(X-120-15) Sketch of Leaves on Twigs 8" × 10½"

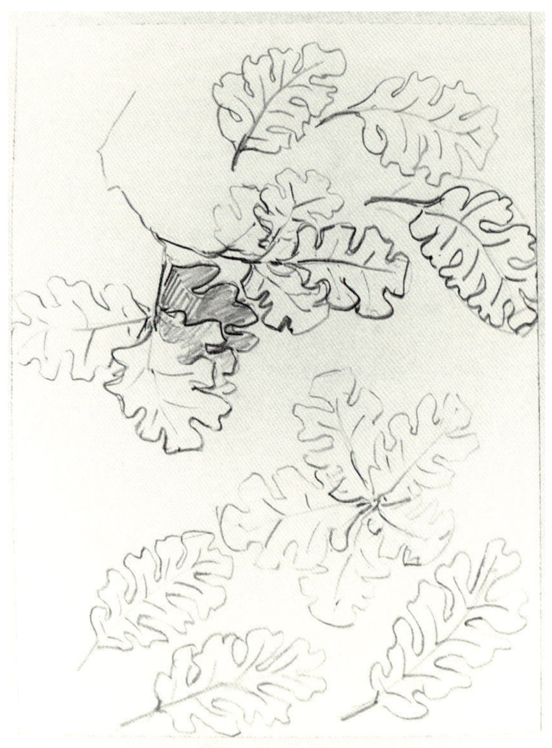

(X-120-11) White Oak Leaves 10½" × 8"

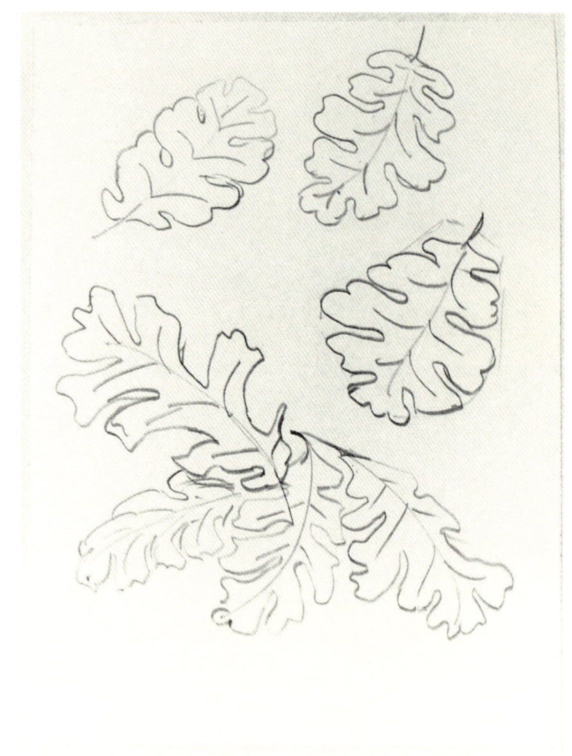

(X-120-10) Leaf Study 10½" × 8"

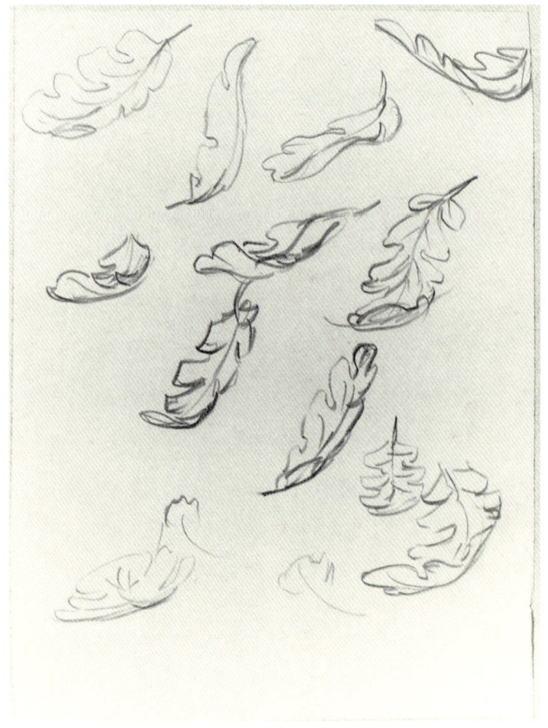

(X-120-12) Oak Leaves at Different Angles 10" × 8"

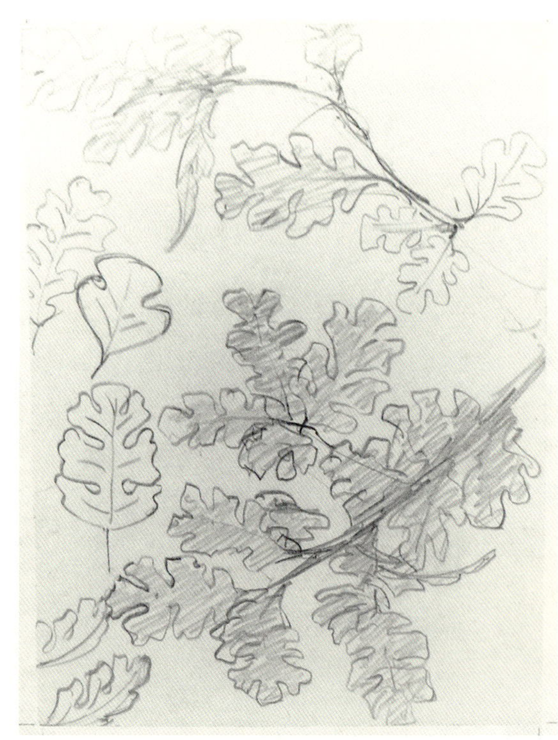

(X-120-17) Oak Leaf Sketches 11" × 8"

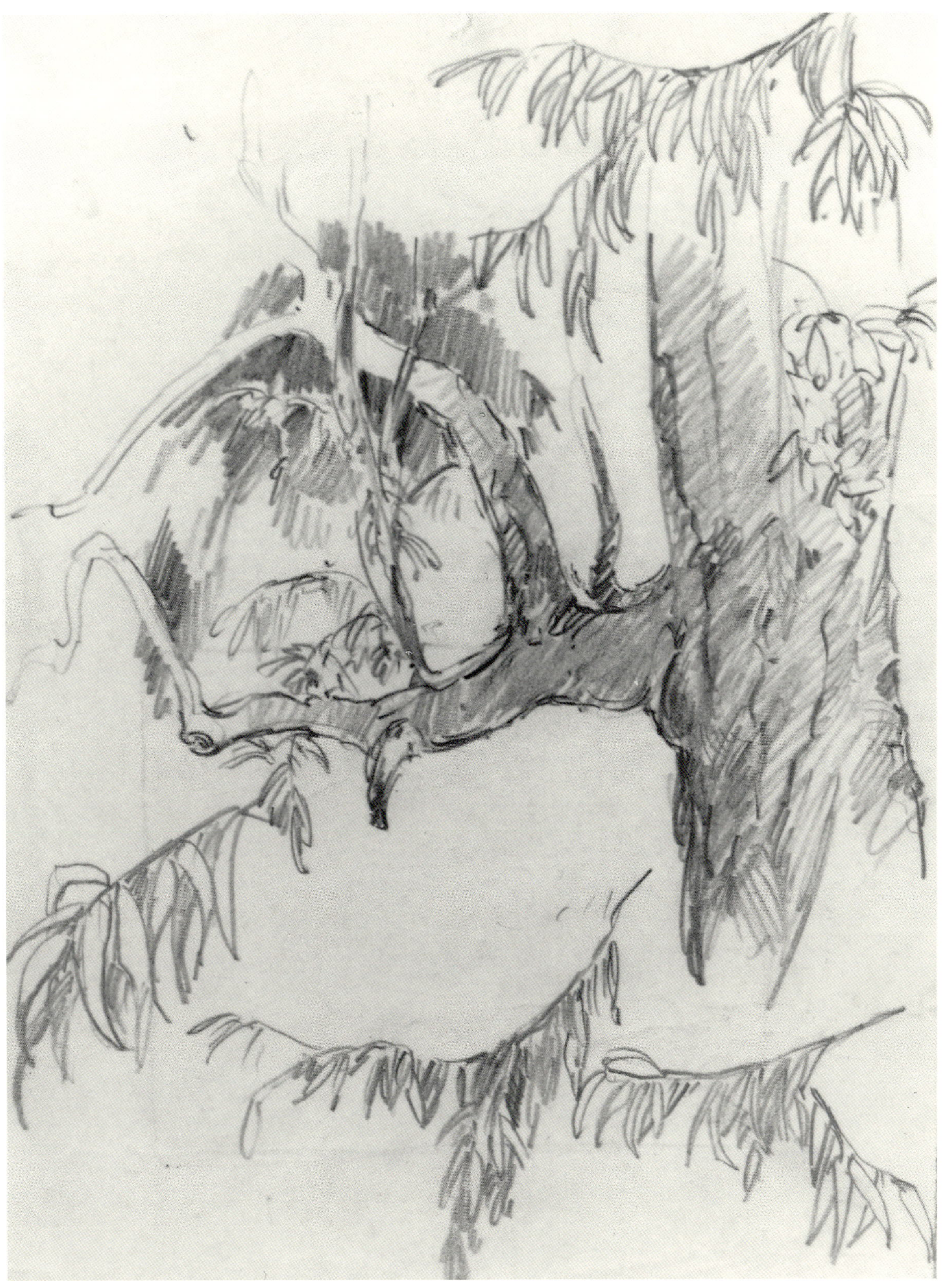

(X-120-14) Tree Study 11" × 8"

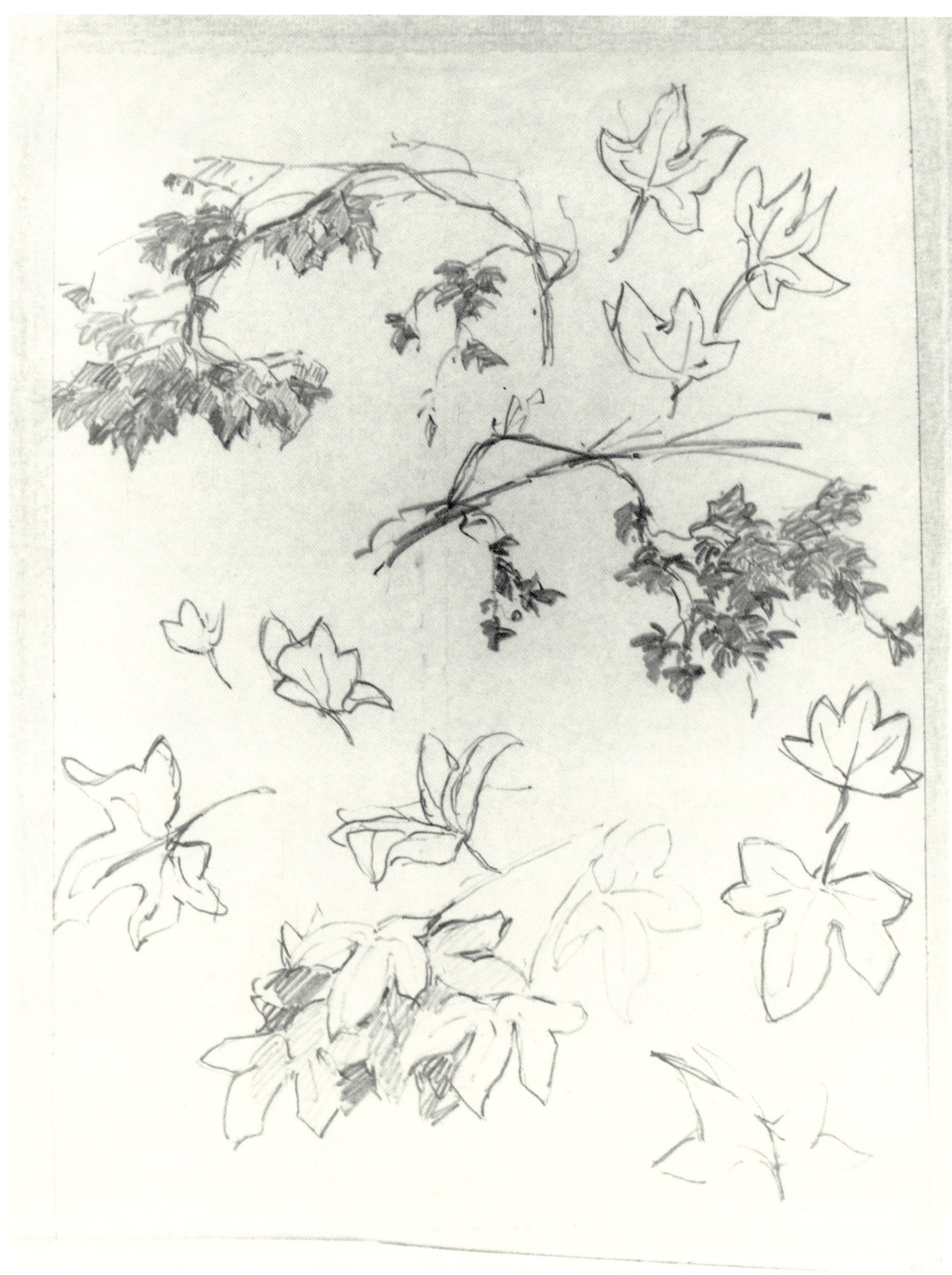

(X-120-9) Leaf Studies 10½" × 8"

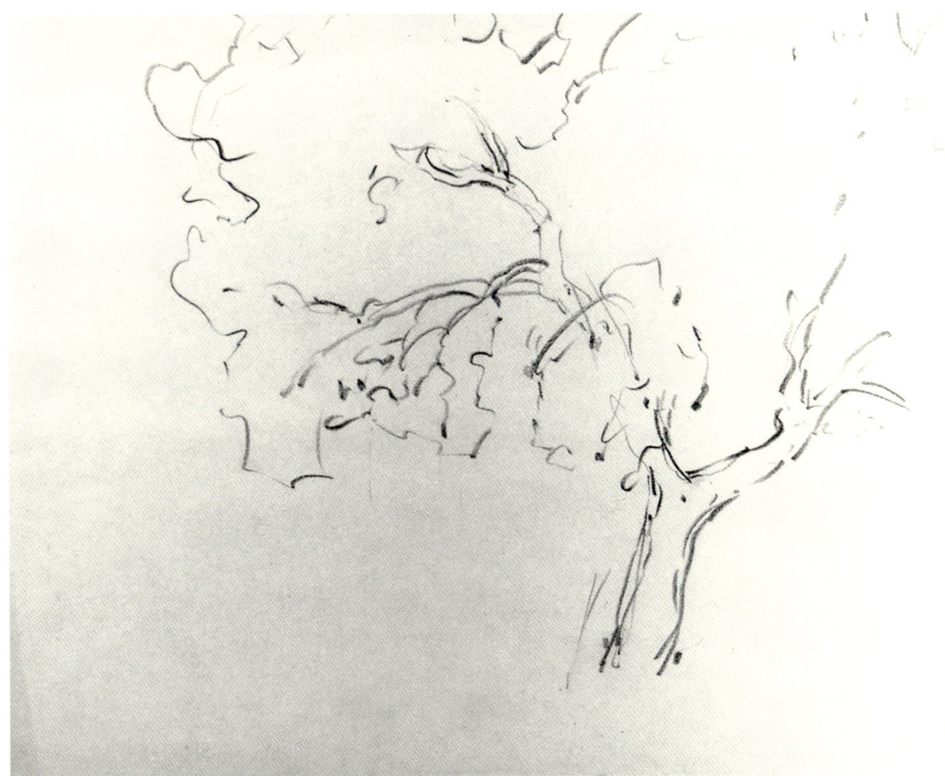

(X-120-8) Tree Sketch 8" × 11"

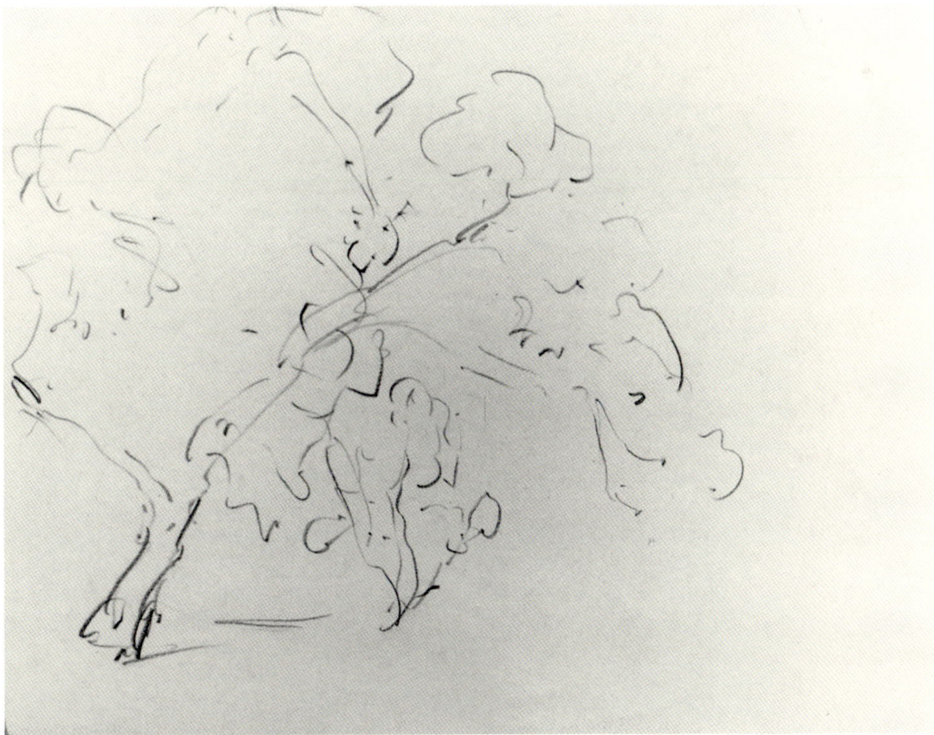

(X-120-6) Tree Study 8" × 10½"

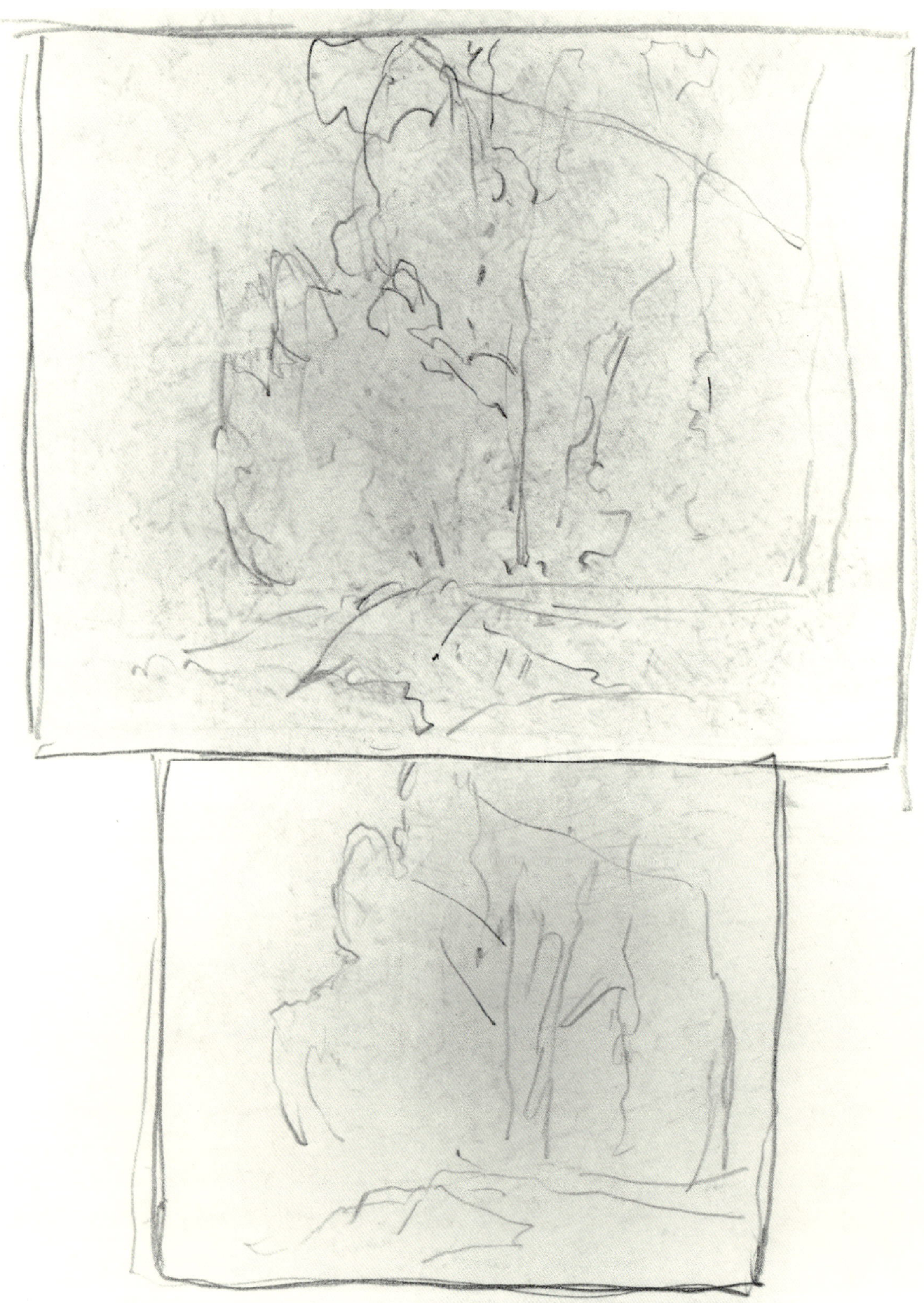

Back of M-36a Trees 8" × 10½"

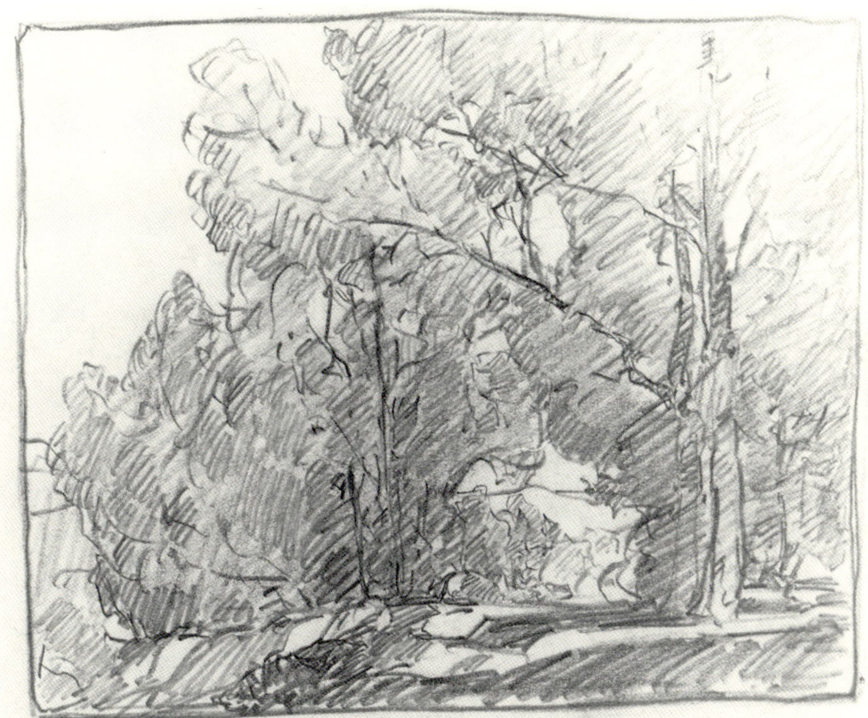

(X-120-21) Sketch of Trees 5½" × 7"

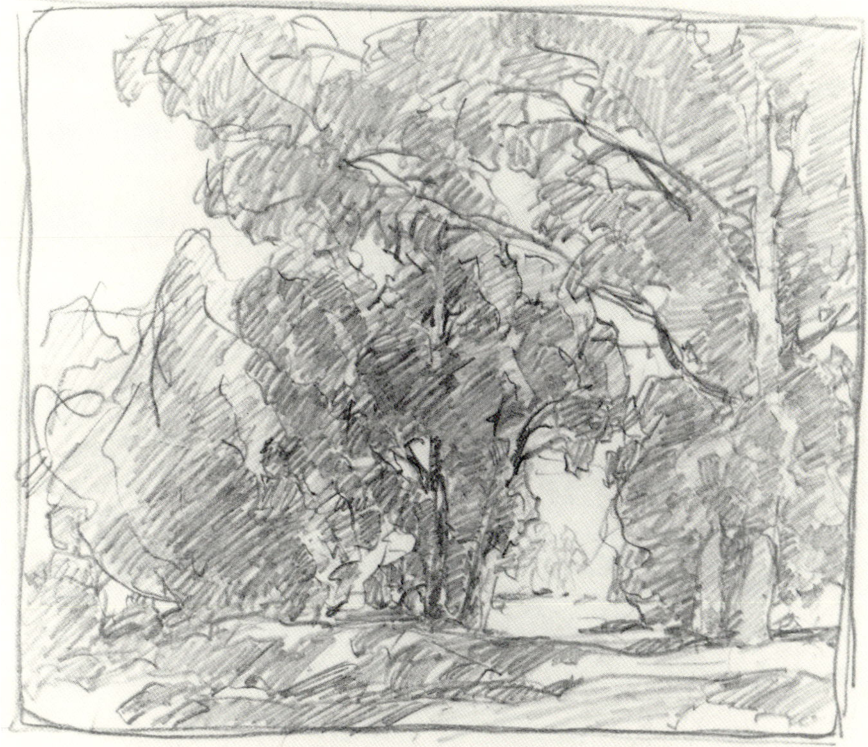

(M-36) Restudy of X-120-21

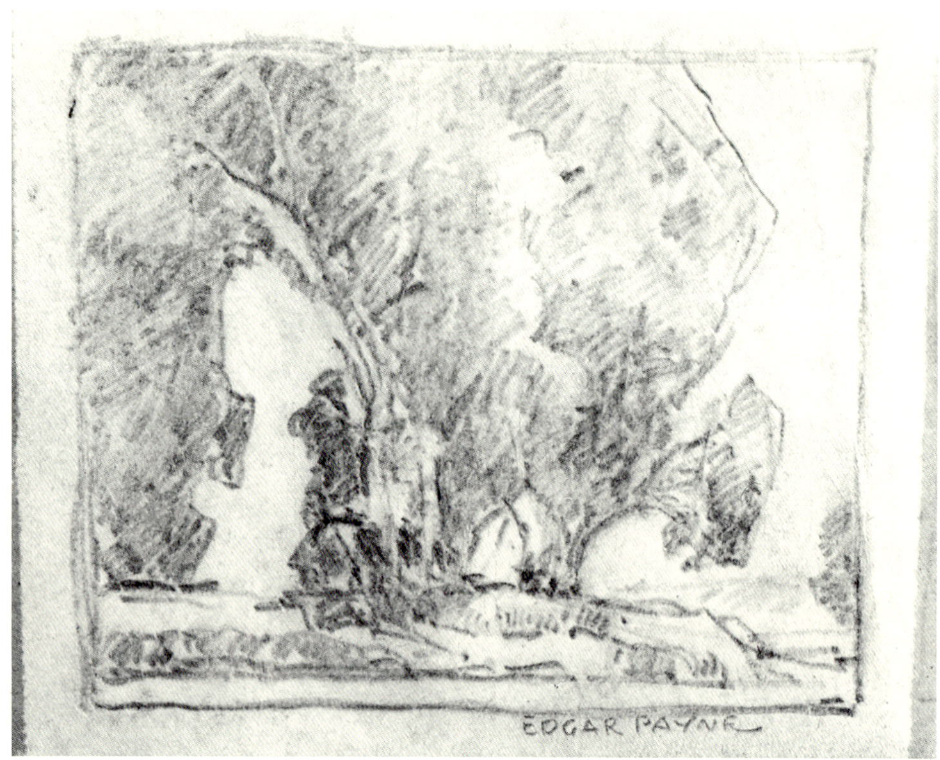

(M-34) Tree with House 3¼" × 4½"

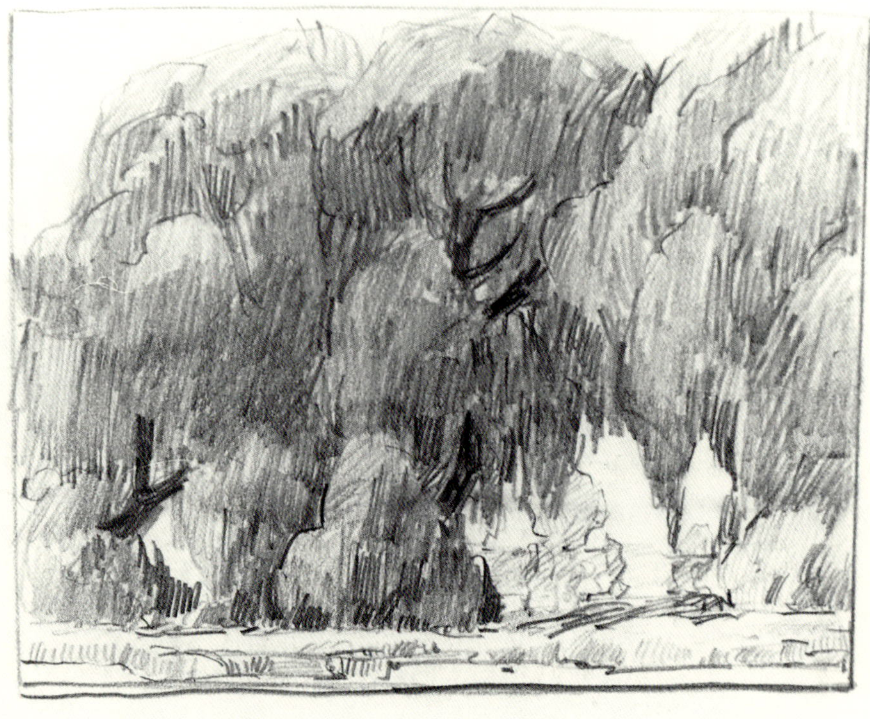

(M-29) Tree Study 5½" × 7"

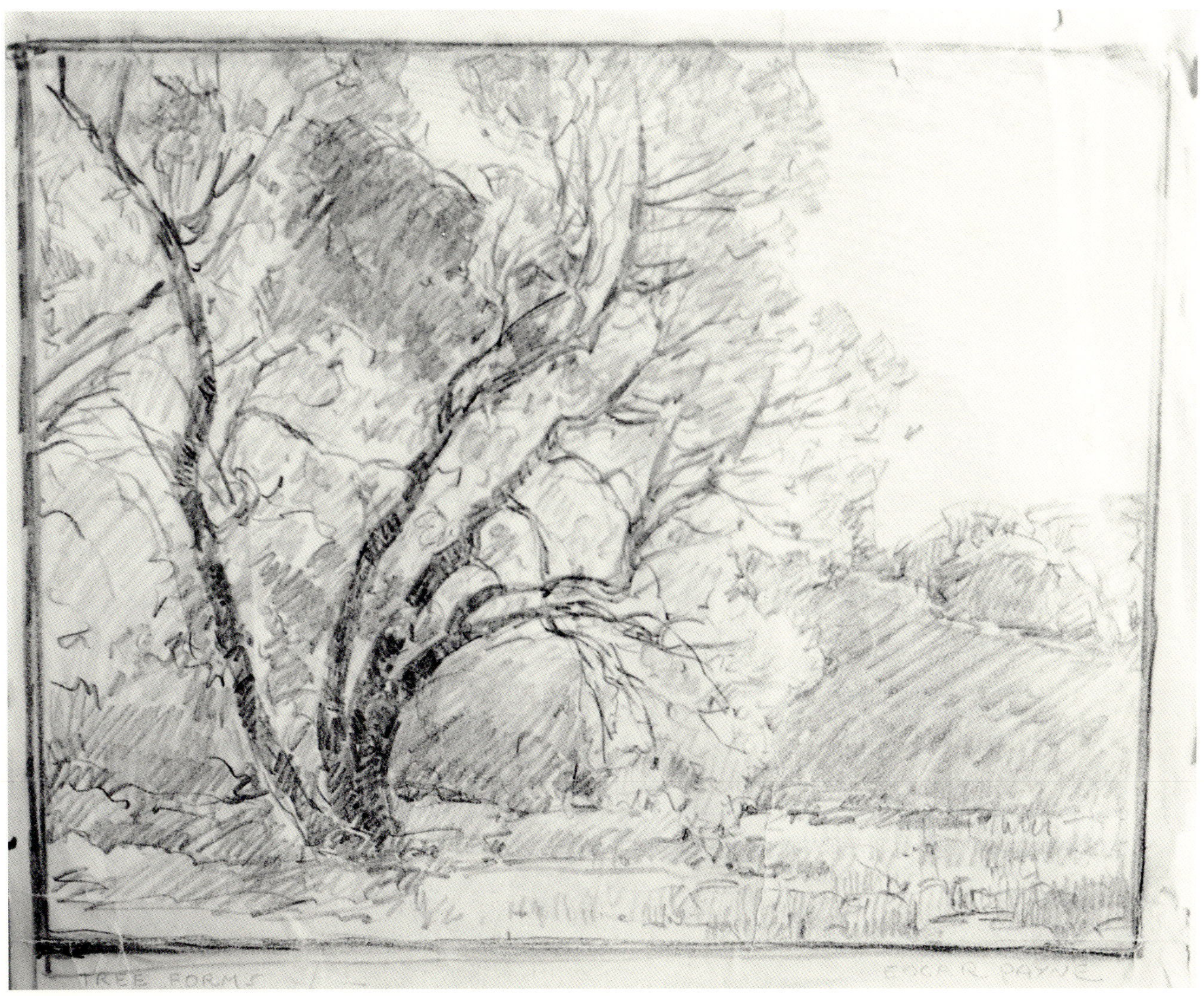

(T-37) Tree Forms 9" × 11"

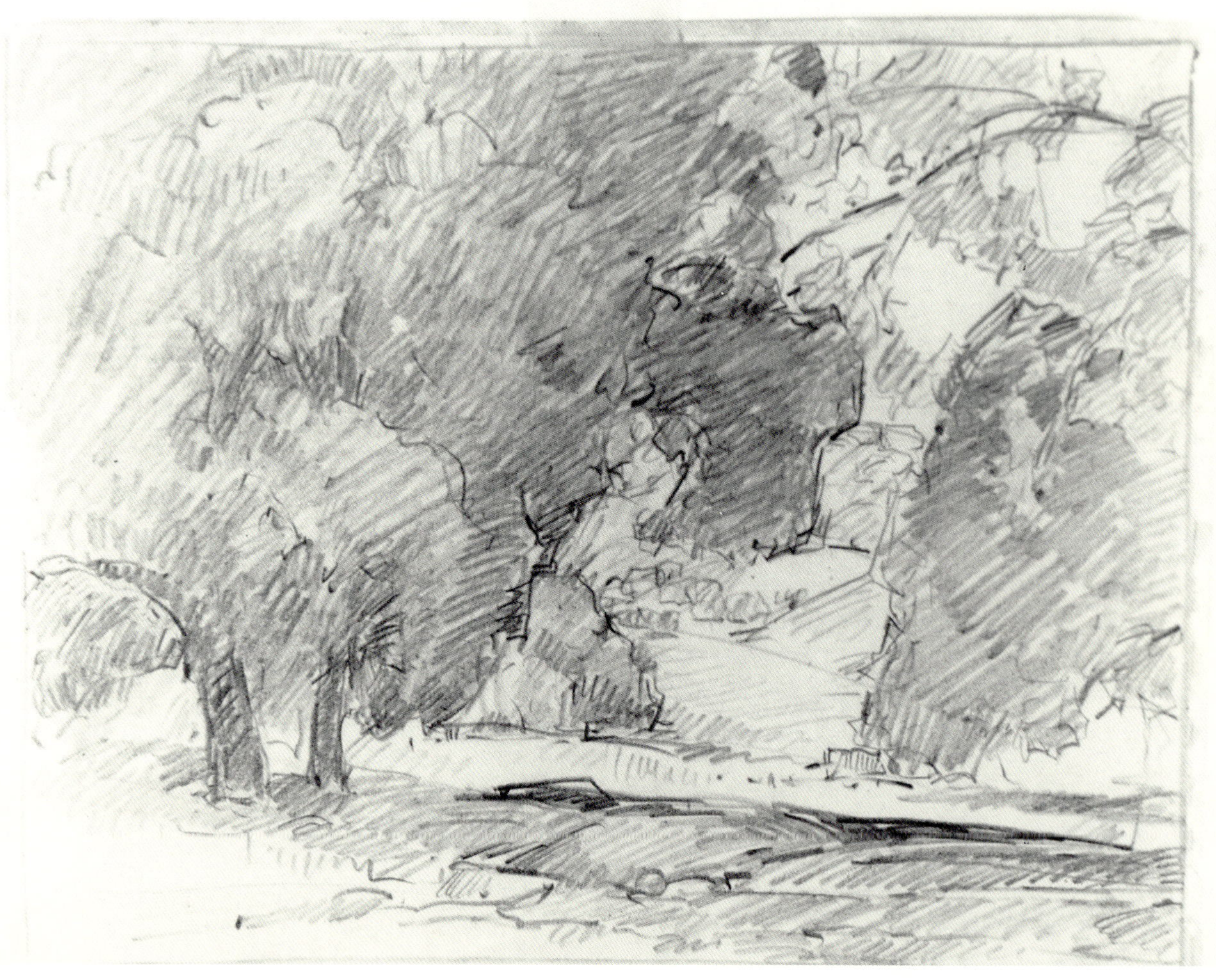

(S-46) Light and Shade Study, Trees 8" × 10½"

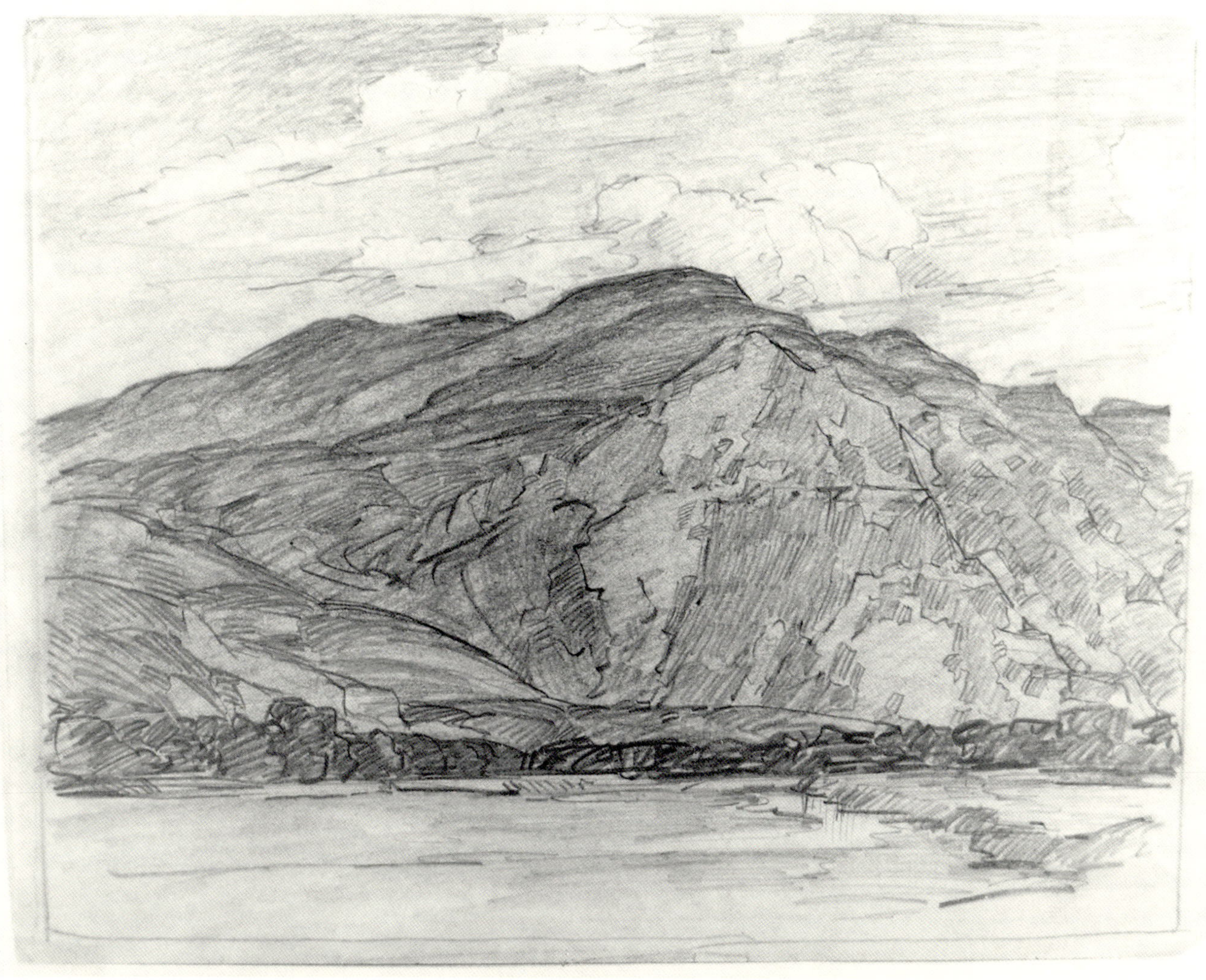

(S-10) Hills in California 8" × 10"

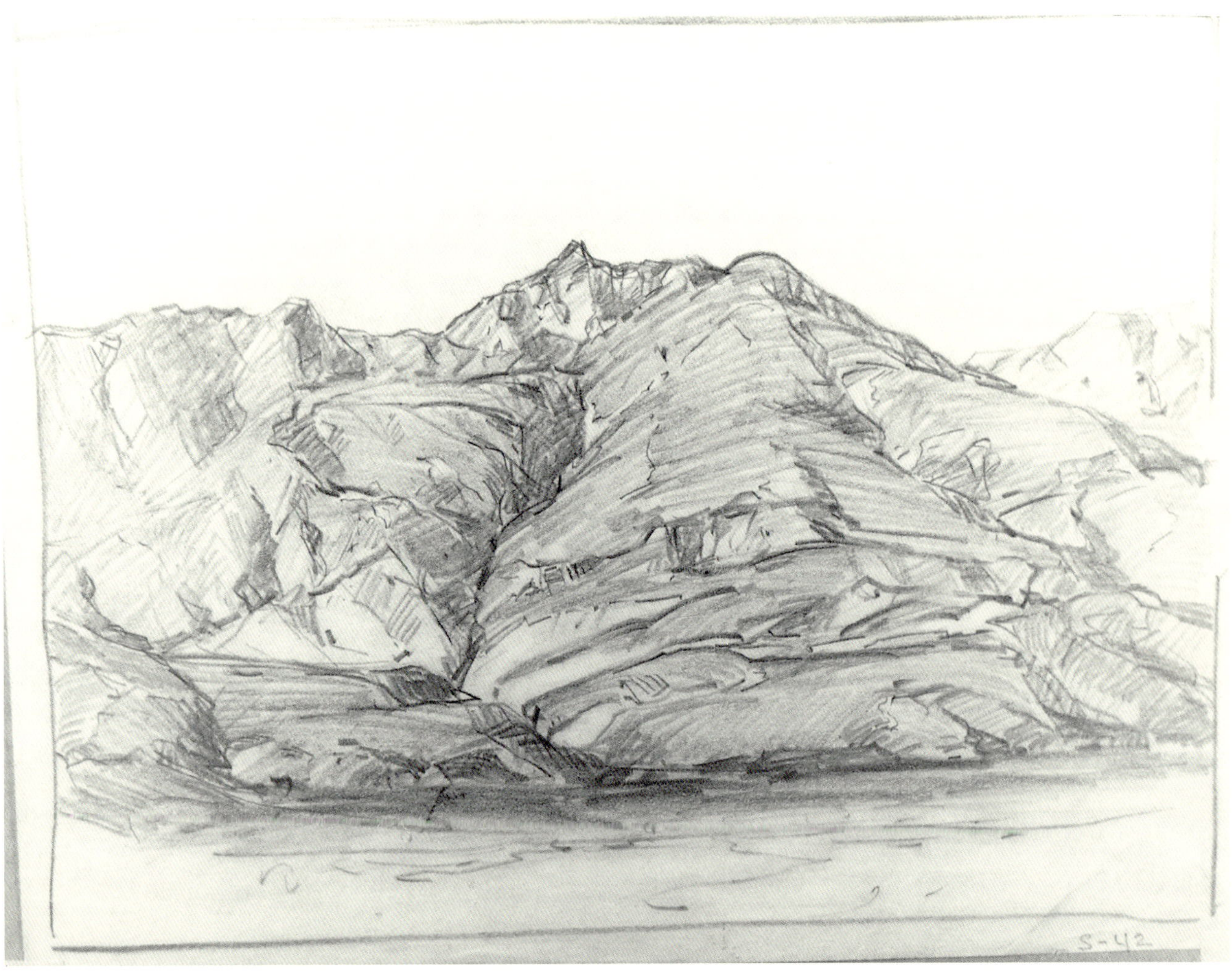

(S-42) California Hills 8" × 10½"

Chapter II

Pencil and Paper Sketches Made in Italy

After a winter in Rome, we drove to Switzerland, but it was too cold to sketch in the mountains, so we took a train to Venice. We did stay awhile in Venice, and I have one small sketch left from there. But Dad heard about the island of Chioggia and the colorful fishing boats there. He was interested in these traditional boats with a history that goes back thousands of years. Now his detailed records of these craft may be of interest, not only to sailboat enthusiasts, but to historians, because the way they were made and rigged may not have often been recorded in such detail.

Later we went to the coast of Brittany, in France, to paint the fishing boats there. I have been told that some persons find the different boats confusing, so I offer some comparisons here. Chioggia (Kee-oh-gee-ah) is near Venice, and I later learned that the rest of the island, beyond the harbor town, is a farming area, growing vegetables for Venice itself. You can find seeds for the striped beets, called Chioggia beets, in seed catalogues.

The fishing boats are quite different because the lagoon in the Adriatic is shallow, and the Atlantic Ocean is something else! The Breton boats, especially the tuna yawls, sailed far out upon the ocean.

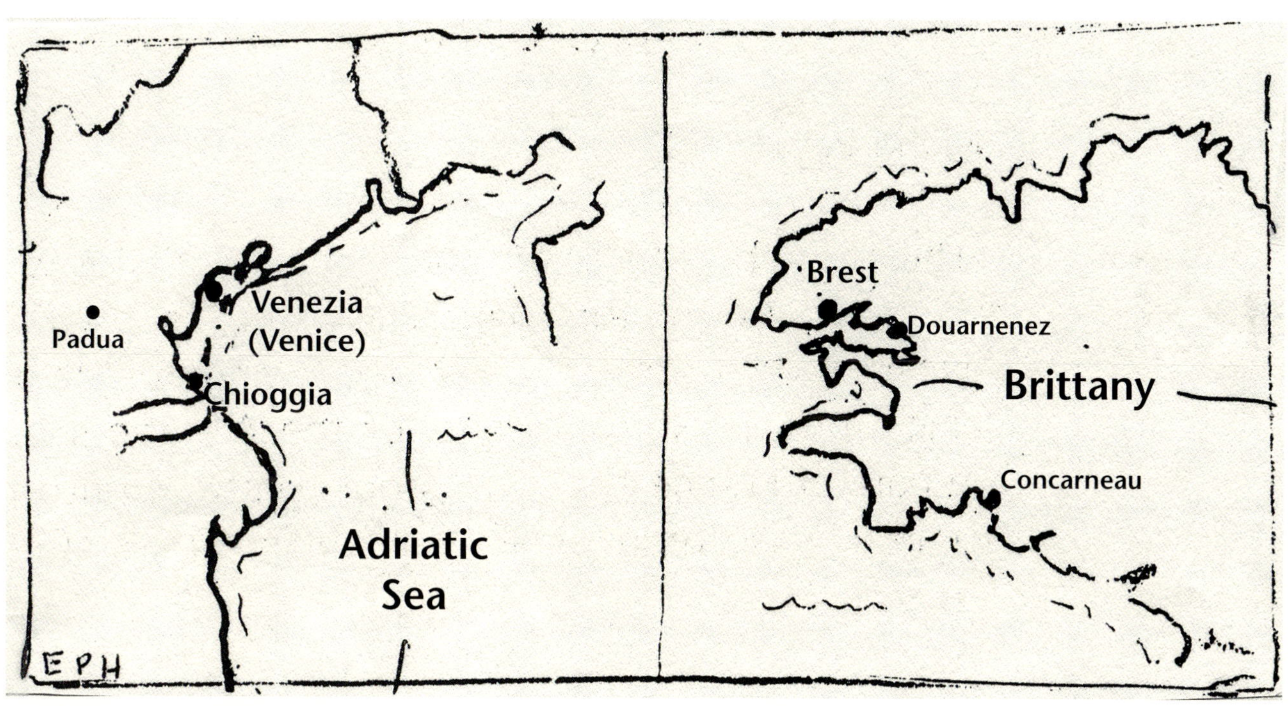

Sketch Maps of Locations (EPH)

The Chioggia fishing boats were lateen rigged. The basic characteristic of this form is that the sail is attached at the top to a boom that can be raised or lowered. This boom crosses the mast, and the angle can be changed to catch the wind. The lateen-rigged boats are very ancient on the Mediterannean, and go back to before classic times. Sometimes this rig is still used today for pleasure boats on quiet waters.

The Brittany boats carried fore-and-aft rigging. There are many varieties of this form, and these can be seen in sailing yachts and other pleasure-sailing boats today. The basic plan is that the sail is attached to the vertical mast by rings, so that the sail slides down to the boom to be furled. There can be other sails, and there is at least a jib, which is triangular, in front of the mast. A yawl has two masts.

At other times, Dad painted a few pictures of the "tall ships" which are square rigged, with booms permanently attached to the masts at right angles to them. Sailors climb the rigging to furl the sails by tying them to these booms. In the Payne notebooks we have left, there are no sketches of such ships.

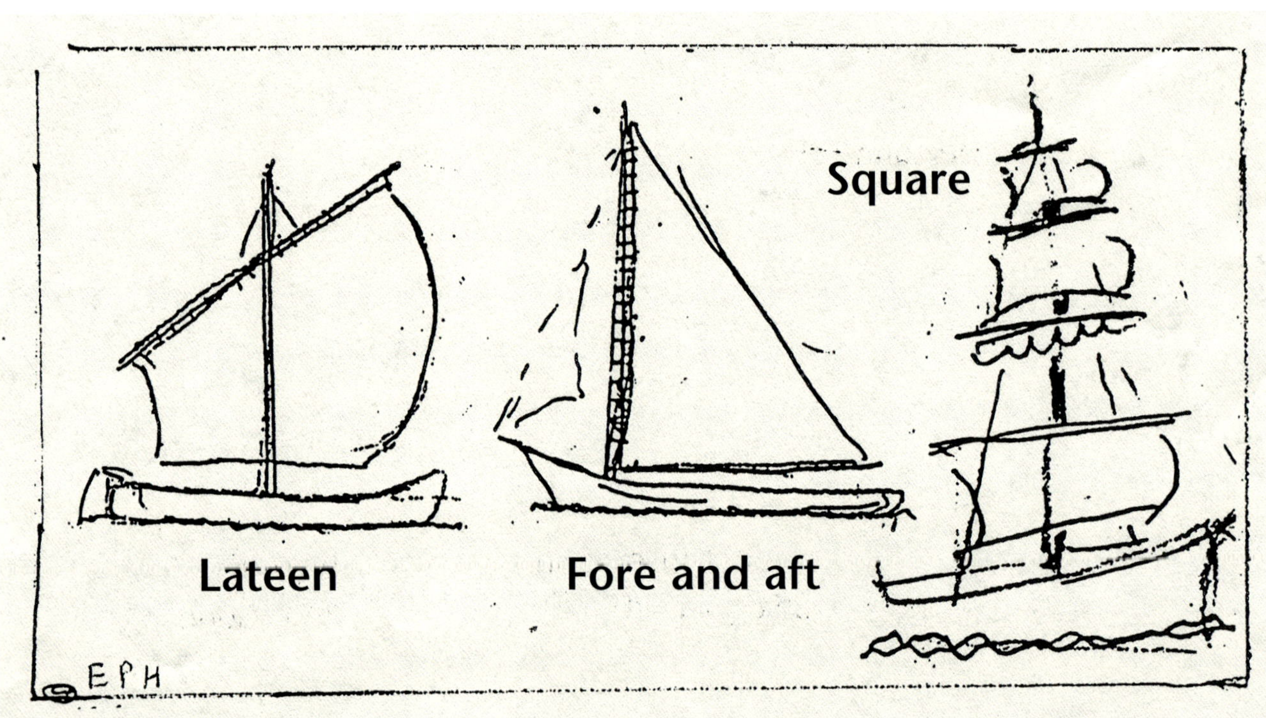

Simplified Sketches of Sail Types (EPH)

Another way to tell the Adriatic lateen-rigged boats from the Breton ones is by the shape of the prow — the front of the boat. The Italian ones are rounded and have two big symbolic "eyes" painted on them. The Breton boats have straight prows, with the jib boom sticking out ahead. The Chioggia boats have big rudders at the stern which could be lifted up when in very shallow water. The rudders are worked by a tiller. Breton yawls are much deeper, with a rudder below the water line. The rudder is controlled by a wheel on the deck.

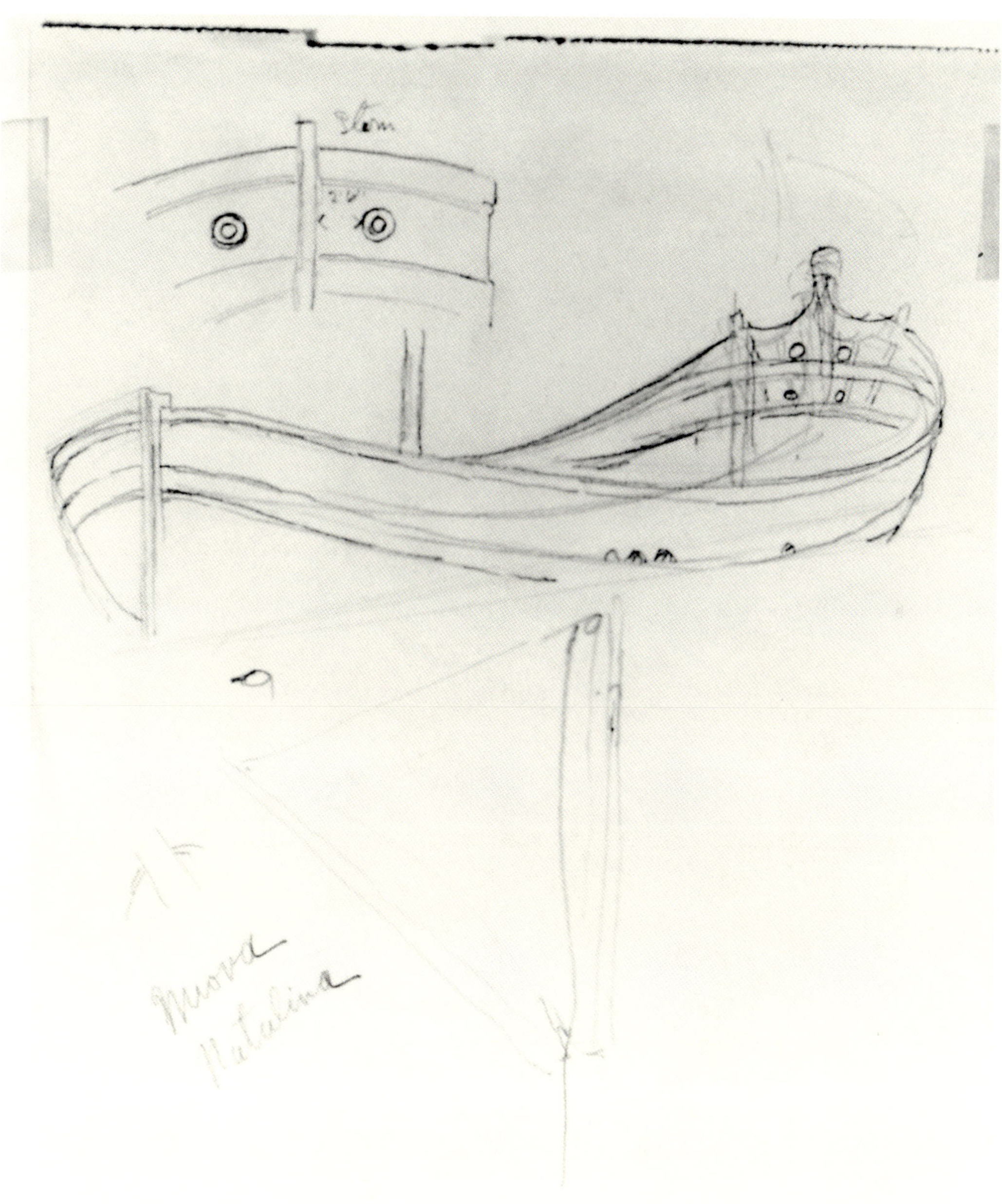

(SL-5) Study of a Chioggia Boat Hull 10" × 8"

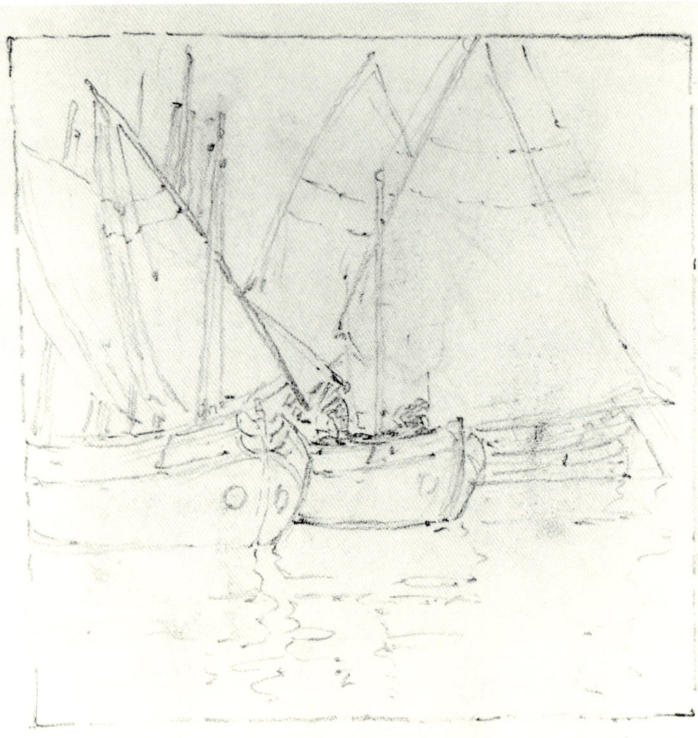

(SL-3) Adriatic Boats, Showing Prows and Sterns 10" × 8"

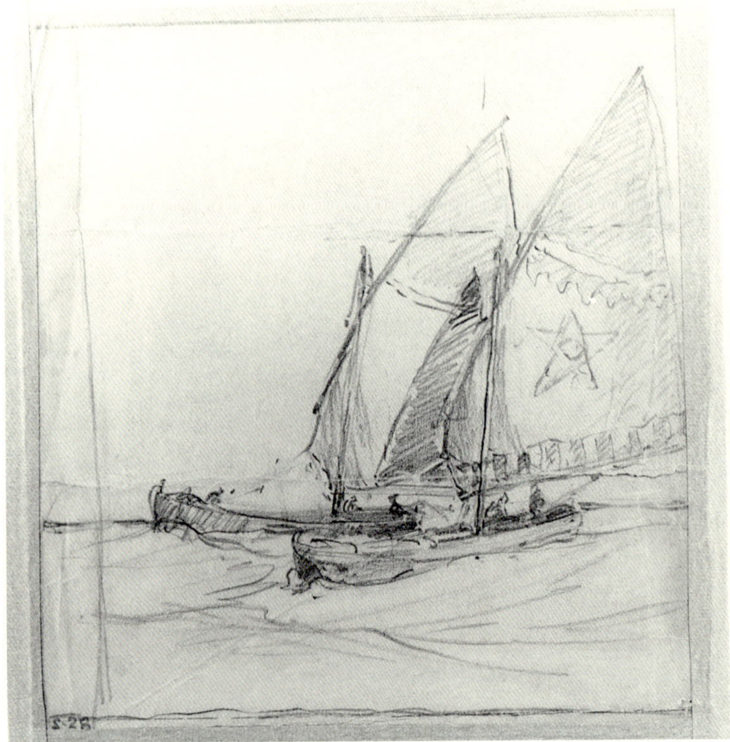

(S-28) Outbound Adriatic Boats 9" × 8½"

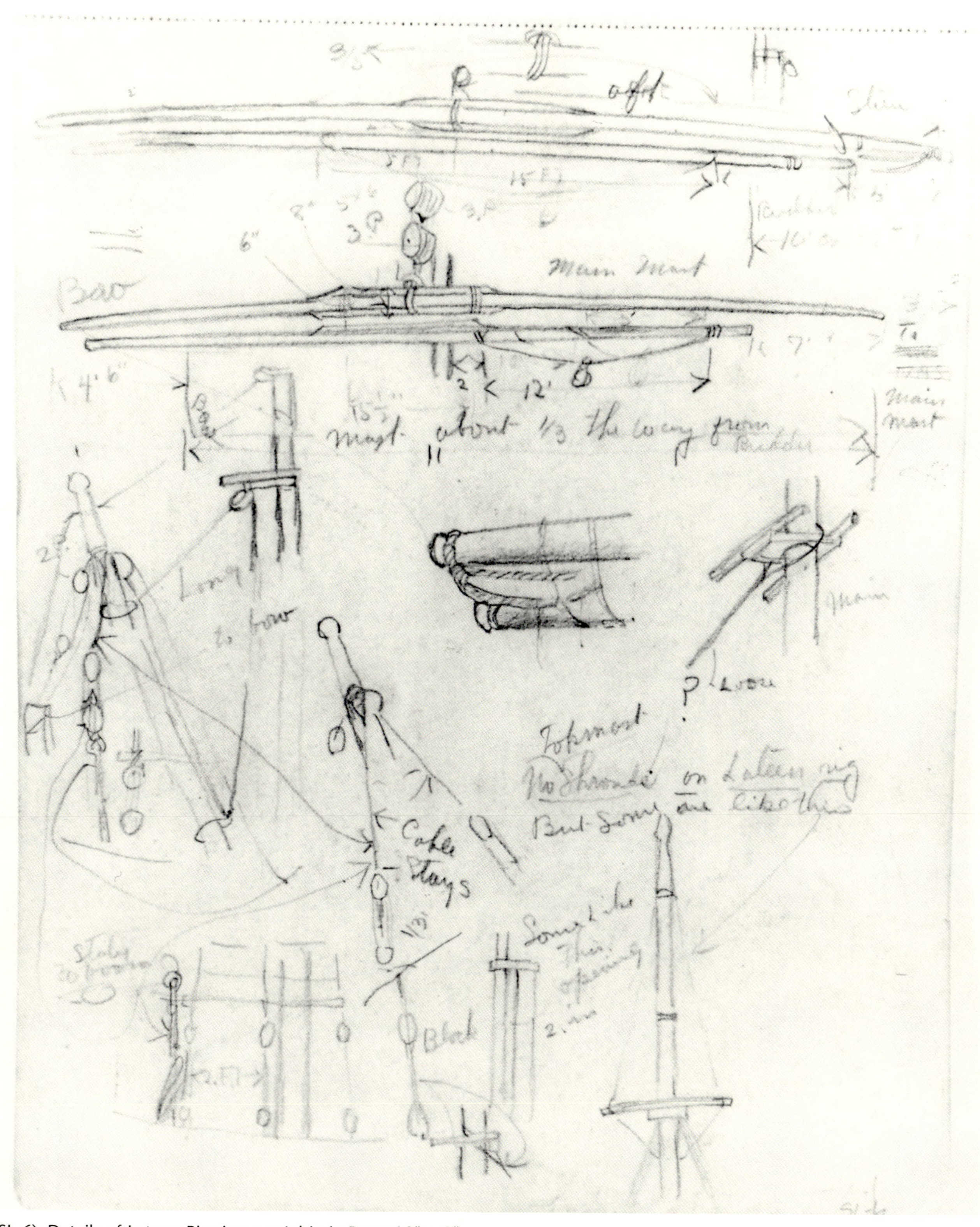

(SL-6) Details of Lateen Rigging on Adriatic Boat 10" × 8"

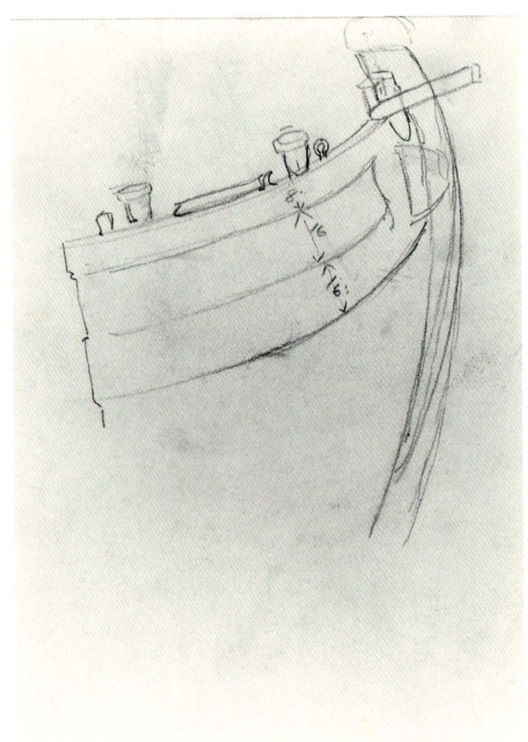

(SL-9) Detail of Prow, Chioggia 10" × 8"

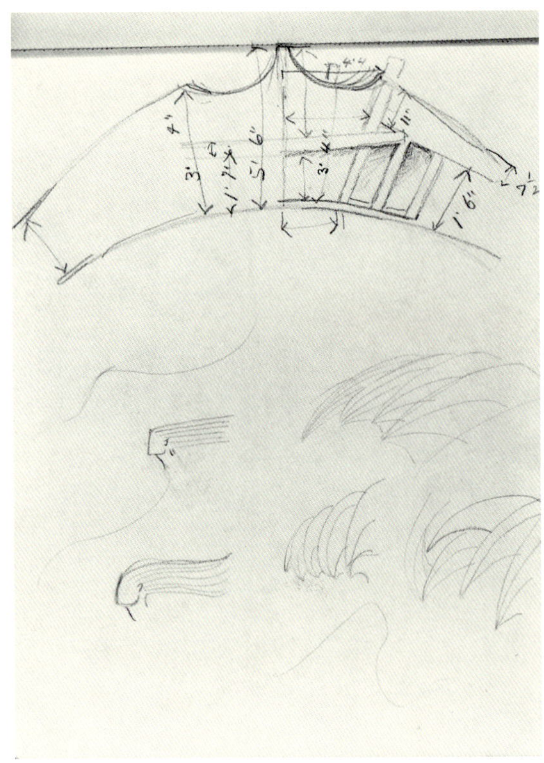

(SL-9b) Detail of Prow from Deck 10" × 8"

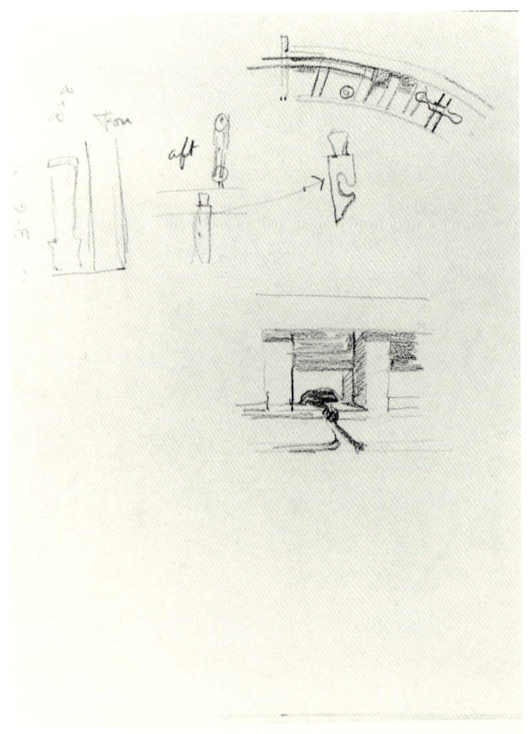

(Z-11) Study of Boat Details, Chioggia 10" × 8"

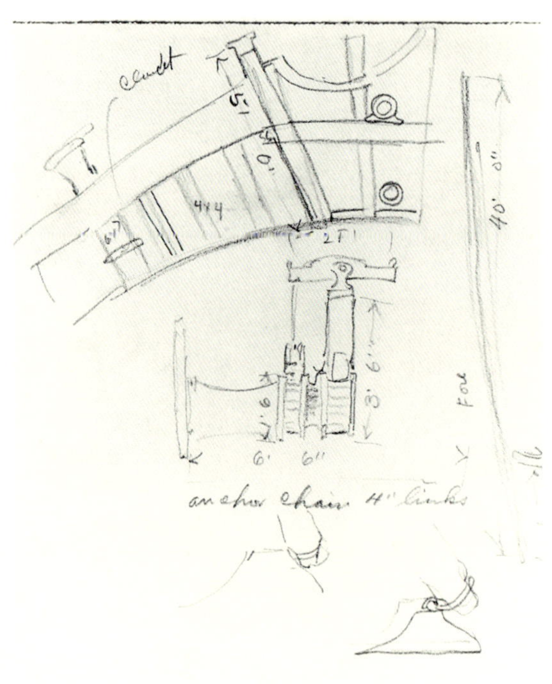

(SL-4) Details of Deck and Rigging 10" × 8"

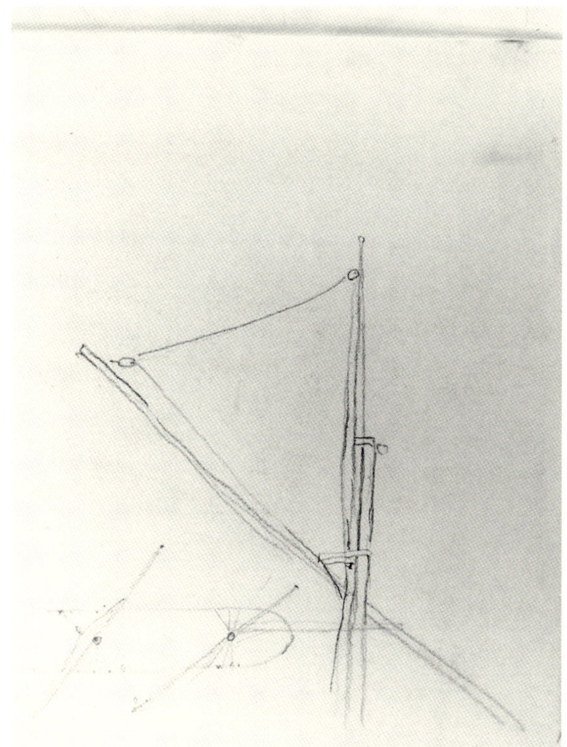

(SL-8a) Sail 10" × 8"

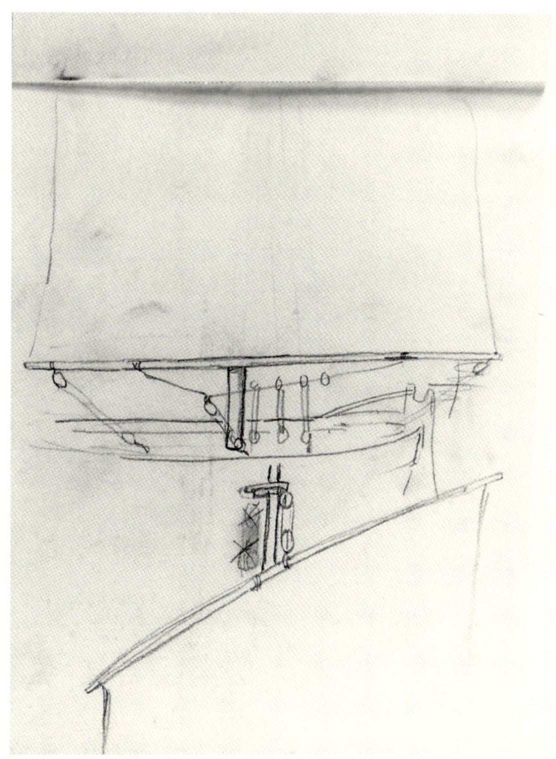

(SL-8b) Details of Rigging 10" × 8"

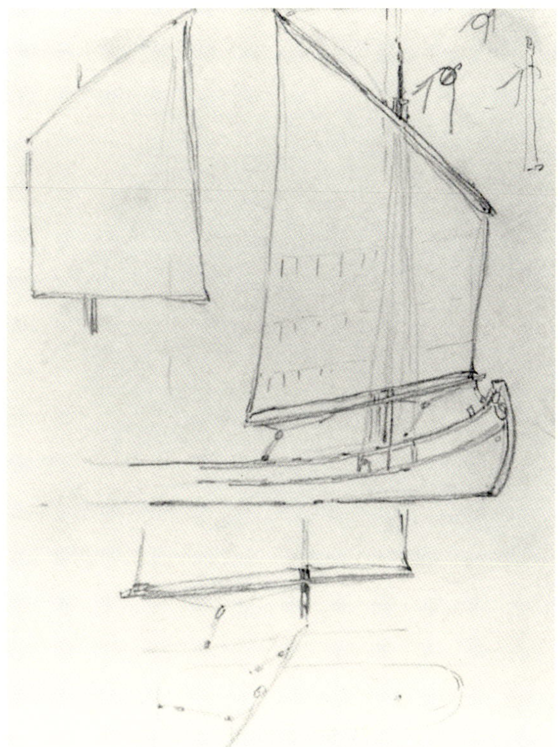

(Z-2) Lateen Sails 10" × 8"

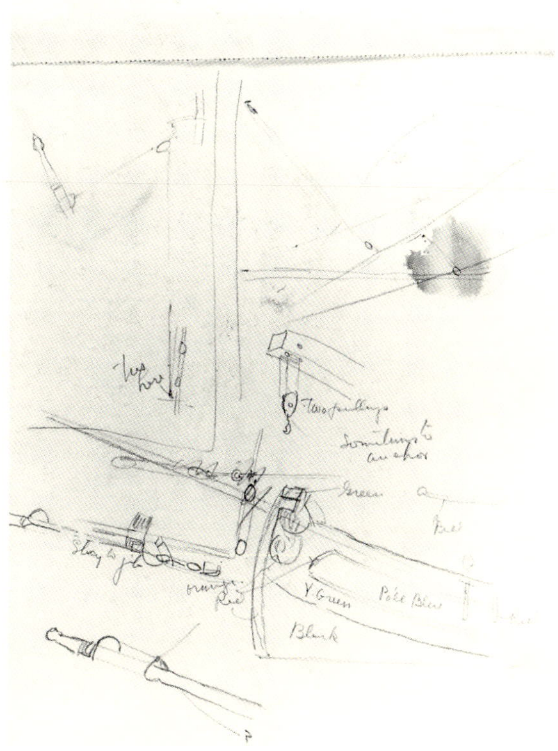

(SL-7) Color Notes for a Chioggia Boat 10" × 8"

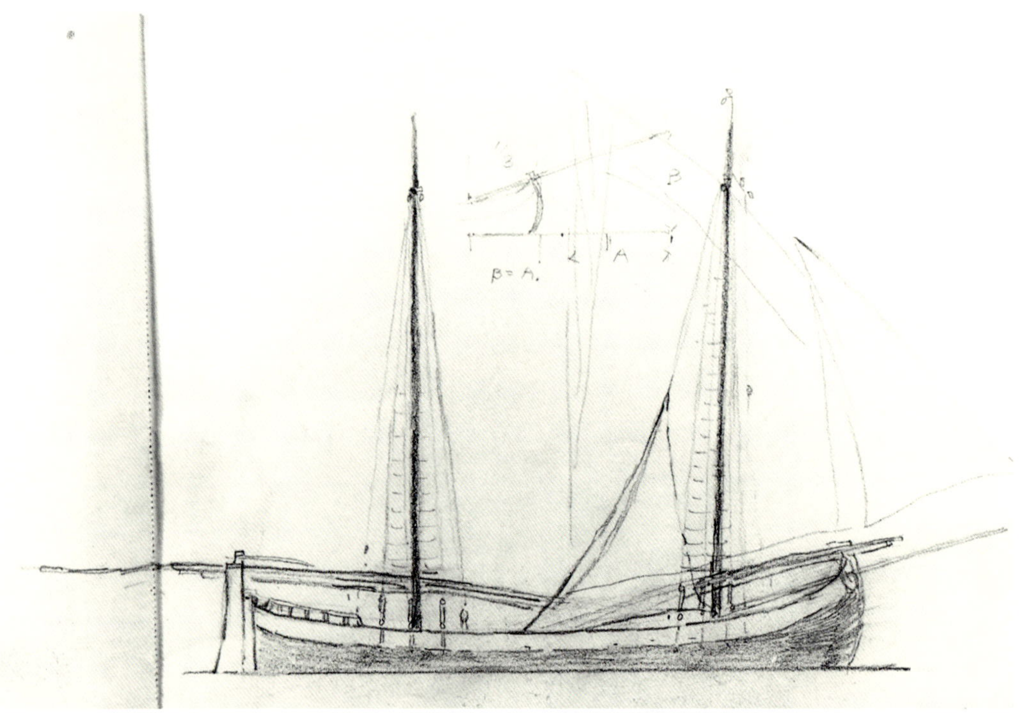

(SL-8) Chioggia Boat Showing Proportions 8" × 10"

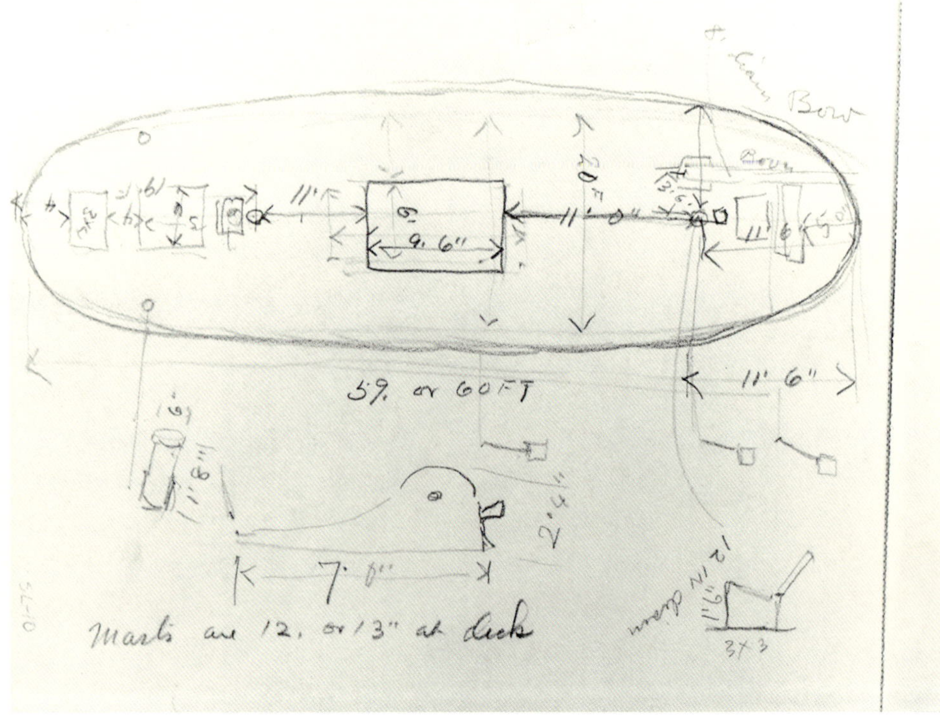

(SL-10) Measurements of Boat Deck 8" × 10"

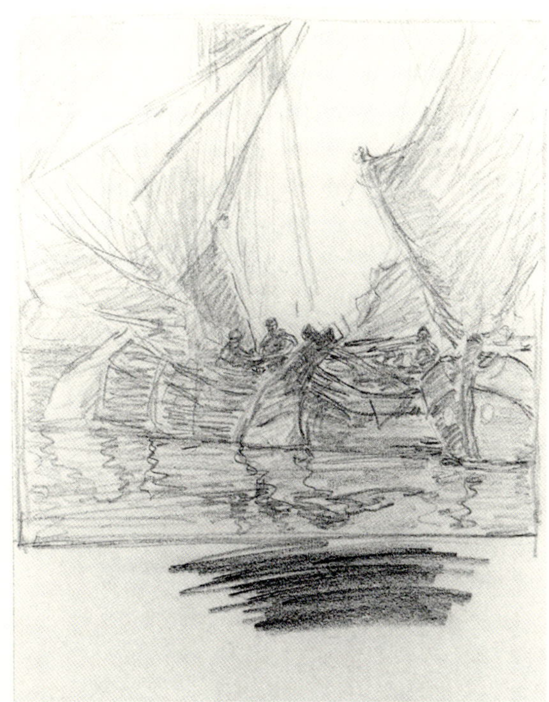

(M-10) Chioggia Boats with Figures 8" × 8"

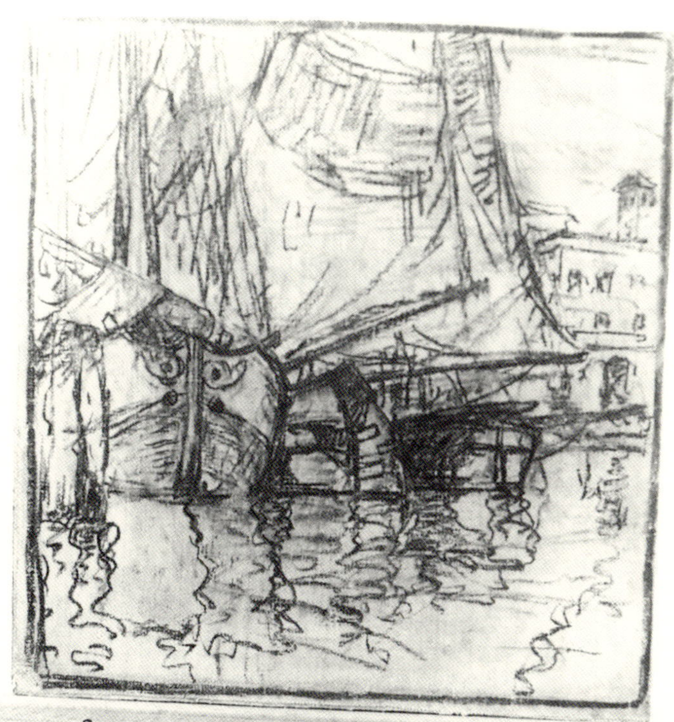

(U-6) Boats in Chioggia Harbor (Charcoal) 13" × 13"

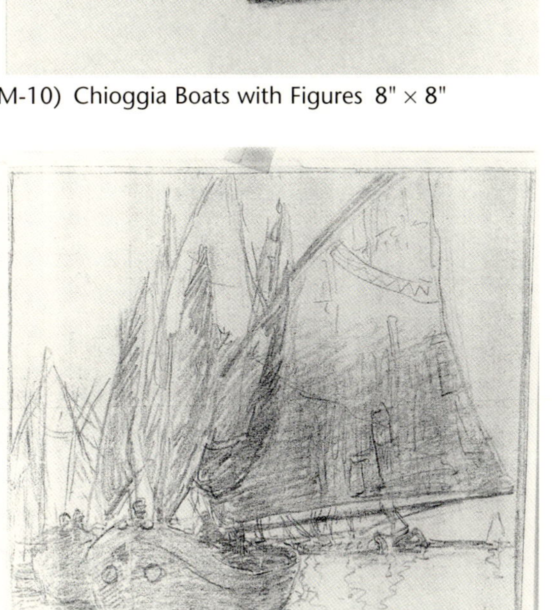

(S-43) Sails: Study in Light and Shade 8½" × 8½"

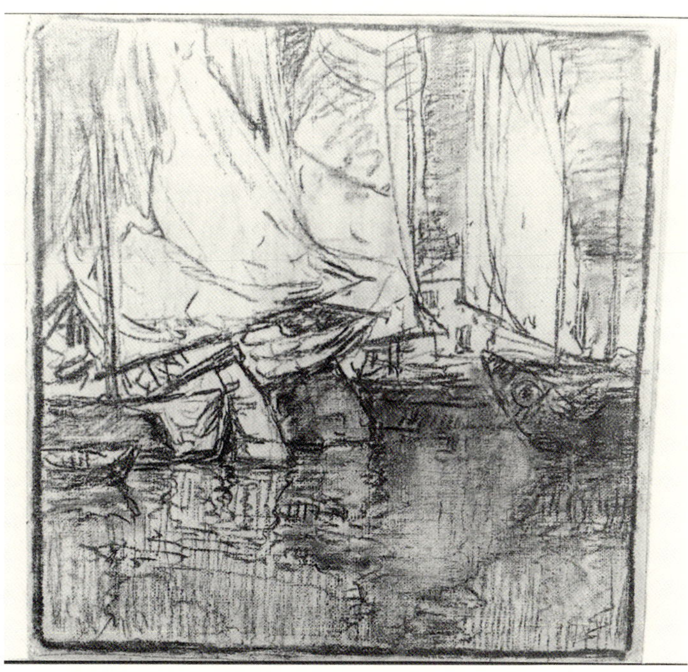

(U-7) Harbor Scene (Charcoal) 13" × 13"

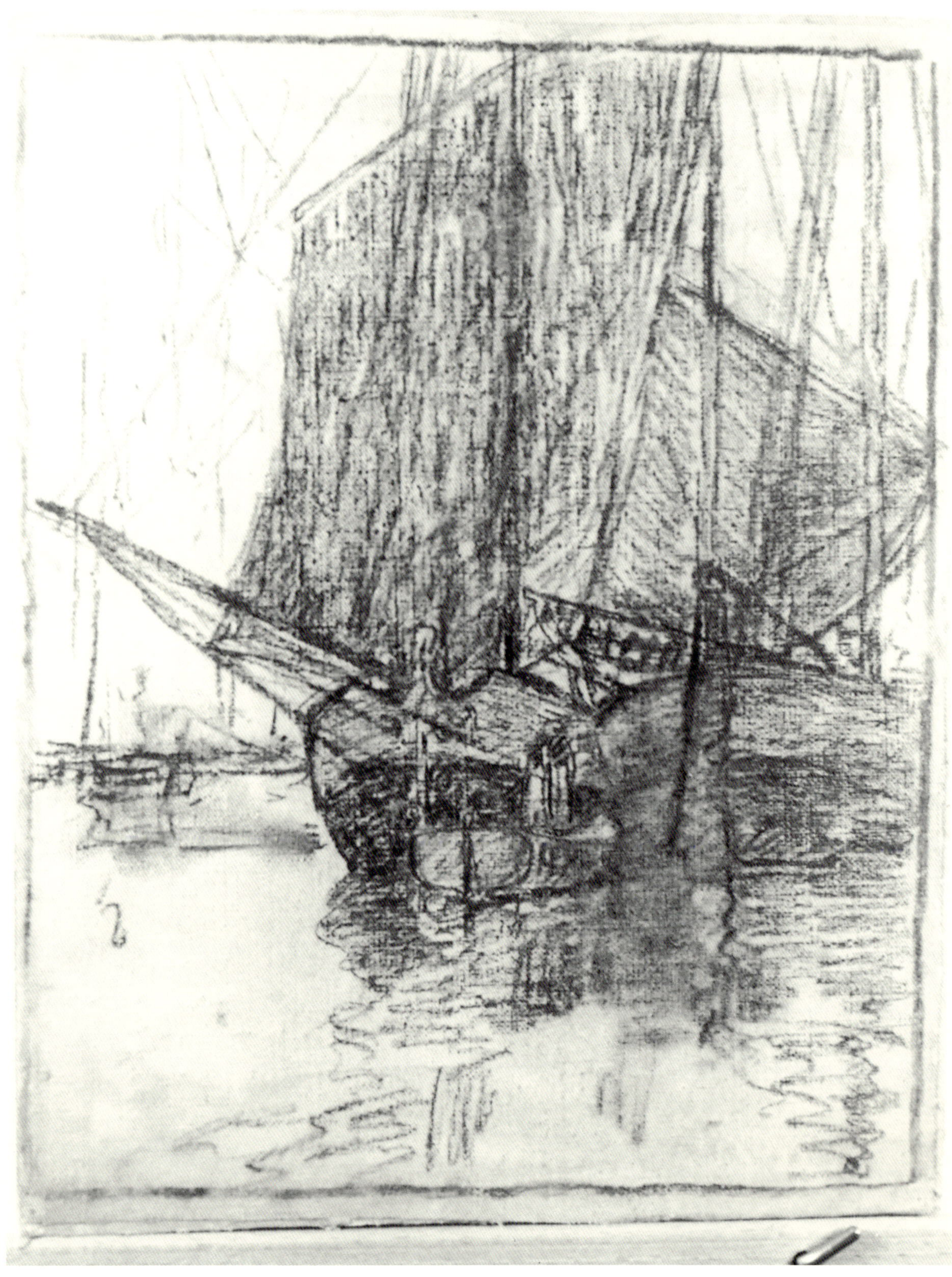

(U-10) Fore and Aft Composition (Charcoal) 15" × 12"

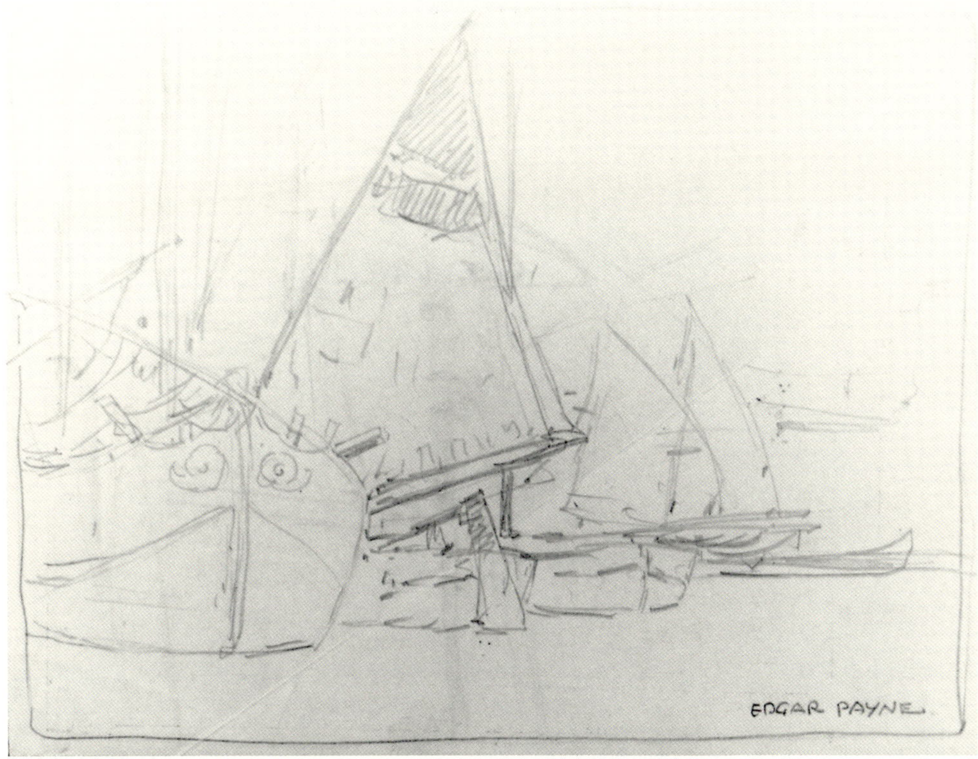

(M-9) Fishing Boats at Rest 8" × 10"

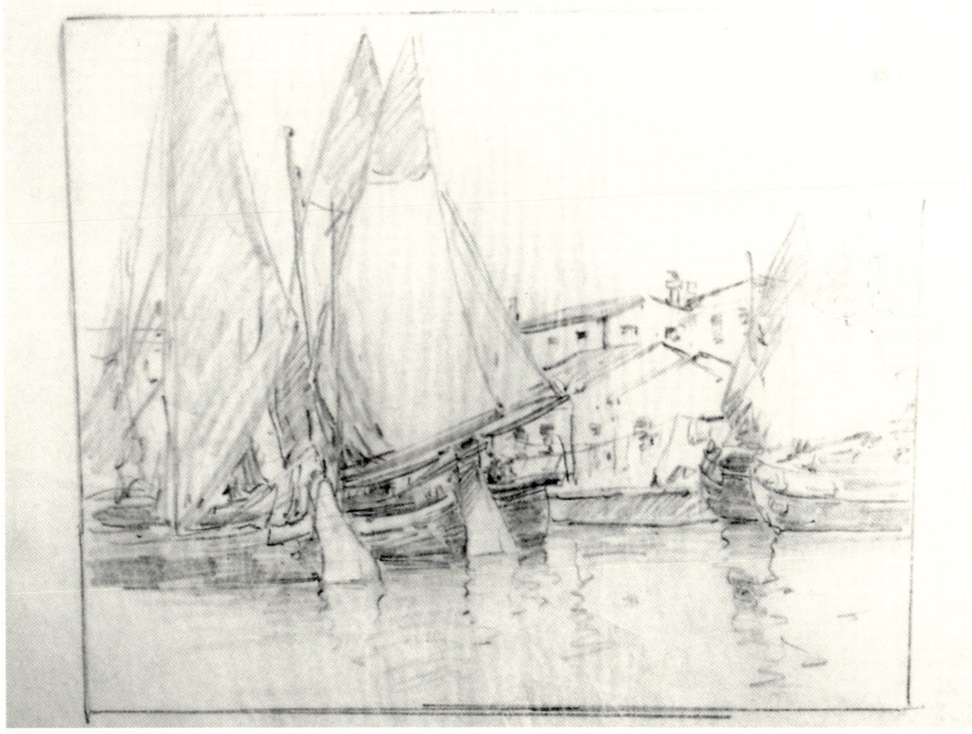

(T-27) Chioggia Boats at Home 10" × 12"

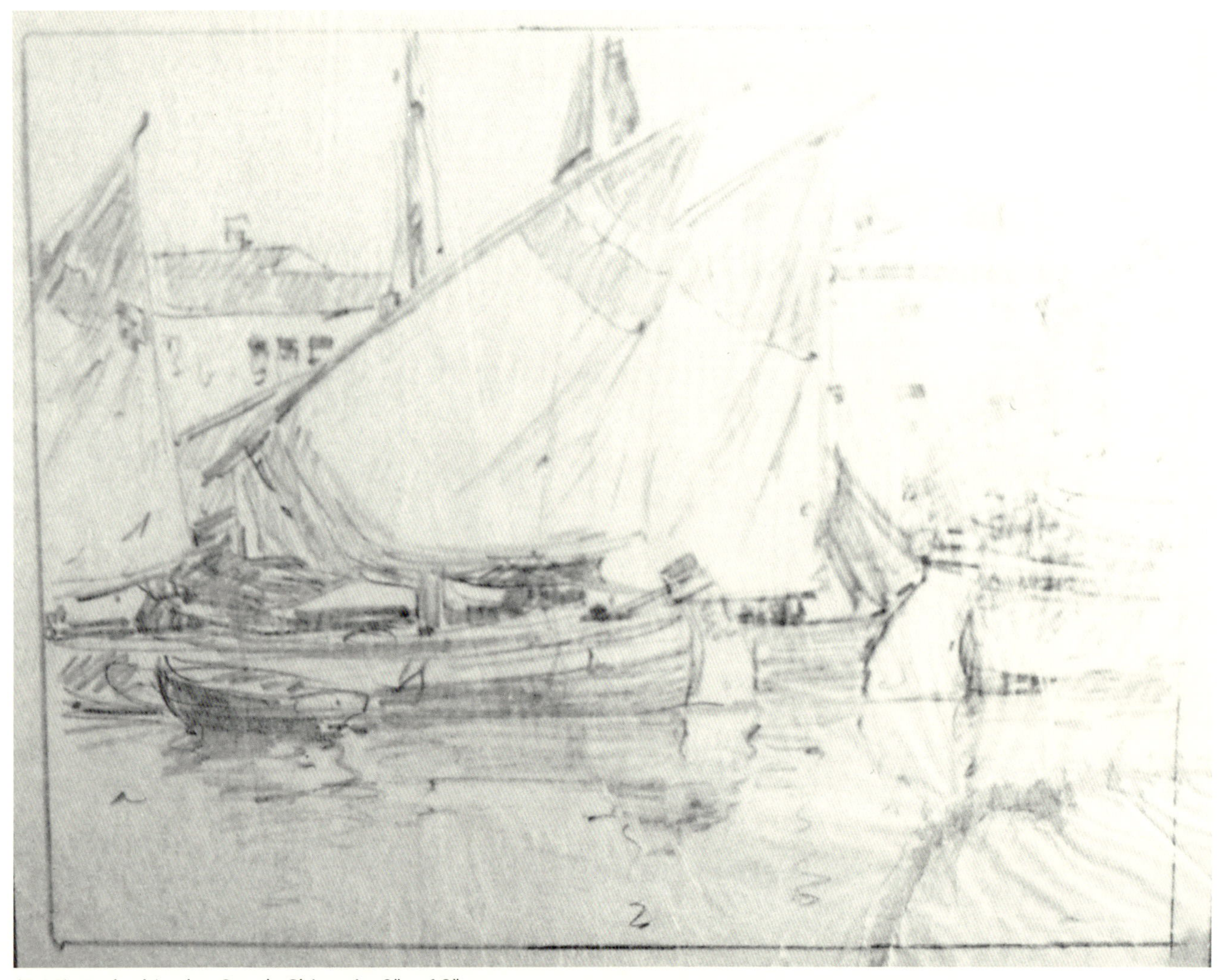

(T-28) Parked in the Canal, Chioggia 9" × 12"

Chapter III

France

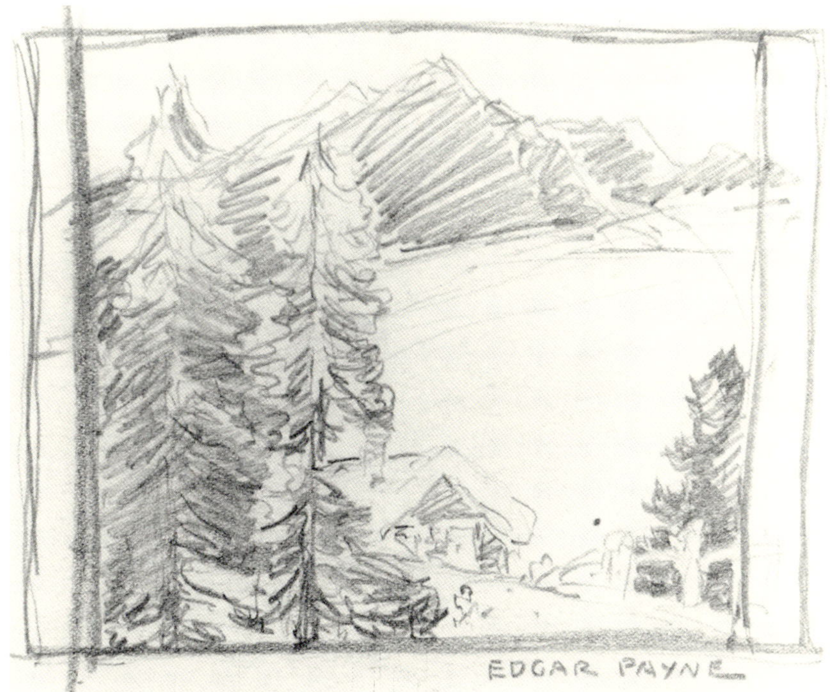

(M-16) Alpine Sketch 4" × 5"

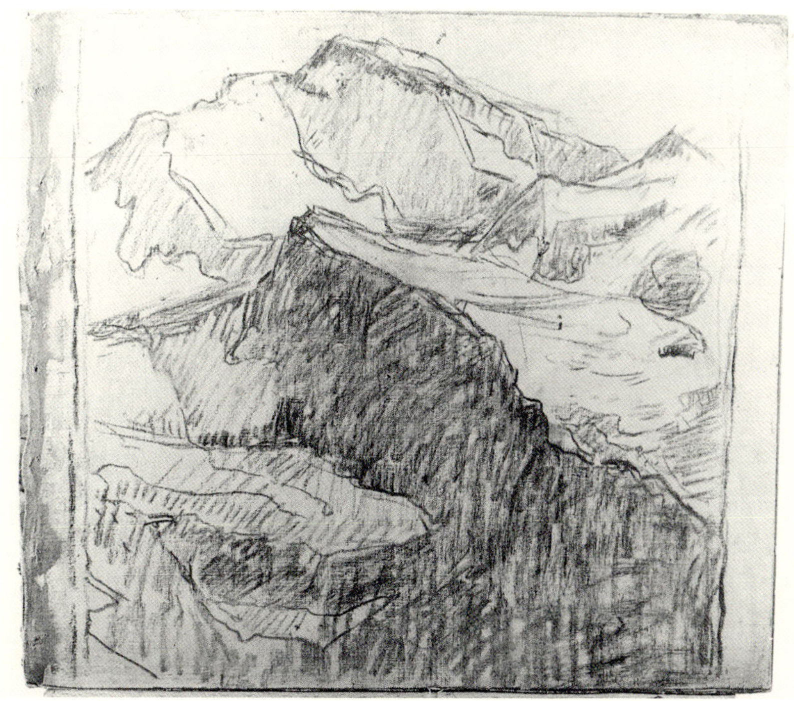

(U-8) Alpine Mountain 13" × 13"

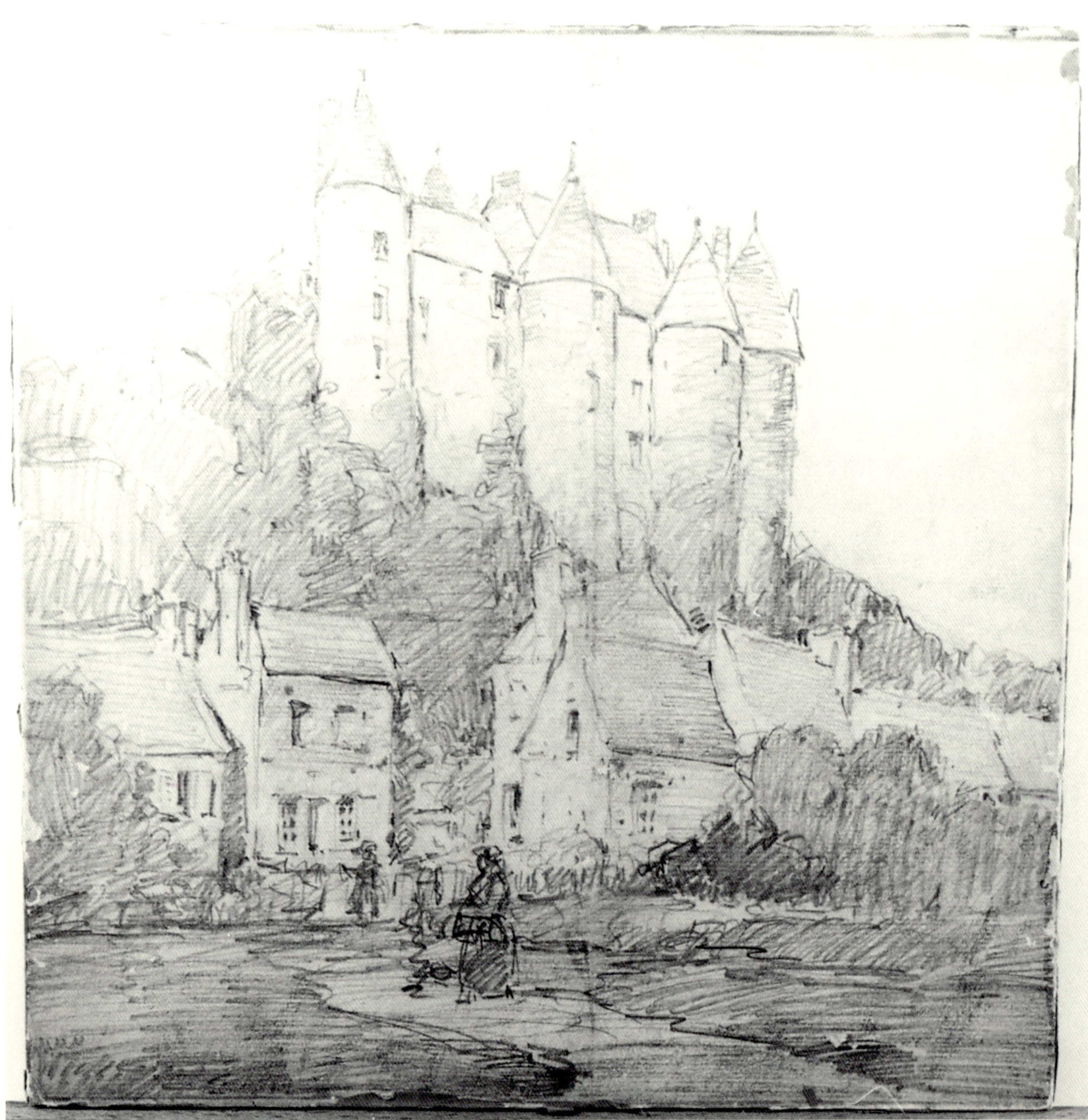

(T-43) Chateau on the Way to Brittany 10" × 10"

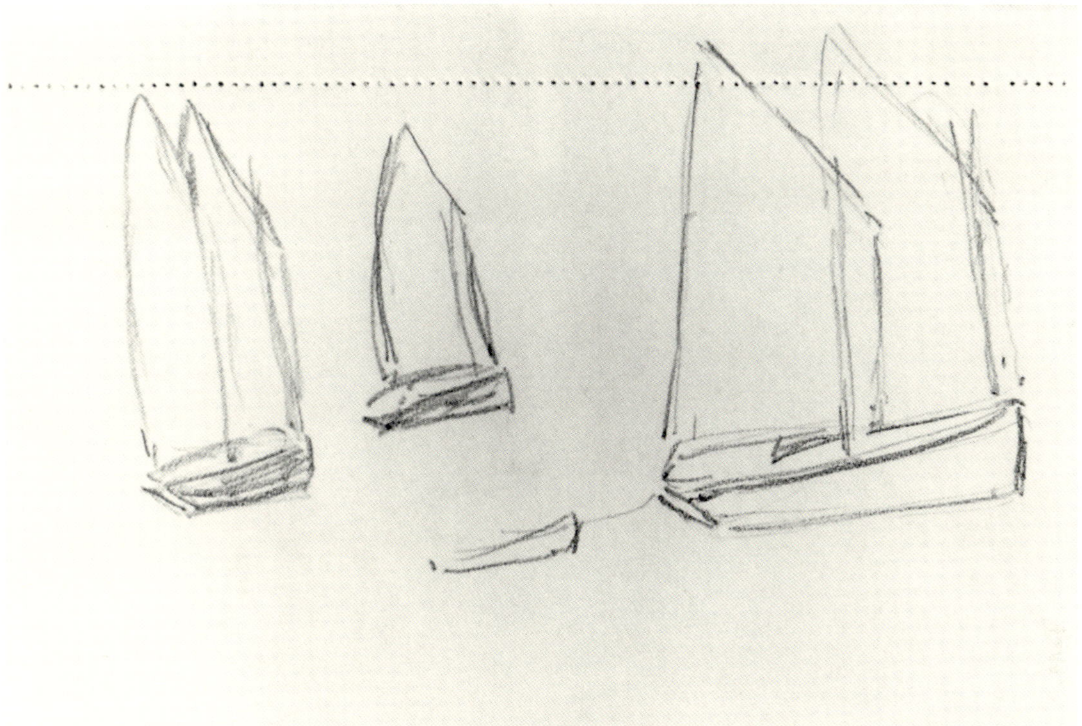

(Z-4) Three Boats, One with Dinghy 3" × 4"

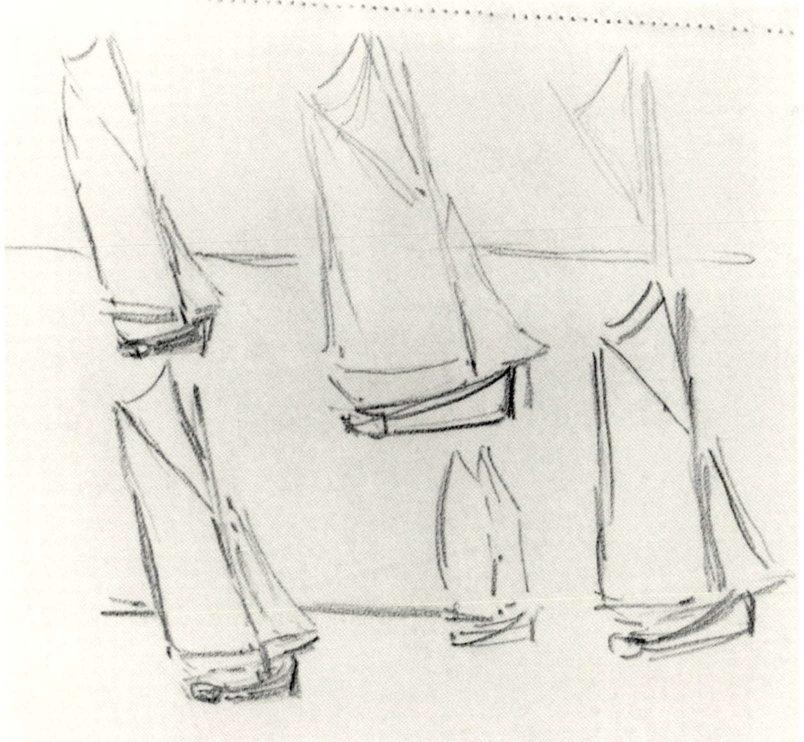

(Z-5) Varieties of Mediterannean Sailing Craft 3" × 4"

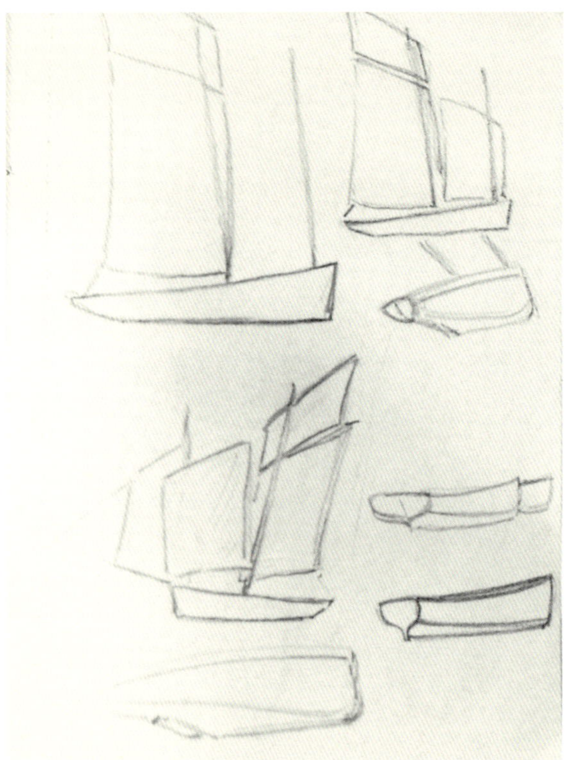
(Z-12) Boat Studies 3" x 4"

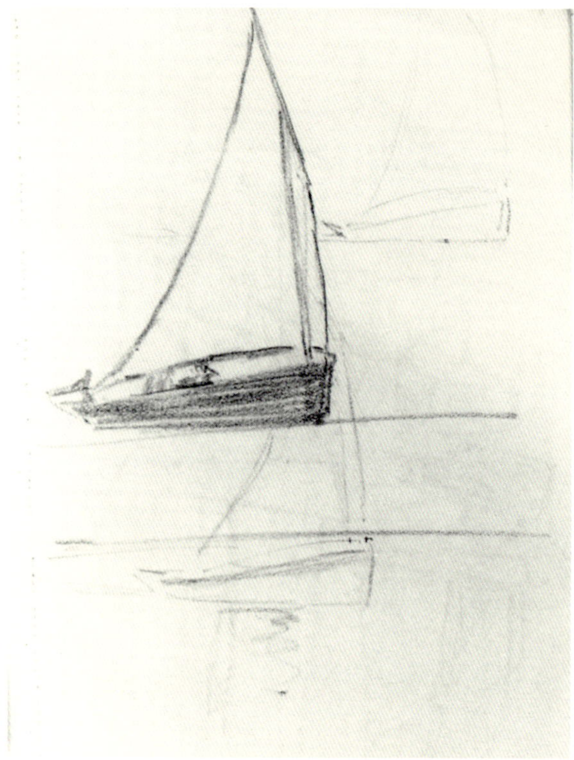
(Z-14) Goëlette, Ancestor of Schooner 3" x 4"

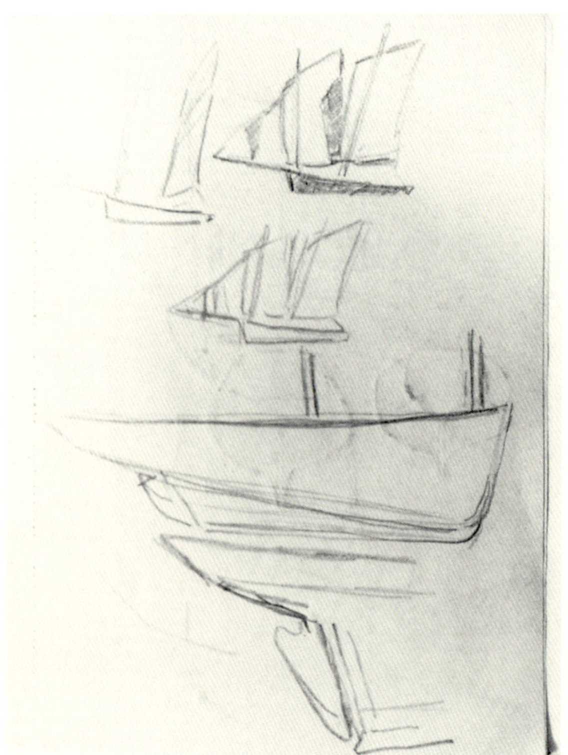
(Z-13) Boats — Small Sketchbook 3" x 4"

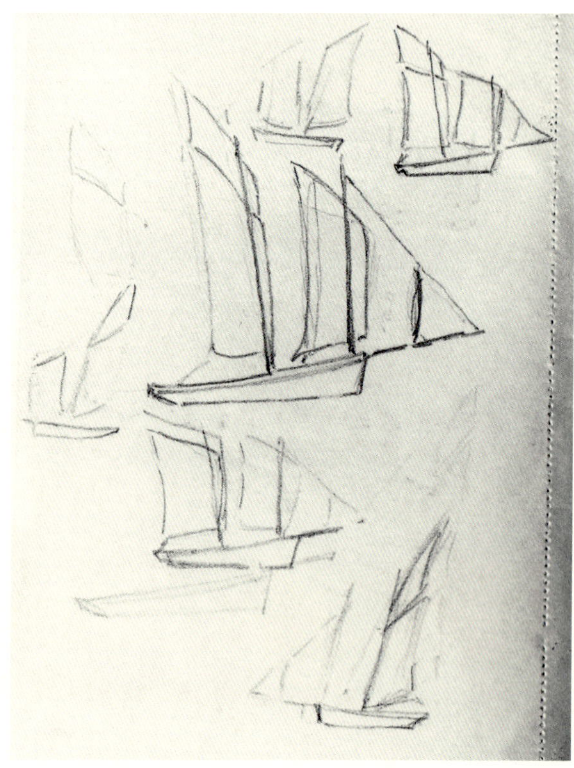
(Z-15) Lugger for Use in Shallower Water 3" x 4"

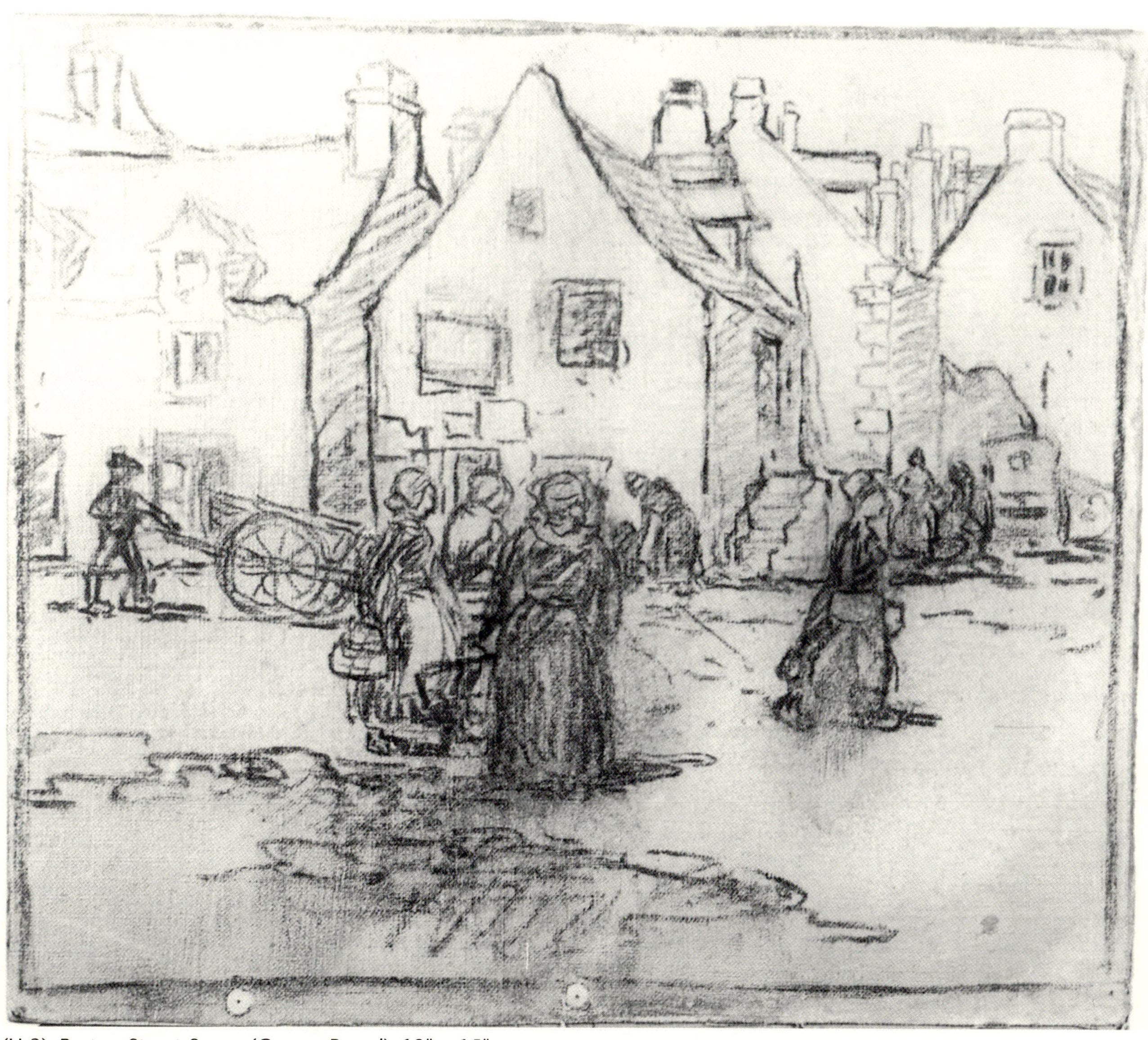

(U-3) Breton Street Scene (Canvas Board) 13" × 15"

Breton Boats

The fishing boats of Brittany were of two kinds. The tuna yawls sailed out into the North Atlantic and trolled for the catch. Breton sardine boats (gaft-rigged sloops) had a single mast with a sail rigged fore and aft, and jib sail. They used blue nets to catch the fish, and often hung these nets to dry when in the harbor.

The tides in Brittany make such an enormous difference that the harbors are often completely without water. The sardine boats had an upright board on each side of the hull to hold the vessel upright in the mud. Once when friends from Chicago made their first trip abroad, they arrived on Concaeneau at night, and got up early to enjoy the harbor they had heard so much about, and were tremendously shocked to find the harbor a sea of mud between the stone docks. Lake Michigan never did that!

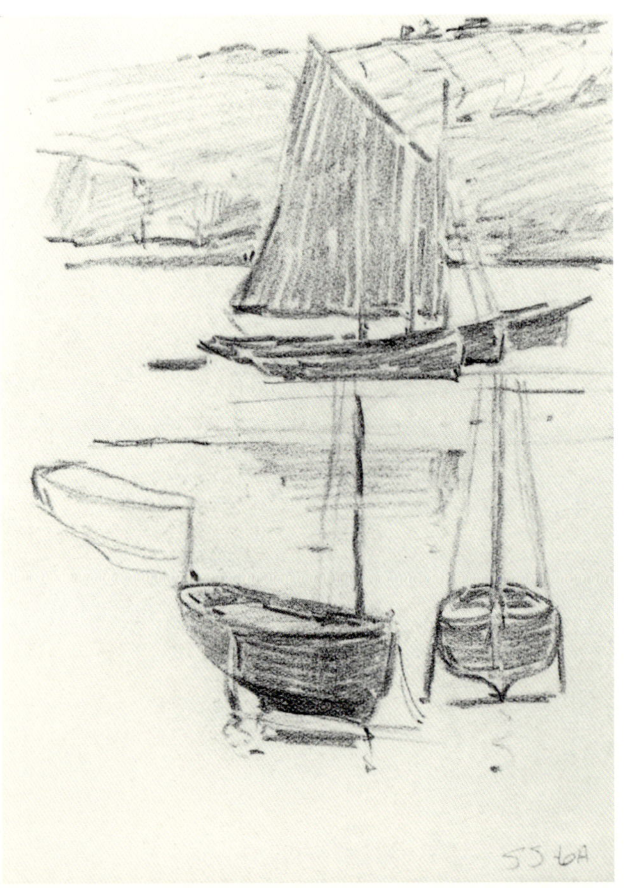

(SS-6a) Breton Sloops at High and Low Tides 6" × 5"

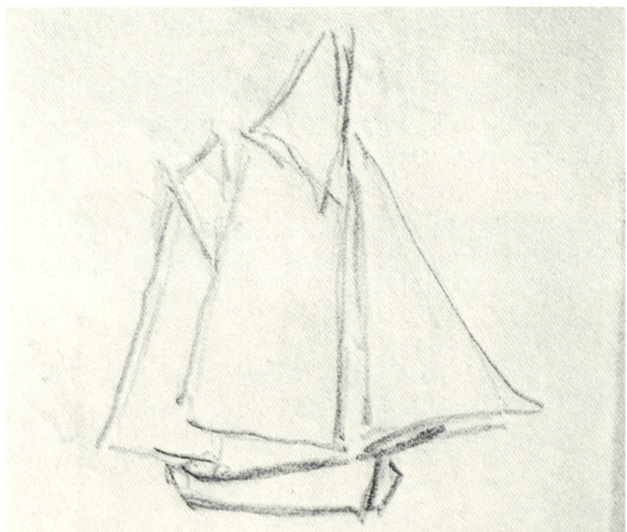

(Z-3) Tuna Yawl 3" × 3"

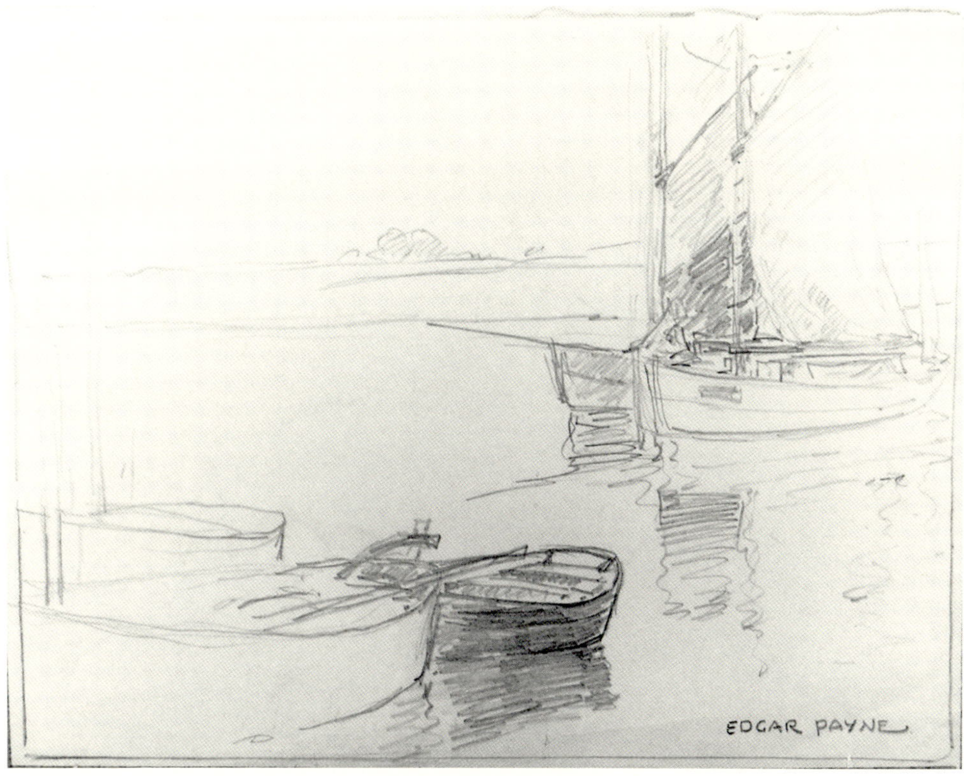

(S-17) Boats in Harbor, Douarnenez 8" × 11"

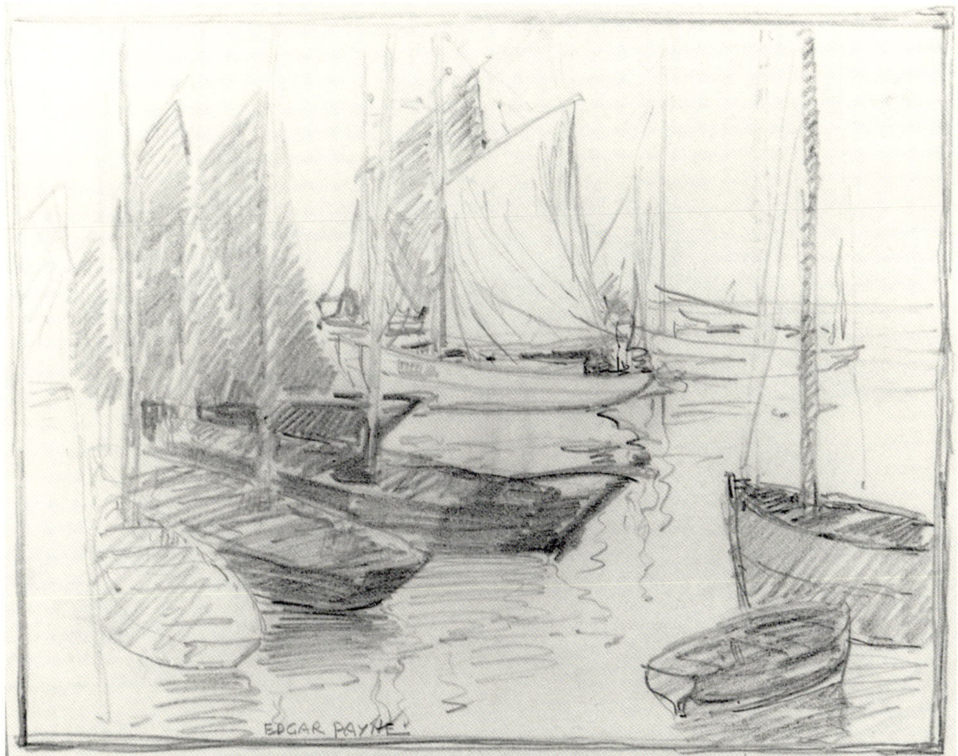

(M-7) Sardine Sloops, Brittany 8" × 11"

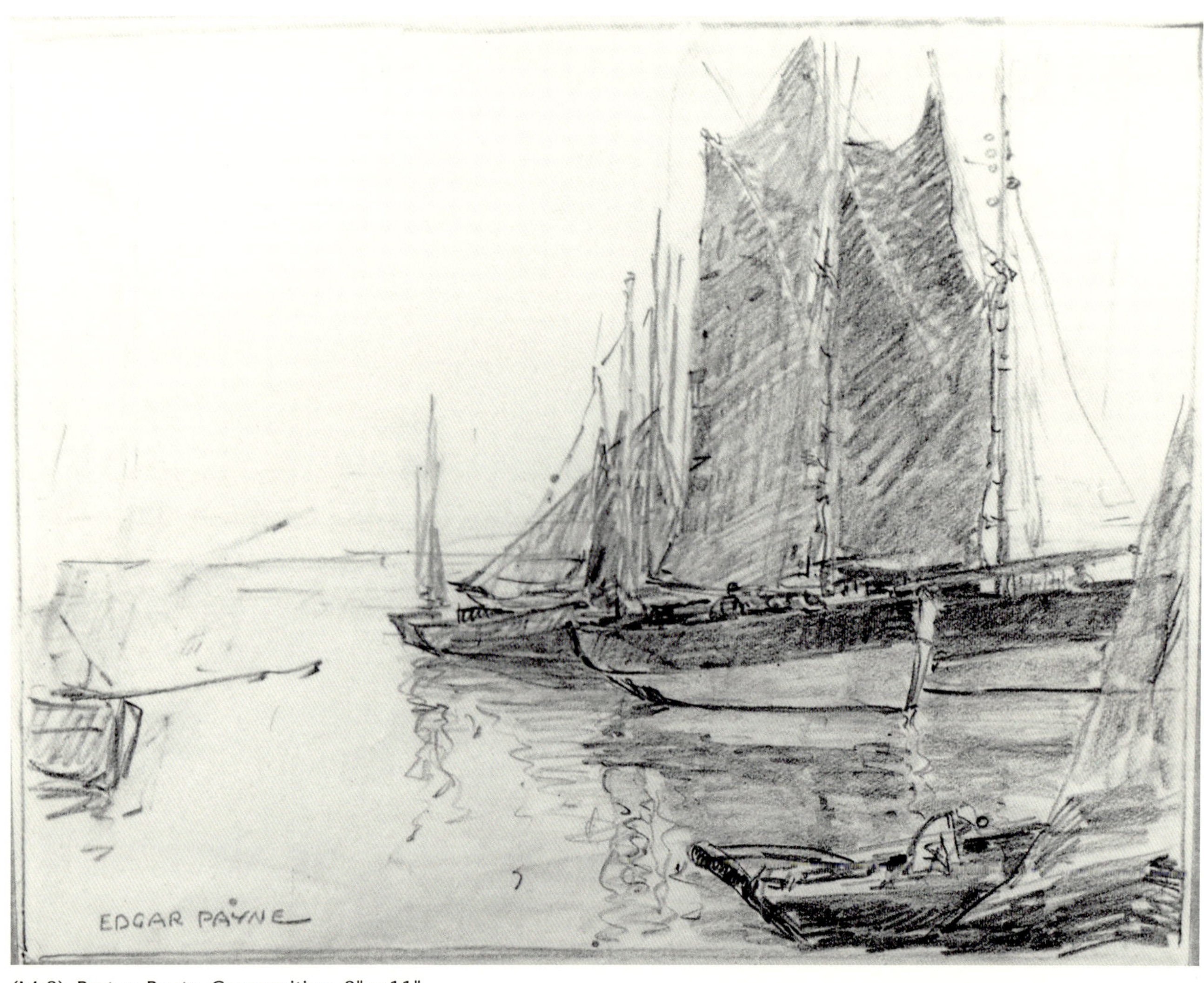

(M-8) Breton Boats, Composition 8" × 11"

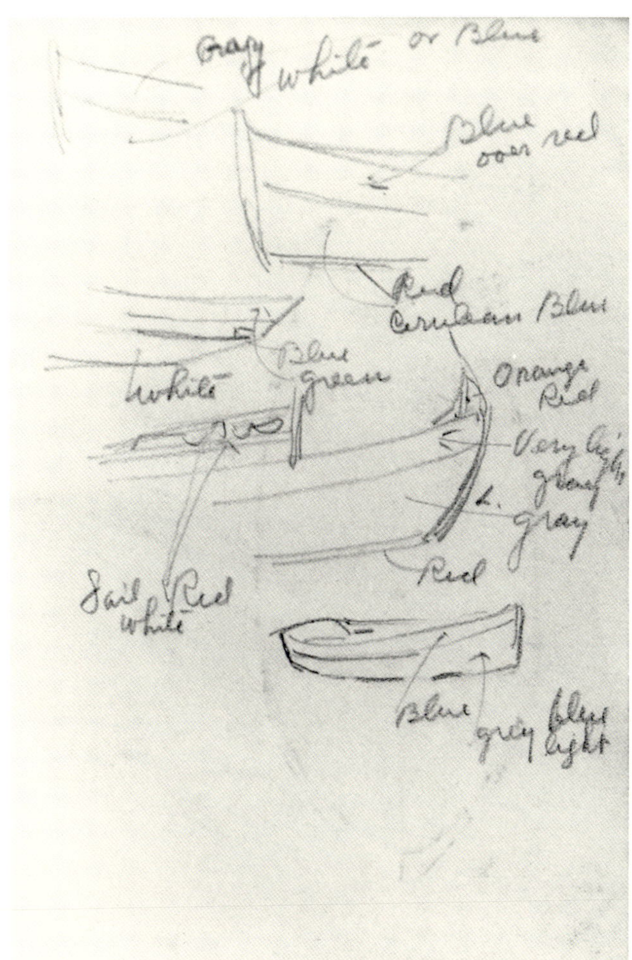

(SS-2a) Color Notes on Breton Boats 6" × 5"

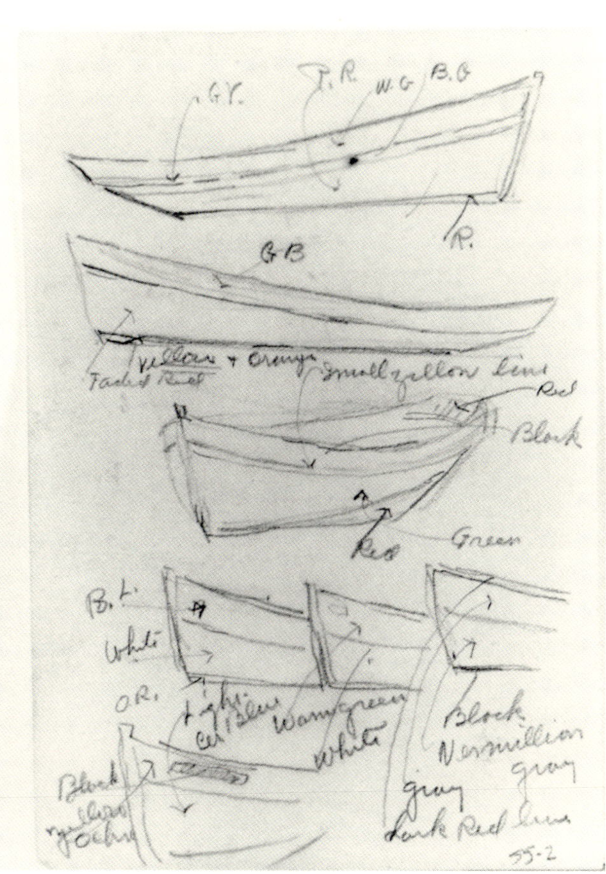

(SS-2) More Color Notes 6" × 5"

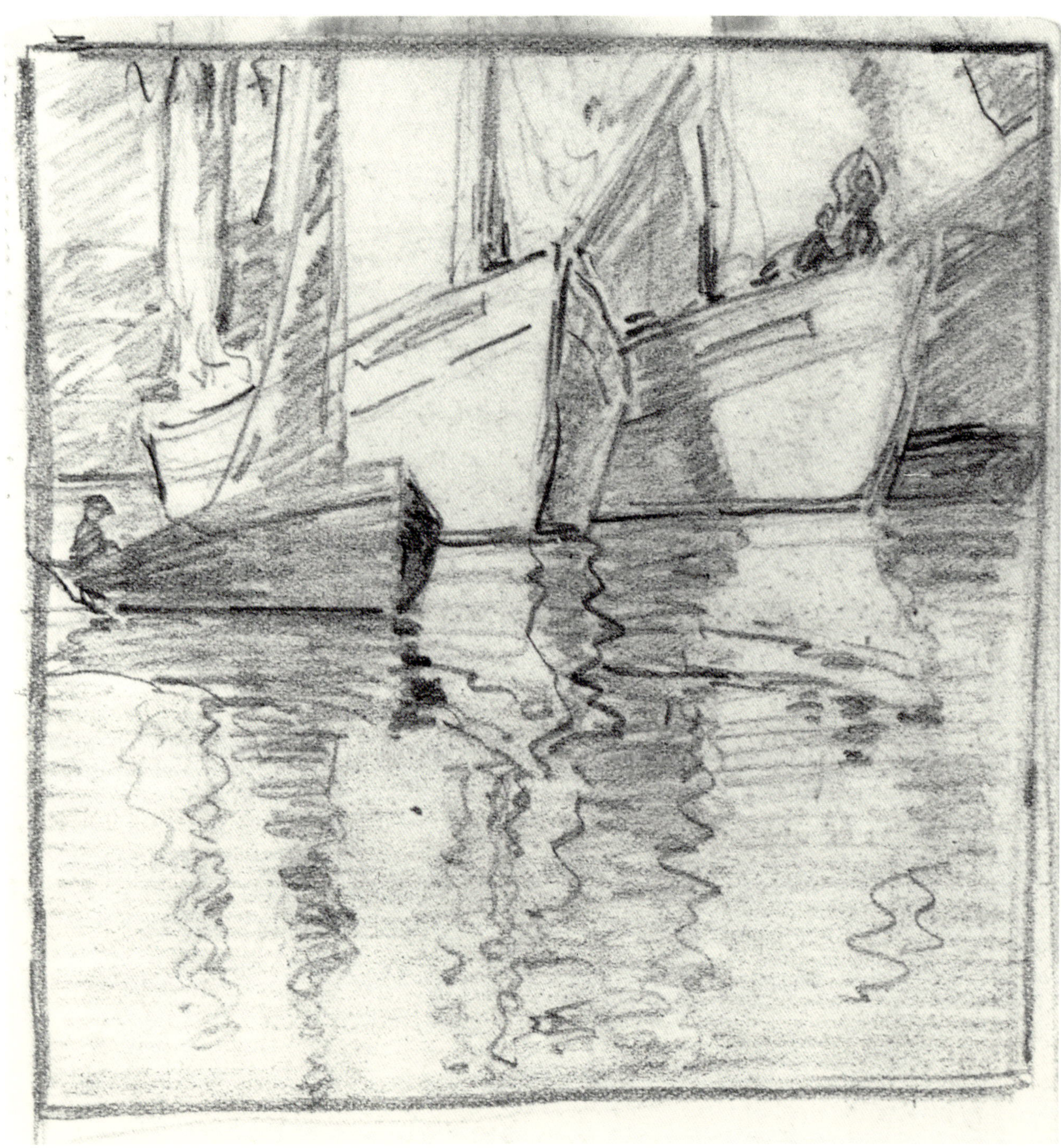

(M-30) Breton Tuna Boats, Showing Prows 4½" × 3½"

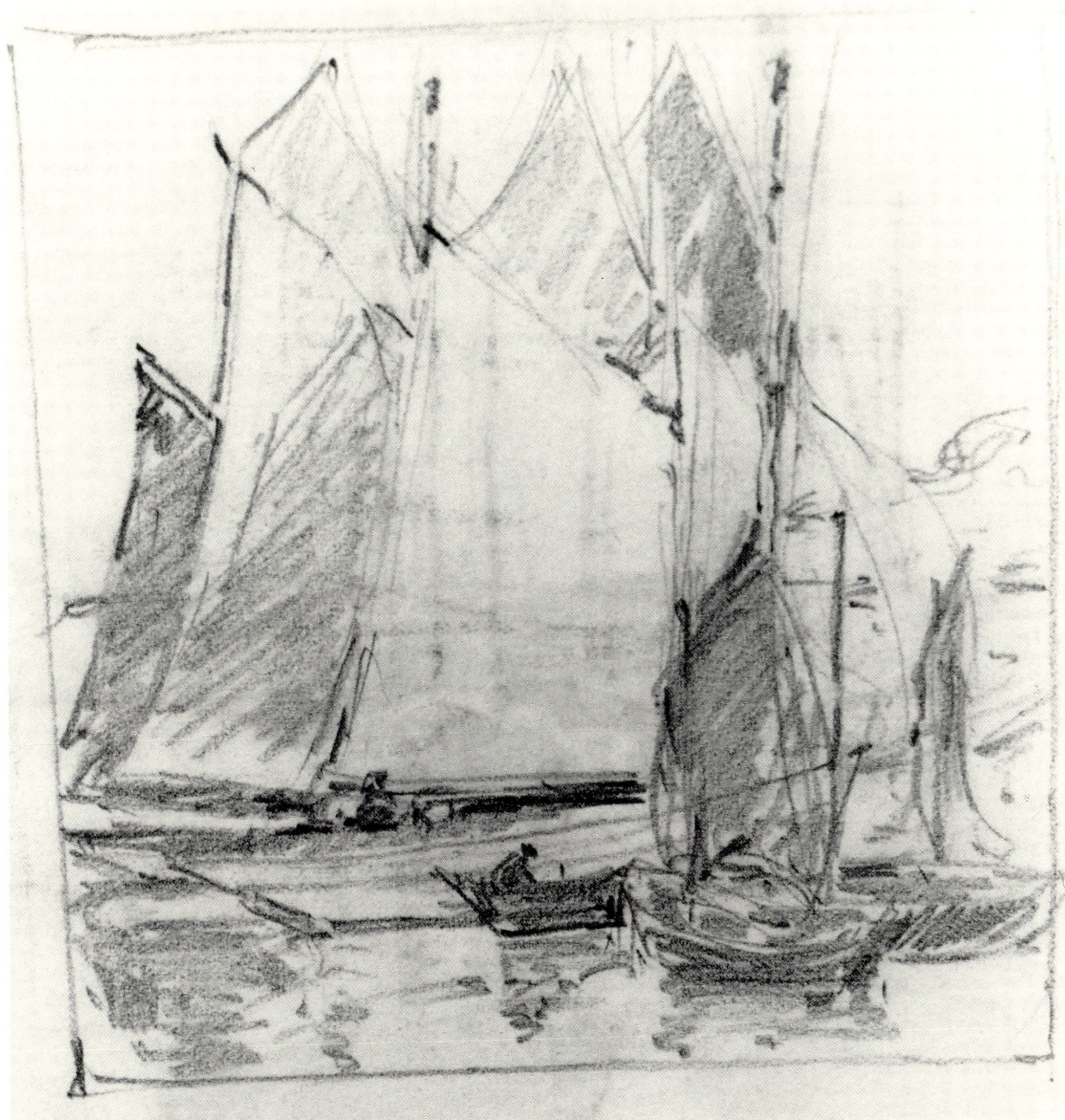

(M-23a) Tuna Yawls and Sardine Boats 4" × 4"

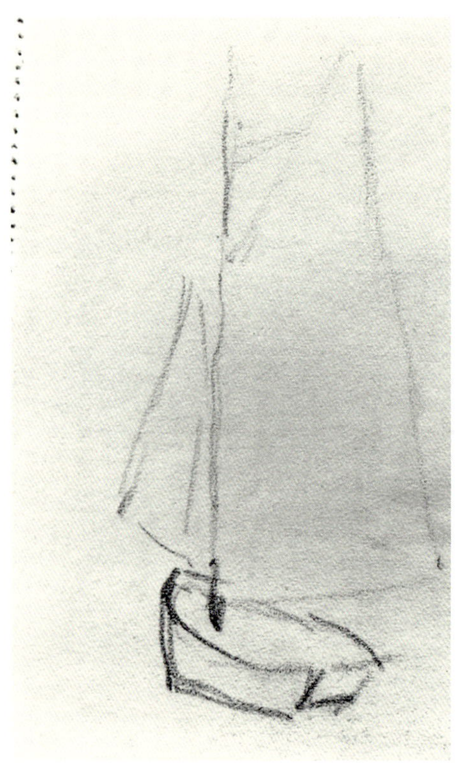

(Z-6) Sloop 3" × 2"

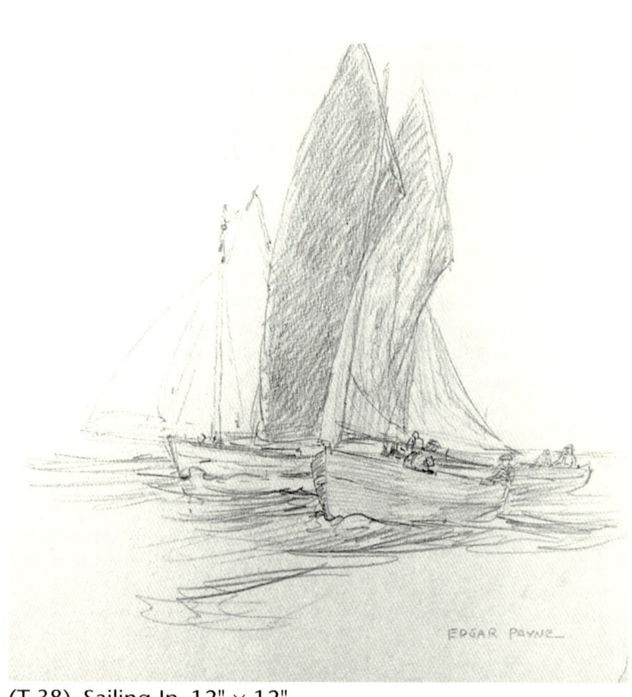

(T-38) Sailing In 12" × 12"

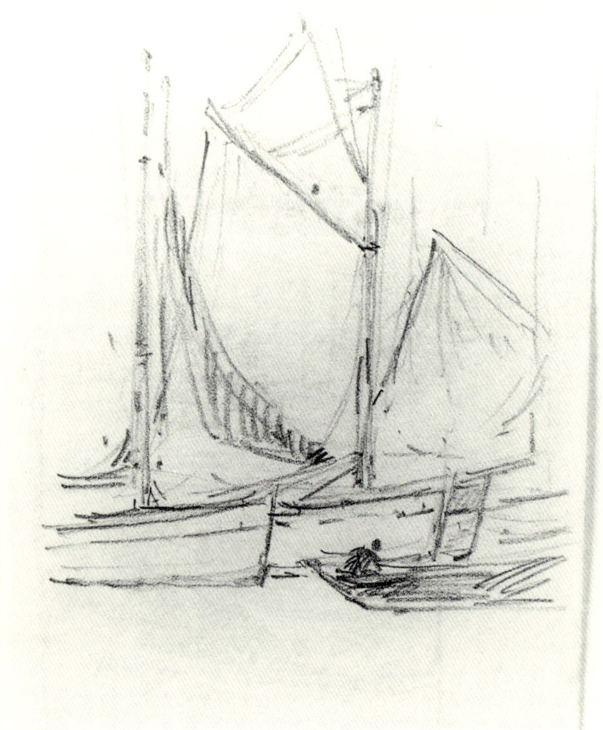

(M-31) In the Harbor 5" × 4"

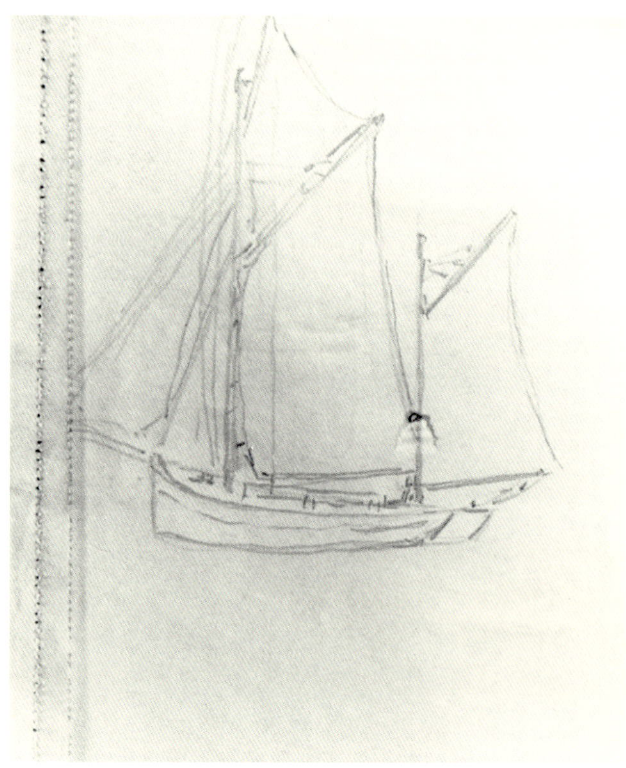

(SS-1) Tuna Boat Showing Sails, Brittany 6" × 5"

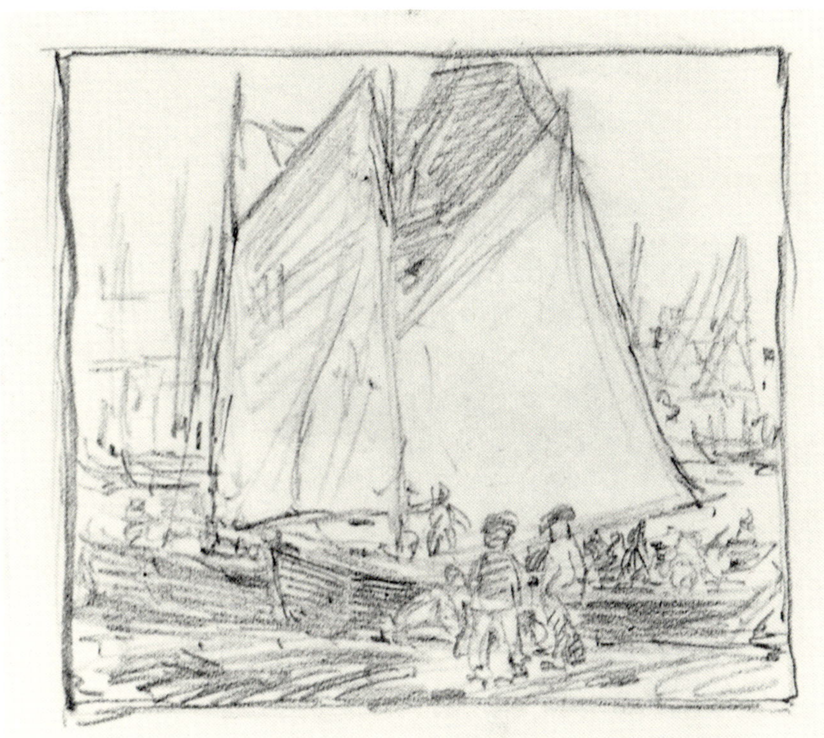

(SS-4a) Breton Boats with Figures 6" × 5"

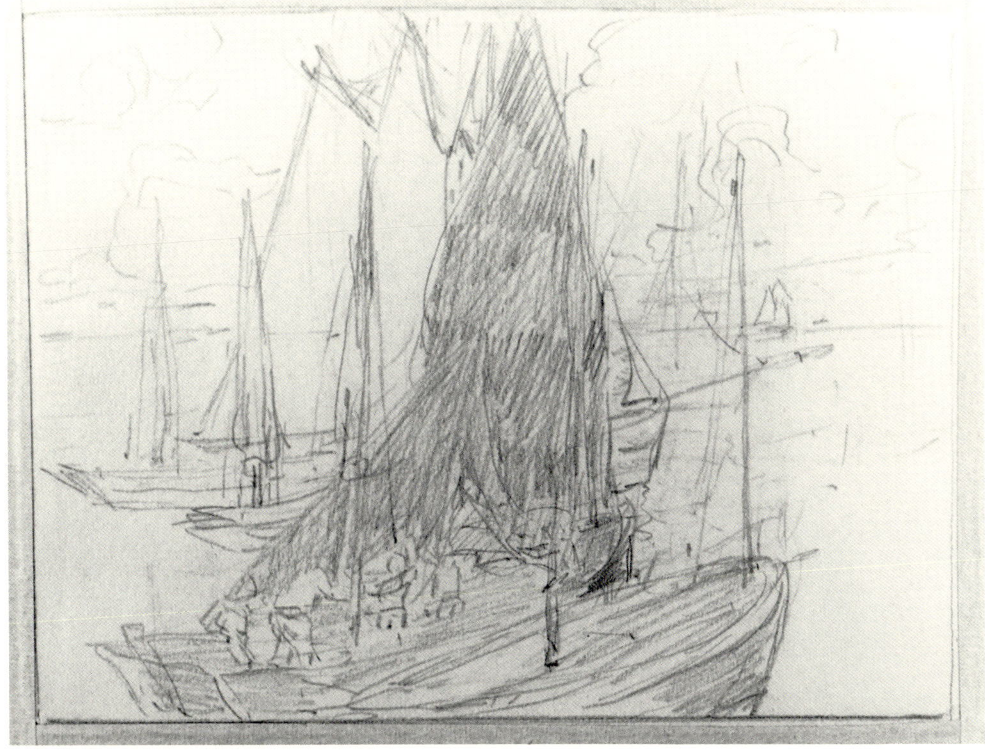

(S-26) Drying Nets, Brittany 7" × 9"

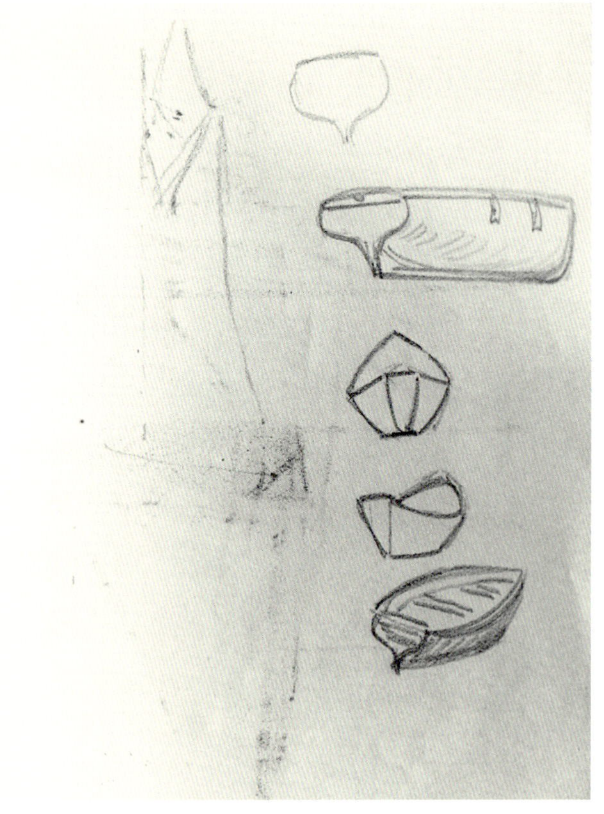

(Z-7a) 3" × 4"

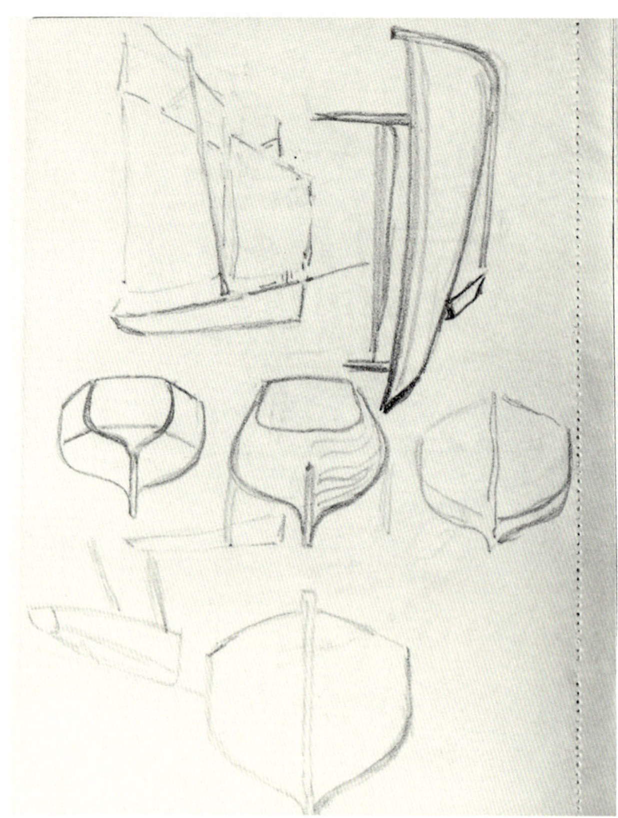

(Z-7c) 3" × 4"

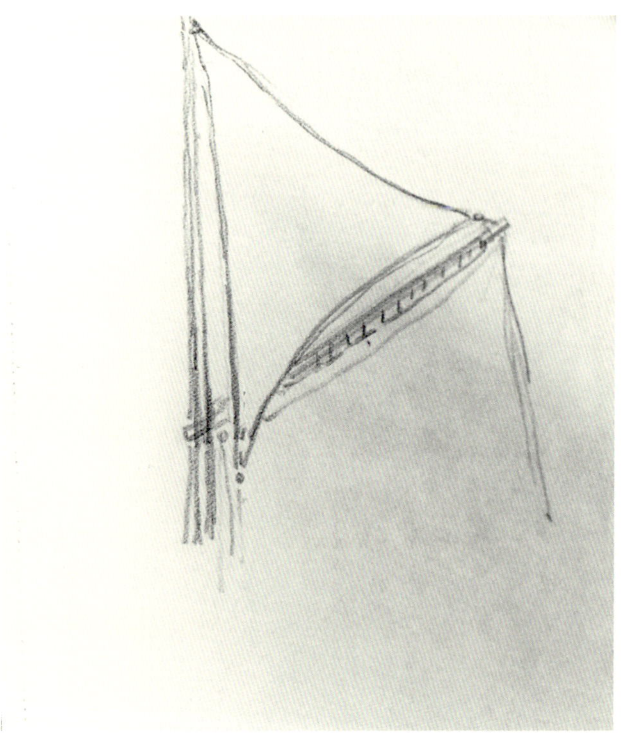

(Z-7b) Notes from a Small Sketchbook 3" × 4"

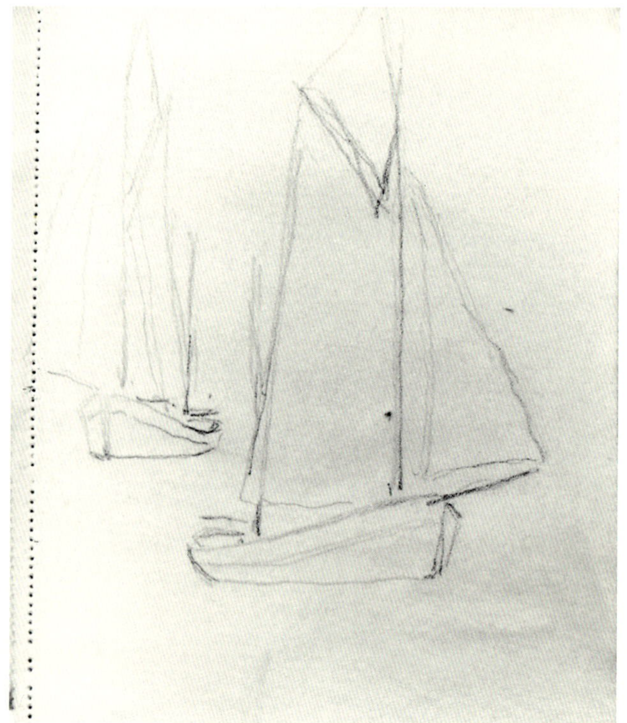

(Z-7d) 3" × 4"

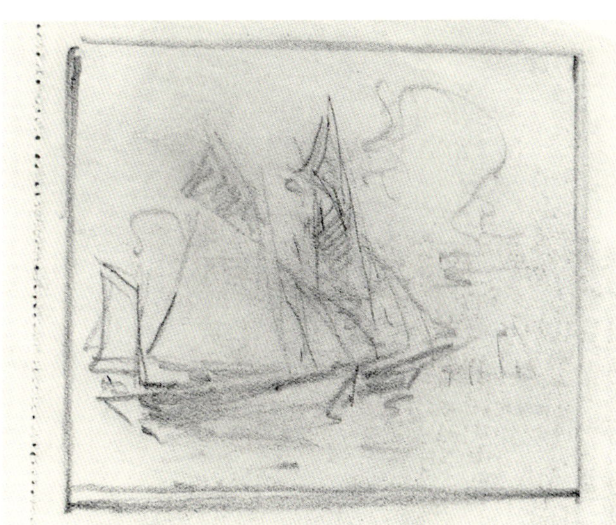

(SS-3) Tuna Yawls Outbound 6" × 5"

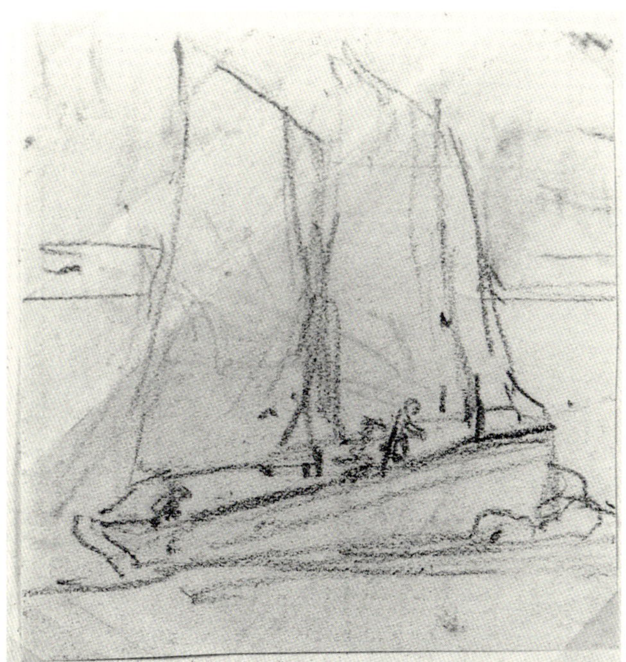

(M-35) Leaving Port 3" × 3"

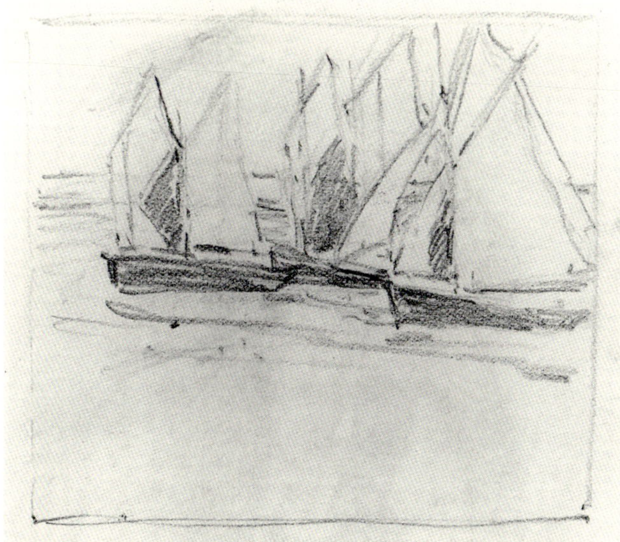

(SS-9) Sardine Boats 6" × 5"

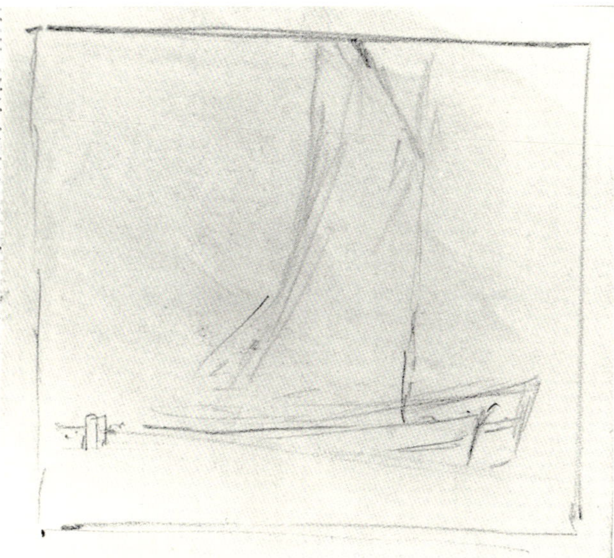

(W-3) Note on Sail Drape 3" × 4"

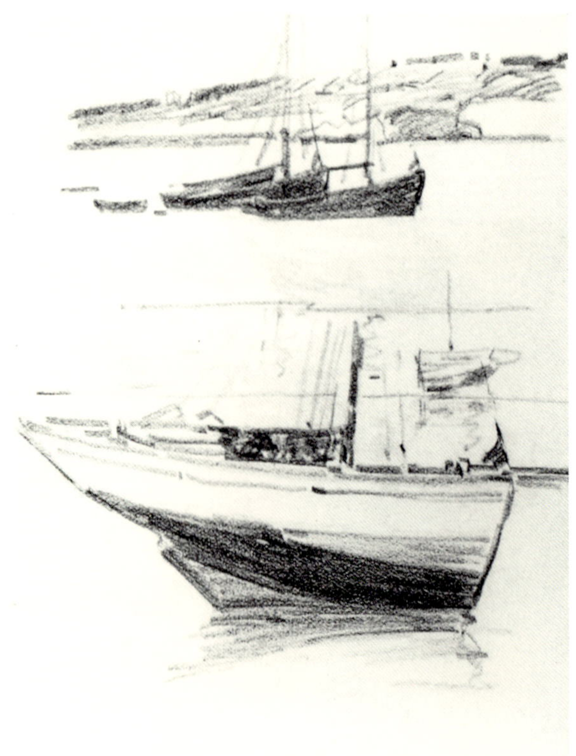

(SS-6) Hull 6" × 5"

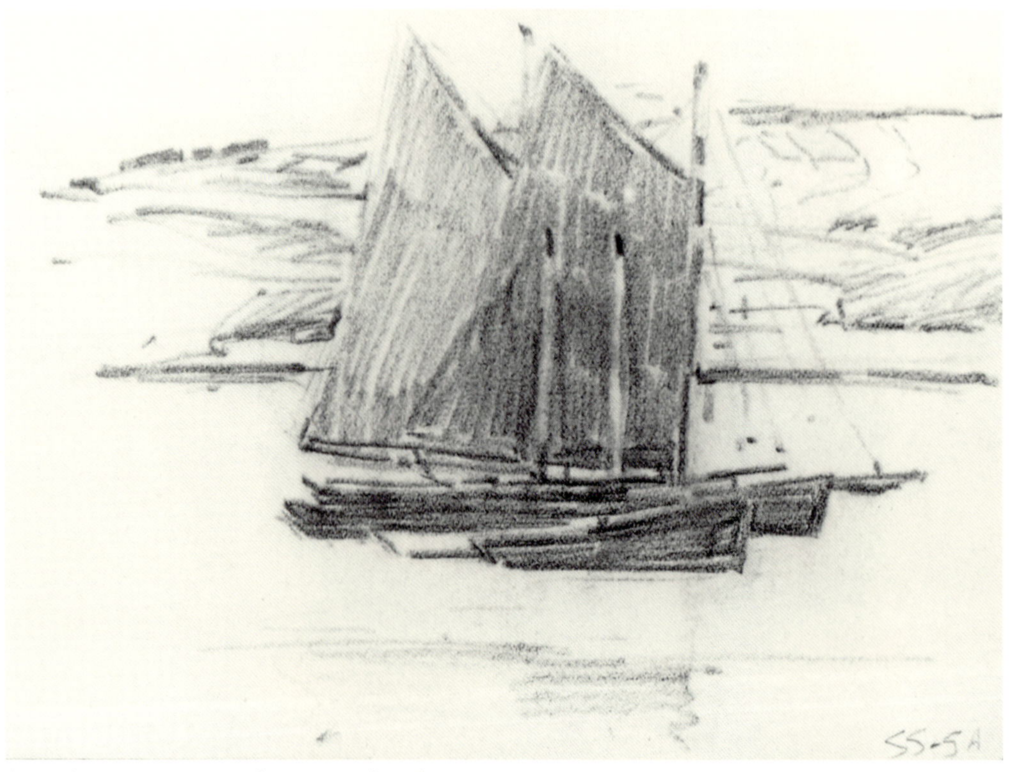

(SS-5a) Douarnenez Harbor Area 5" × 6"

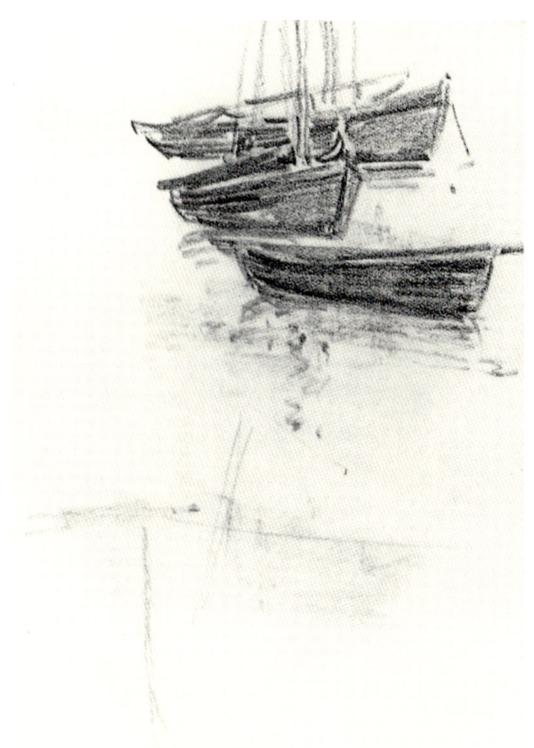

(SS-7a) Study of Hulls 6" × 5"

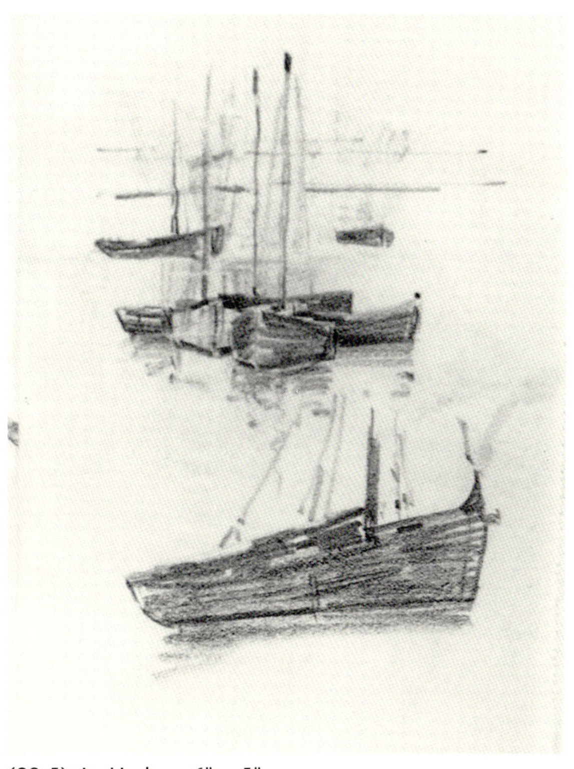

(SS-5) In Harbor 6" × 5"

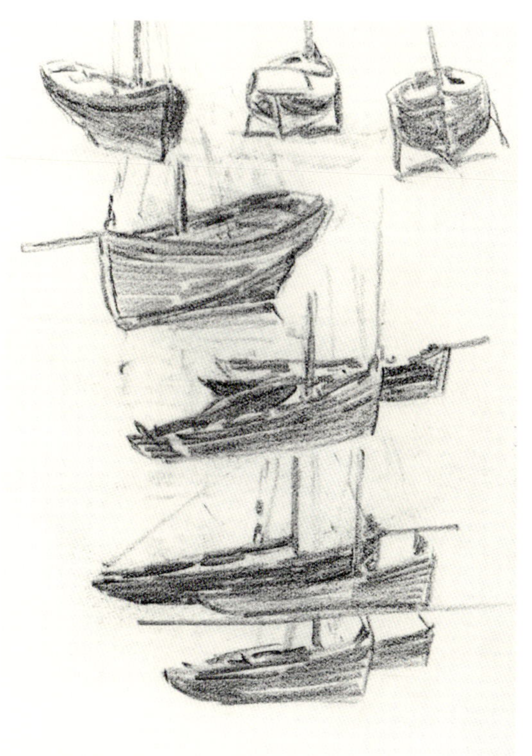

(SS-7) Sardine Boats in Harbor 6" × 5"

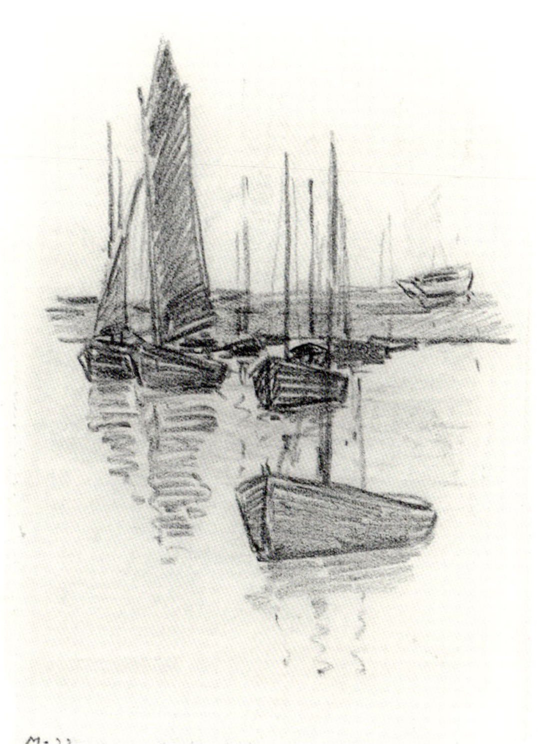

(M-23) Sloops in Quiet Water 6" × 5"

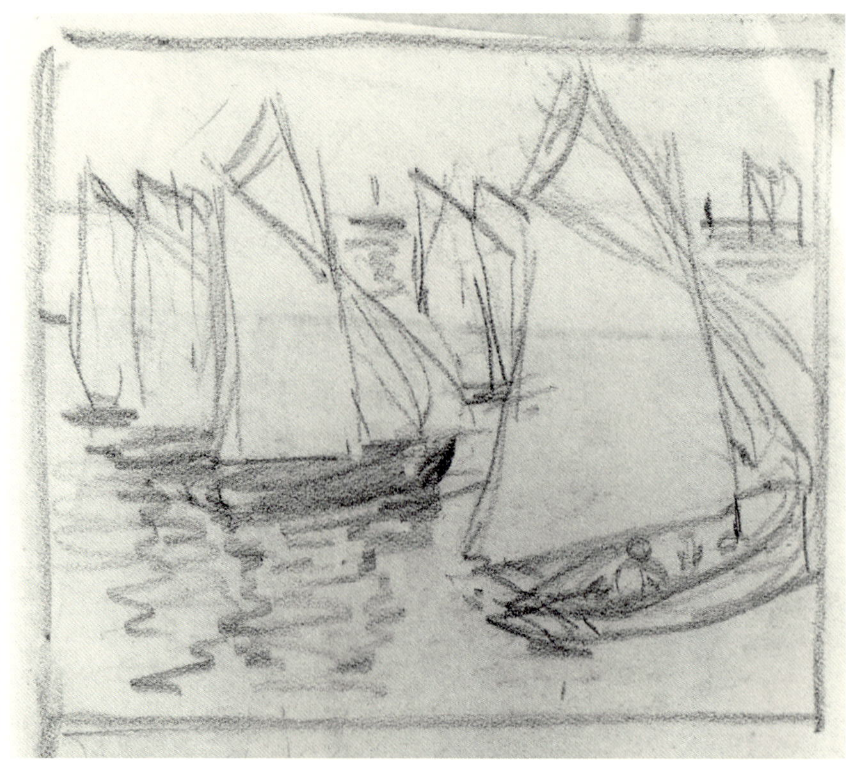

(M-30b) Back of M-30 Outbound 4" × 3"

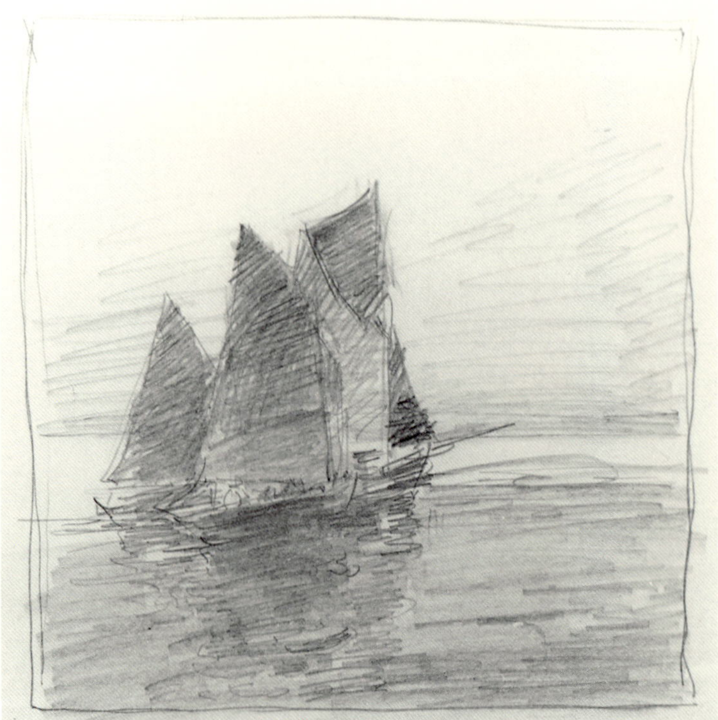

(S-19) Breton Boats in Shadow 8" × 8"

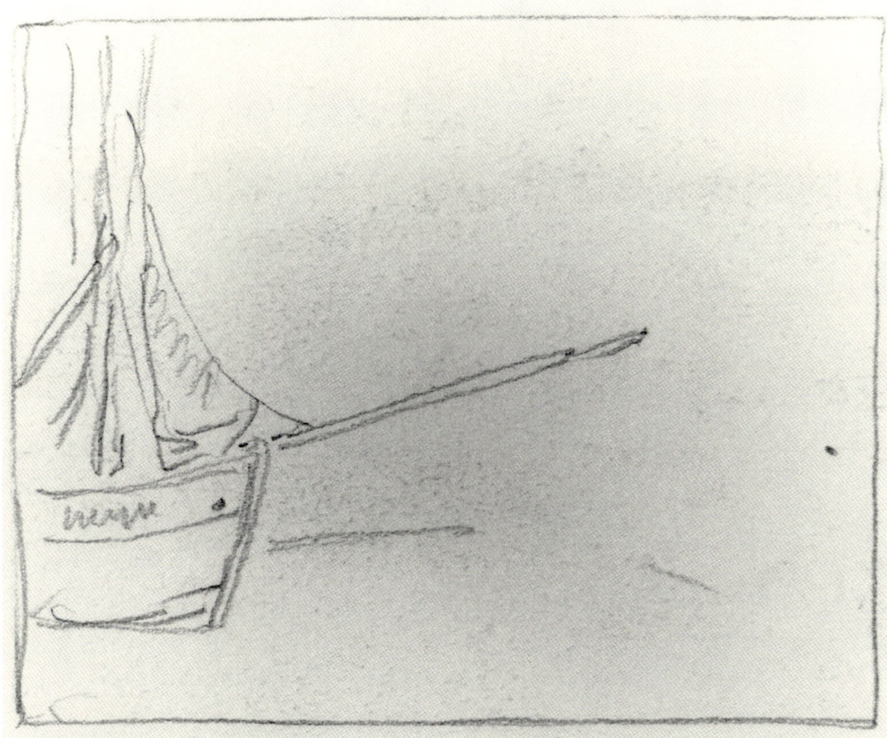

(S-43b) Back of S-43 Quick Sketch of Prow 8" × 8"

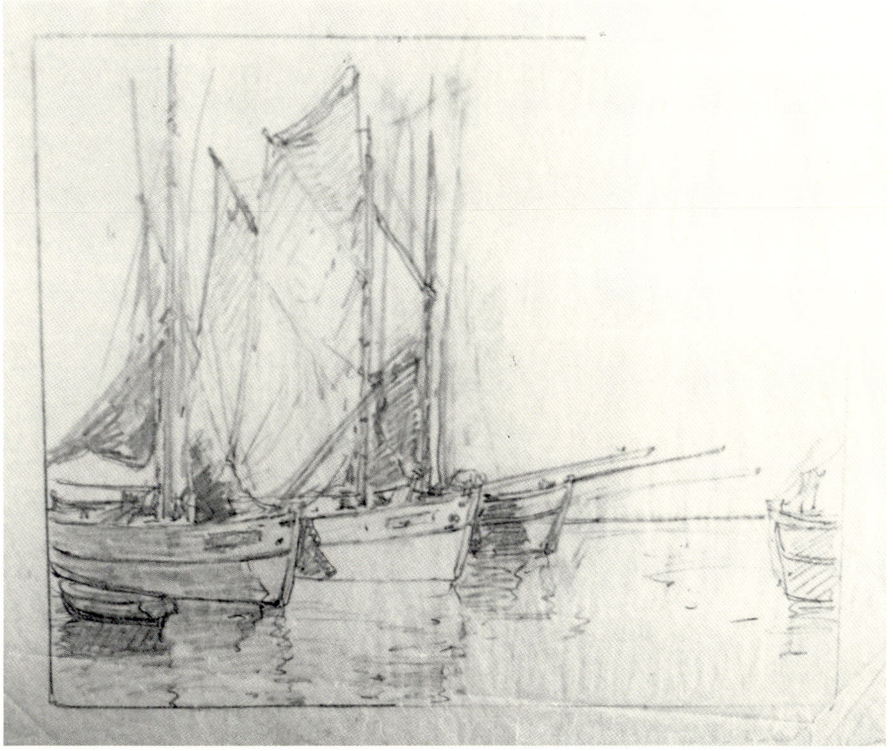

(T-20) Breton Tuna Boats 12" × 14"

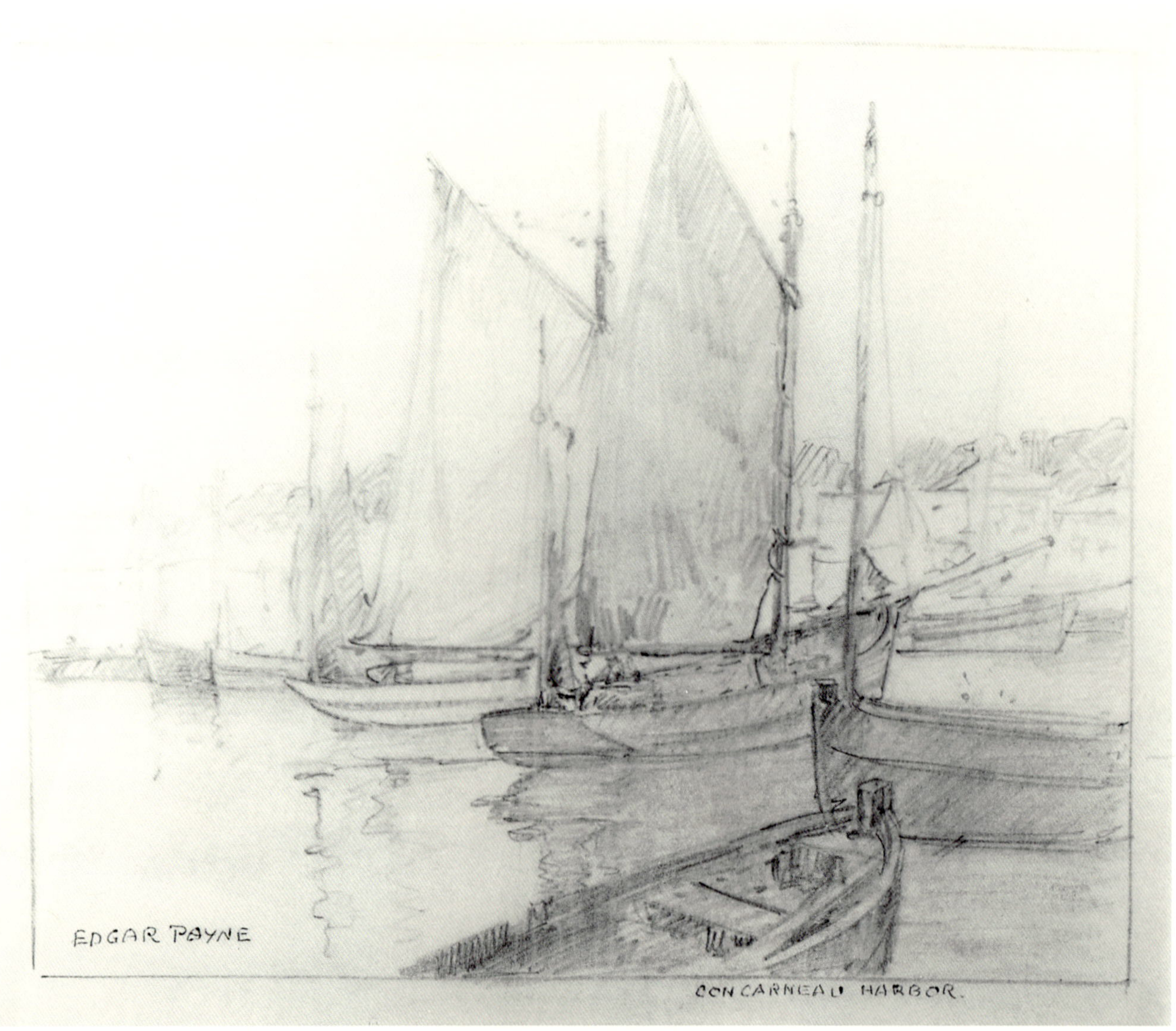

(T-26) Concarneau Harbor 10" × 12"

In the winter of 1925–26, he used the details he had learned to make a model of a Breton Tuna Yawl. Mother made the sails. This was long before one could buy plastic model parts, and the pulleys were made with a drill by a dentist friend, George Brandriff. Brandriff was interested in art, a "Sunday painter" and while Dad did not formally teach at that time, he was willing to take a talented individual with him on sketching excursions and "give a few pointers." George Brandriff later quit dentistry and became a fulltime artist. His works are still well-known today.

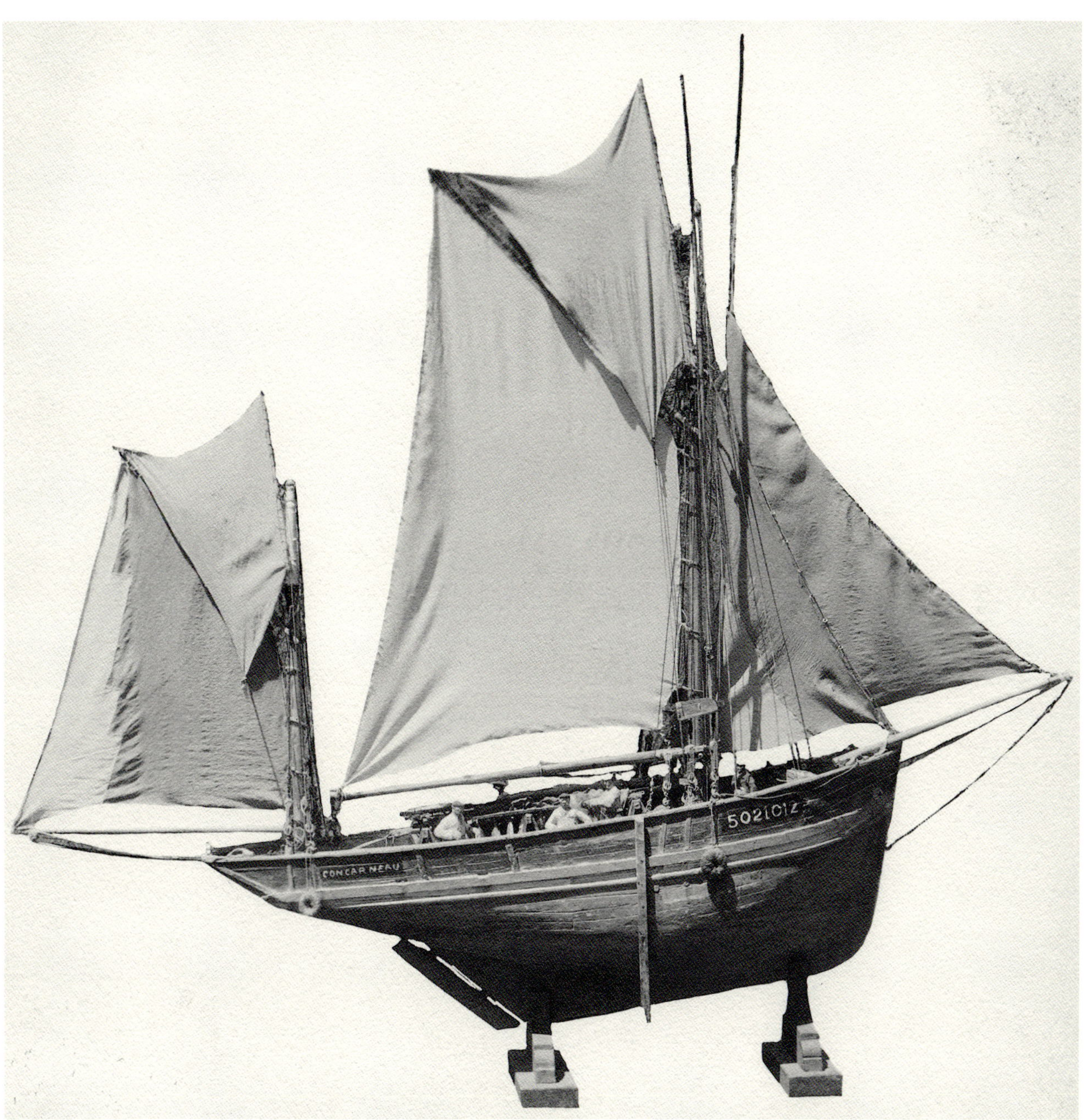

Photograph of Payne's Model of Breton Tuna Boat

While landscapes and seascapes were my father's main interest, he often included figures, and sometimes for the sake of the composition. So we find in the field notes drawings of Breton fishermen (farmer's clothes were different) and the women in the harbor towns. In each town in Brittany at that time, women still wore the traditional clothes and the coif on their heads that were different for each area. We spent most of the time in Brittany in Concarneau, but also visited Douarnenez. Wooden shoes — *sabots* — were worn by all.

Dad's sketches are mostly of fishermen, and you can see what they wore in the follwing sketches. The color of the main garments were, in Concarneau, mostly what is still called "Breton red," often very patched. The caps were large navy berets. In France the edge of the beret was always tucked under, not worn outside as sometimes seen in this country, and in Brittany the front was pulled forward to shade the eyes.

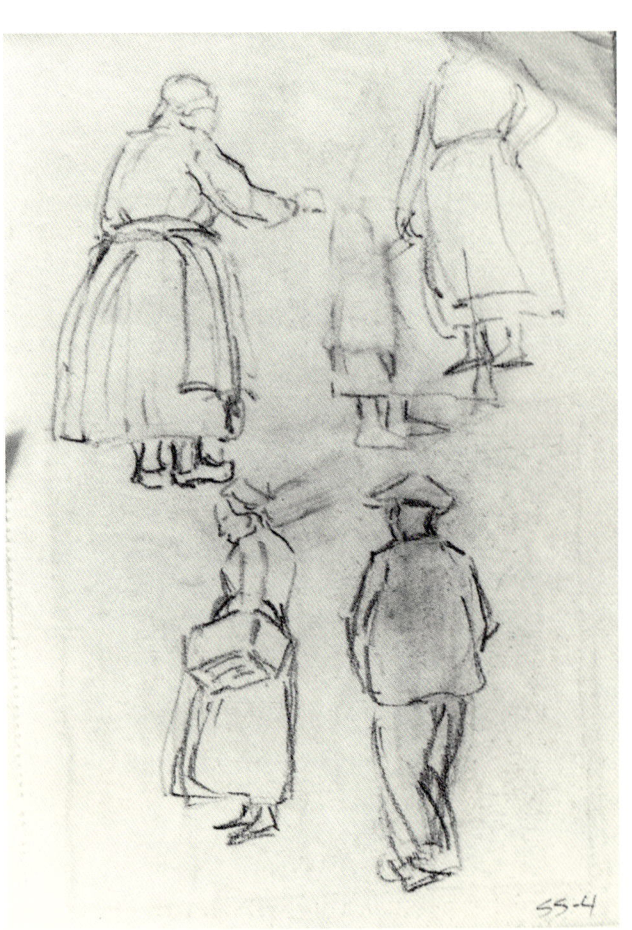

(SS-4) Breton Women and Fishermen 6" × 5"

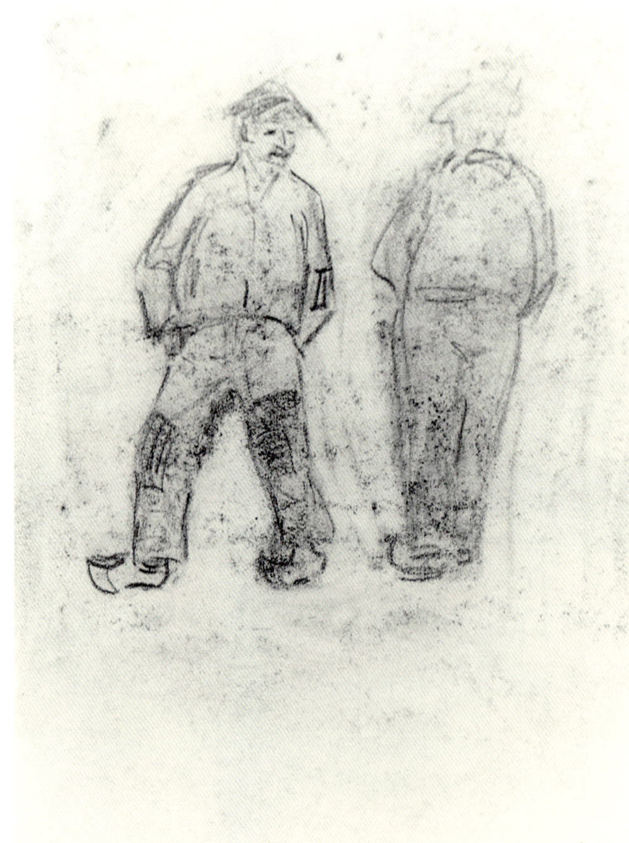

(SS-9a) Breton Sailors in Sabots (Wooden Shoes) 6" × 5"

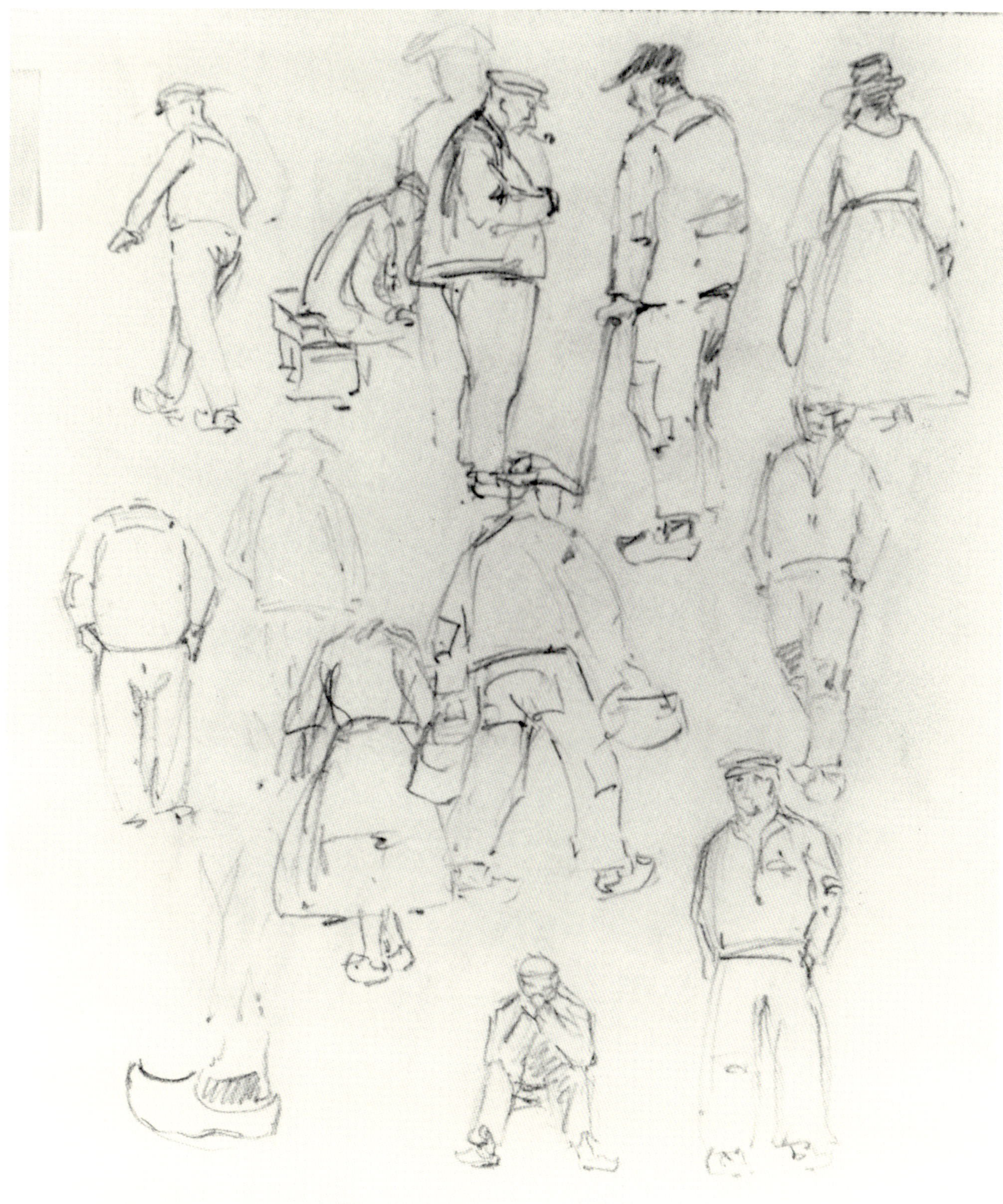

(SL-1) Sketches of Figures 10" × 8"

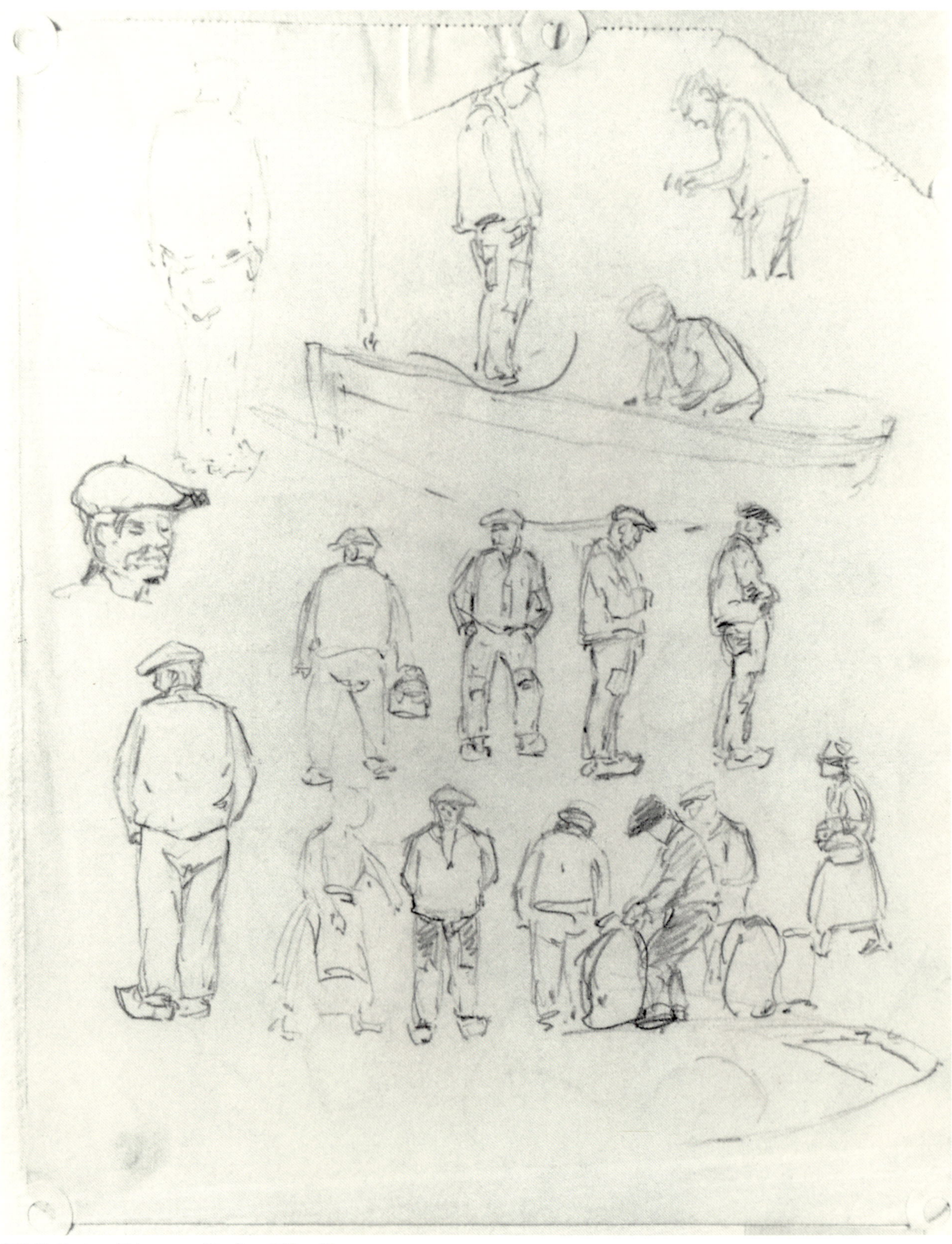

(T-12) Breton Fishermen Studies 10" × 8"

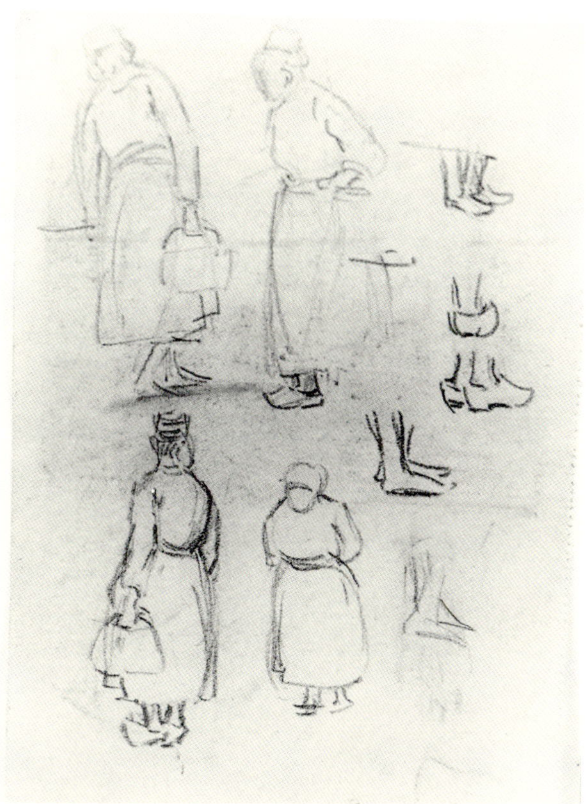

(SS-8a) Sketches of Breton Women 6" × 5"

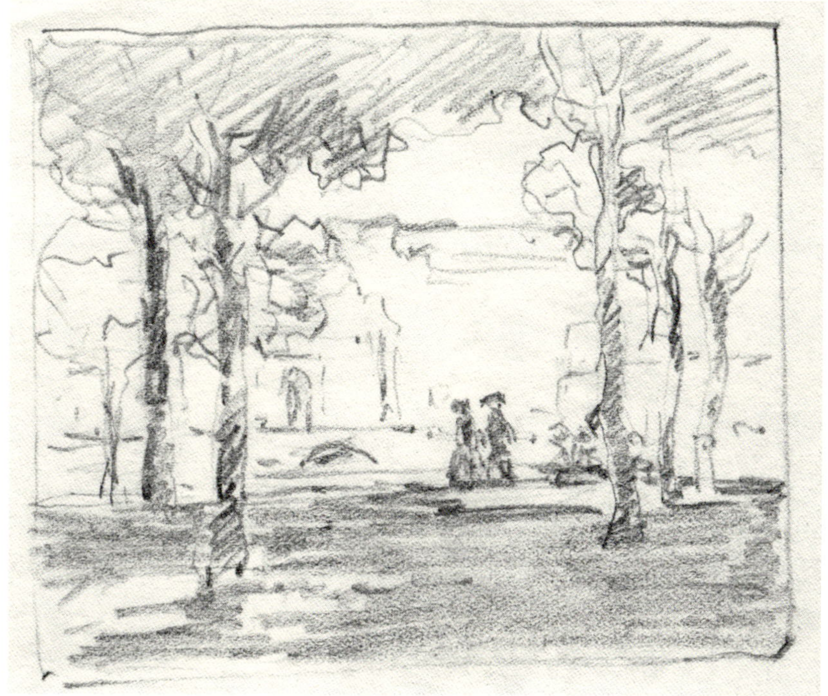

(SS-8) Note — Breton Square 6" × 5"

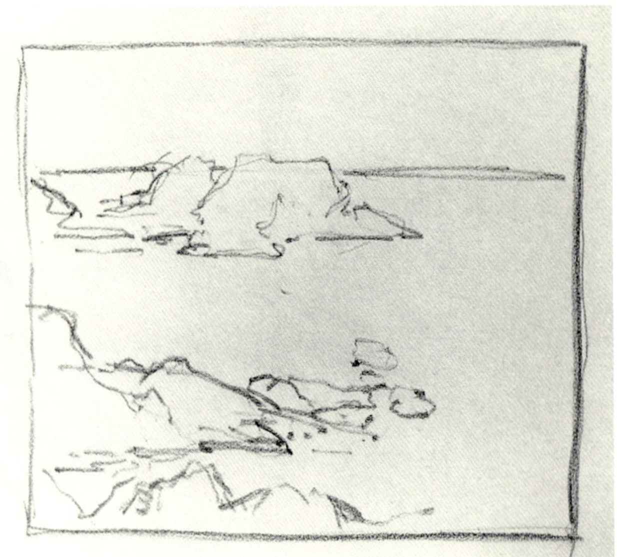

(Z-10) Note on Brittany Shore 4" × 4"

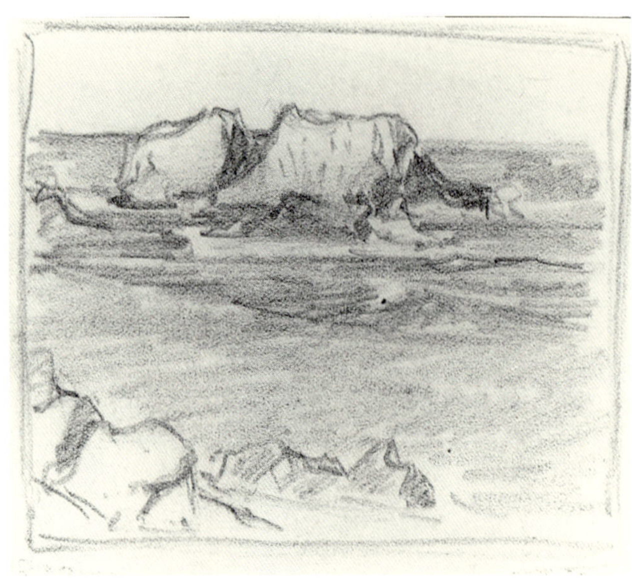

(M-33) Development of note on Brittany Shore 4" × 4"

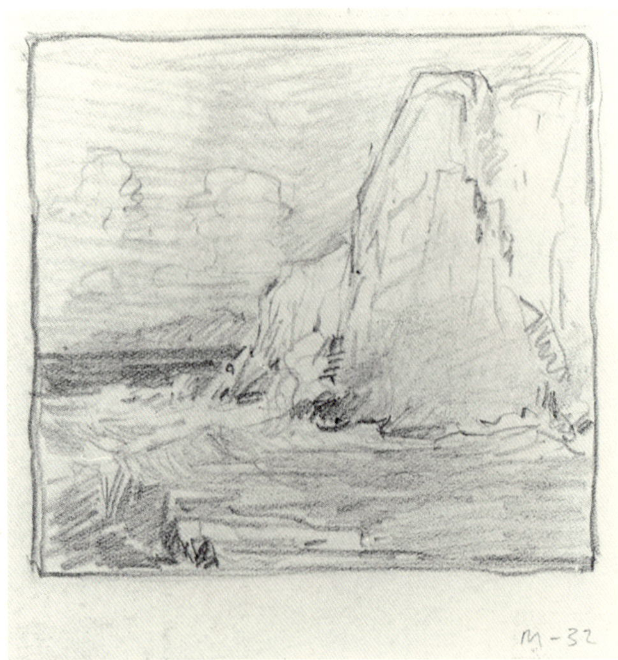

(M-32) Cliff, Brittany 4" × 4"

Chapter IV

California Mountains (the Sierra Nevada)

When we first went to the Sierras — I believe it was in 1917 or 1918 — there were no roads from the east into the mountains. We packed in on horseback from one of the little towns in Owens Valley, after traveling for three days from Los Angeles in a Model T Ford across unpaved desert roads, sleeping on the sand at night. I have been told that Dad was the first of the California painters to paint in the mountains there.

This first trip was to celebrate the completion of the Congress Hotel murals, which were shipped to Chicago. His helpers on the project were Jack Wilkinson Smith, Peter Neilson, Grayson Sayre and Conrad Buff. Mother had kept track of all the materials on the project. This was the first of many trips Dad took into the High Sierras, and I believe these mountains were the place he loved above all others. Mountains had a spiritual quality for him, and his paintings show it.

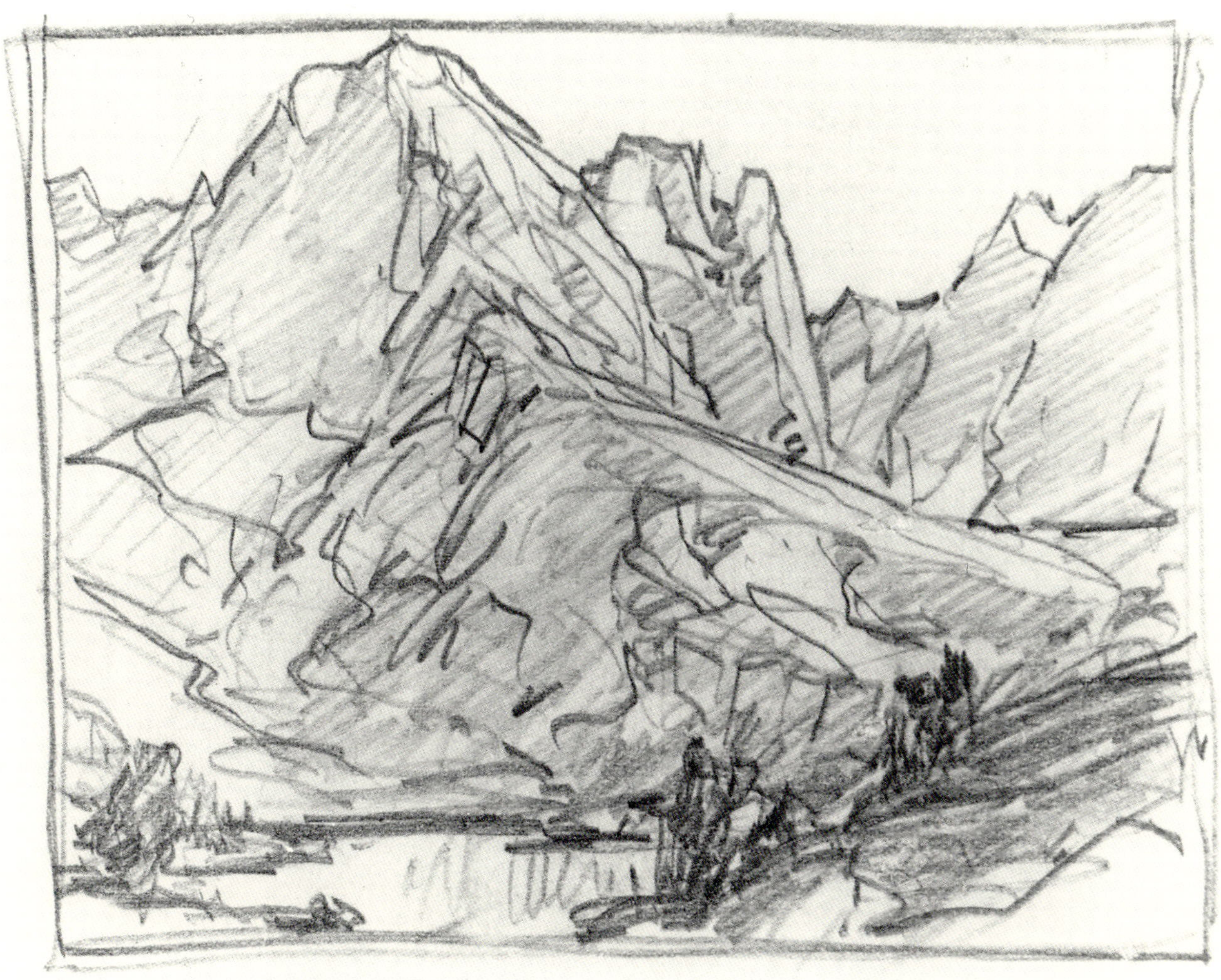

(X-120-22) Sierra Scene 3" × 4"

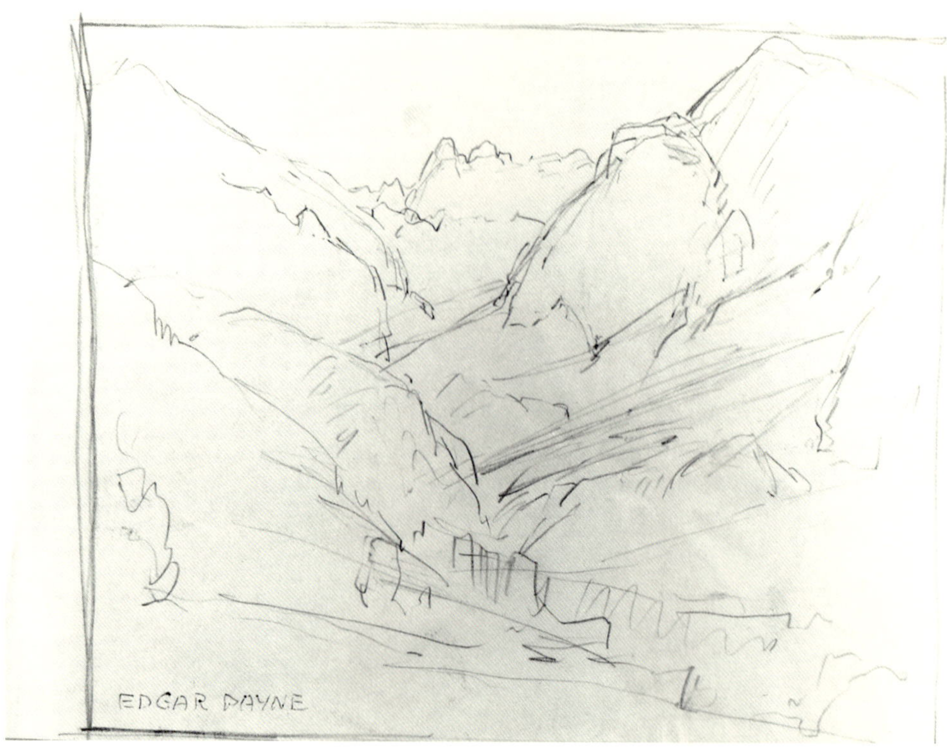

(M-1) Sierra Composition 8" × 10"

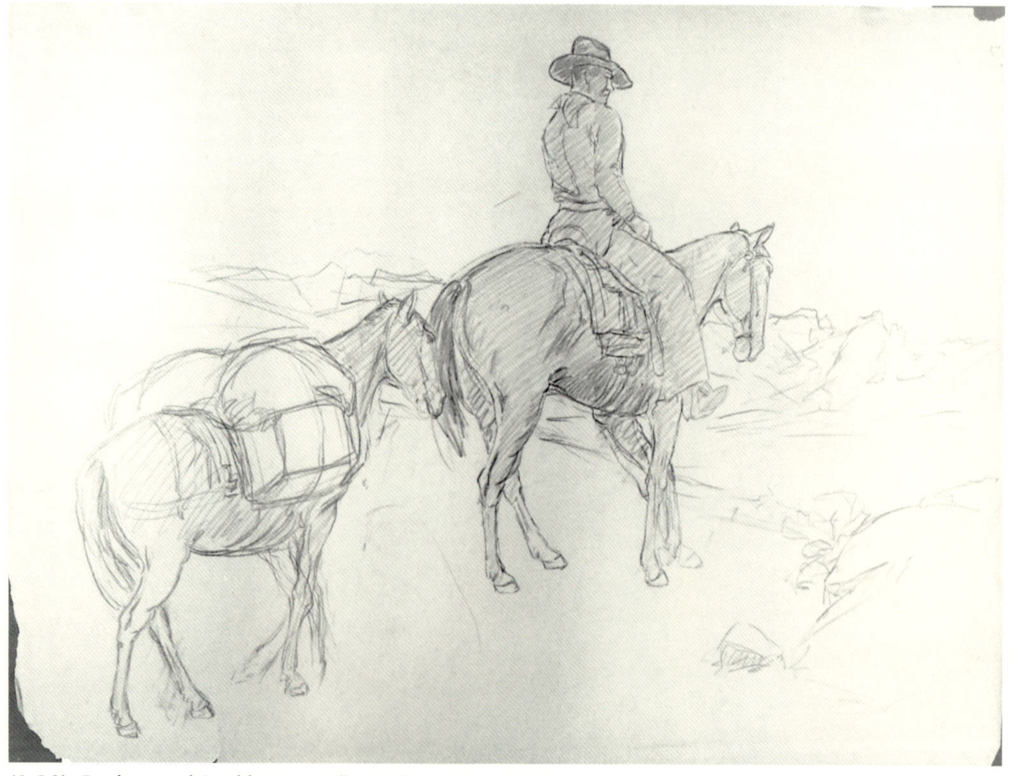

(S-30) Packer and Packhorse 17" × 24"

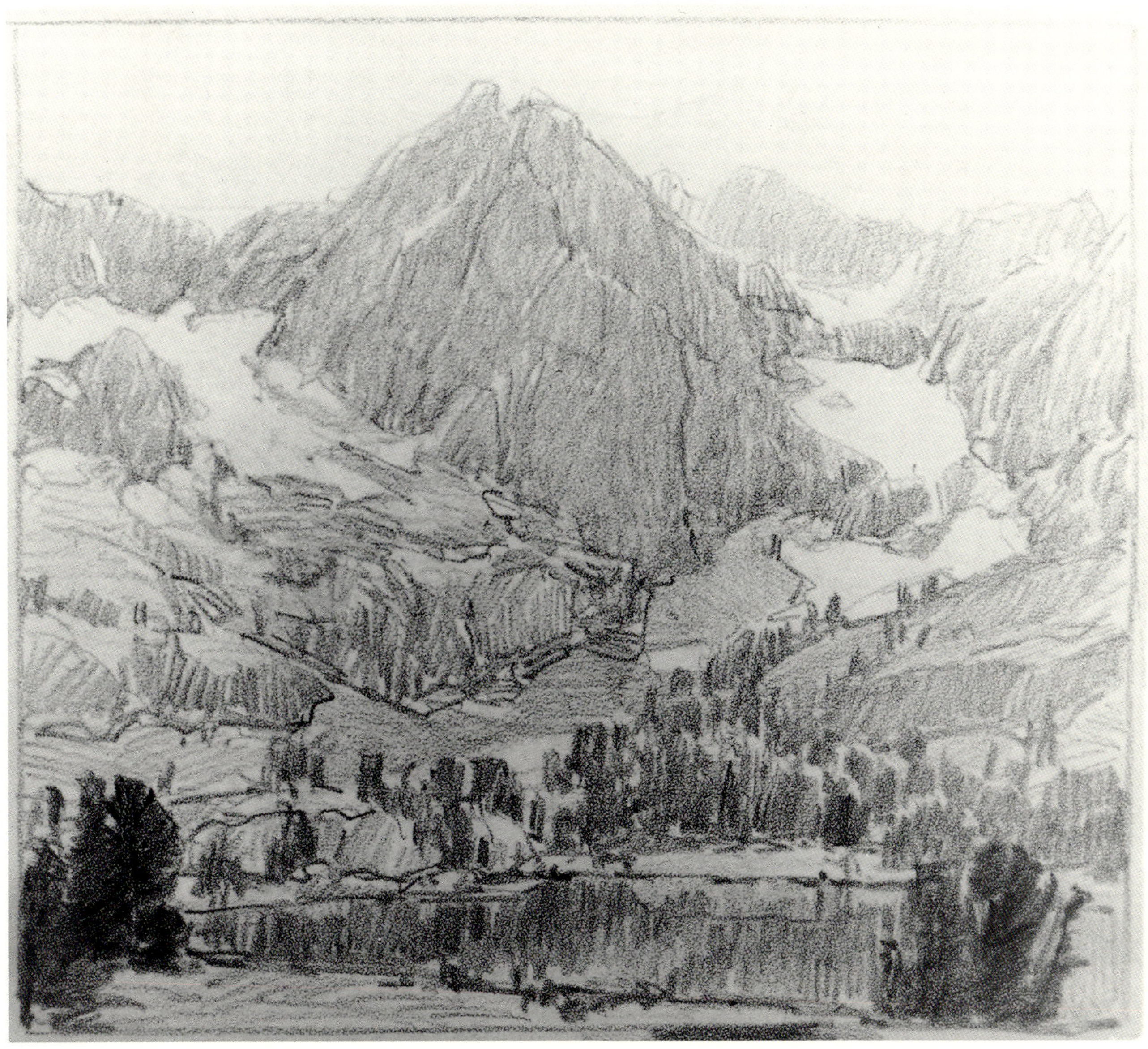

(S-36) Sierra Peak 8" × 9"

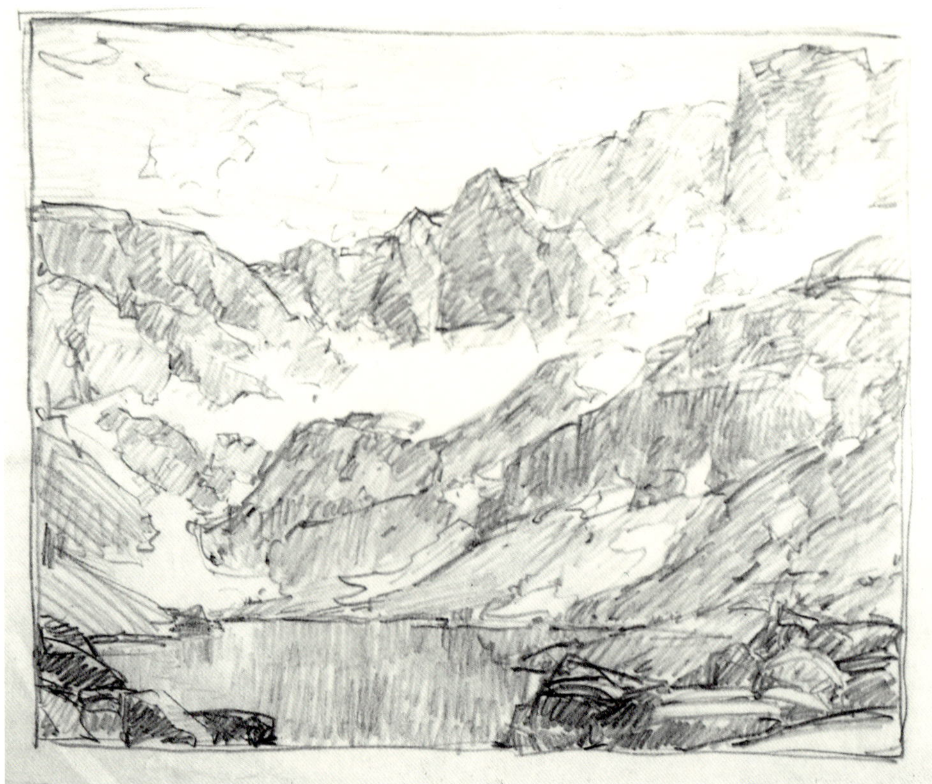

(S-12) Sierra Lake 8" × 10¼"

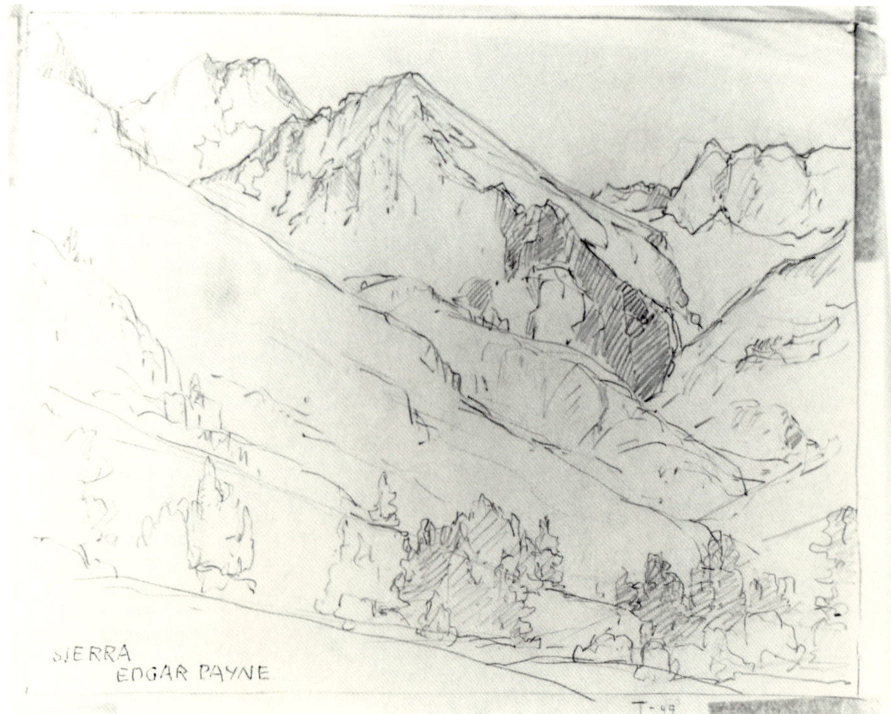

(T-49) Sierra 8" × 10"

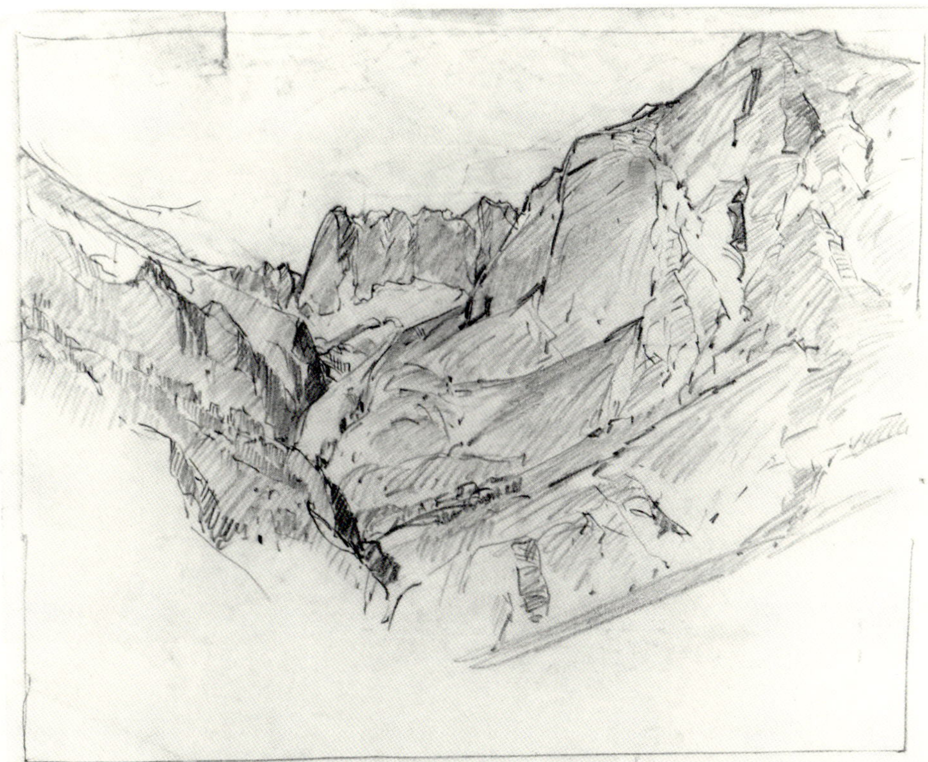

(M-17) Sierra Canyon 8" × 10"

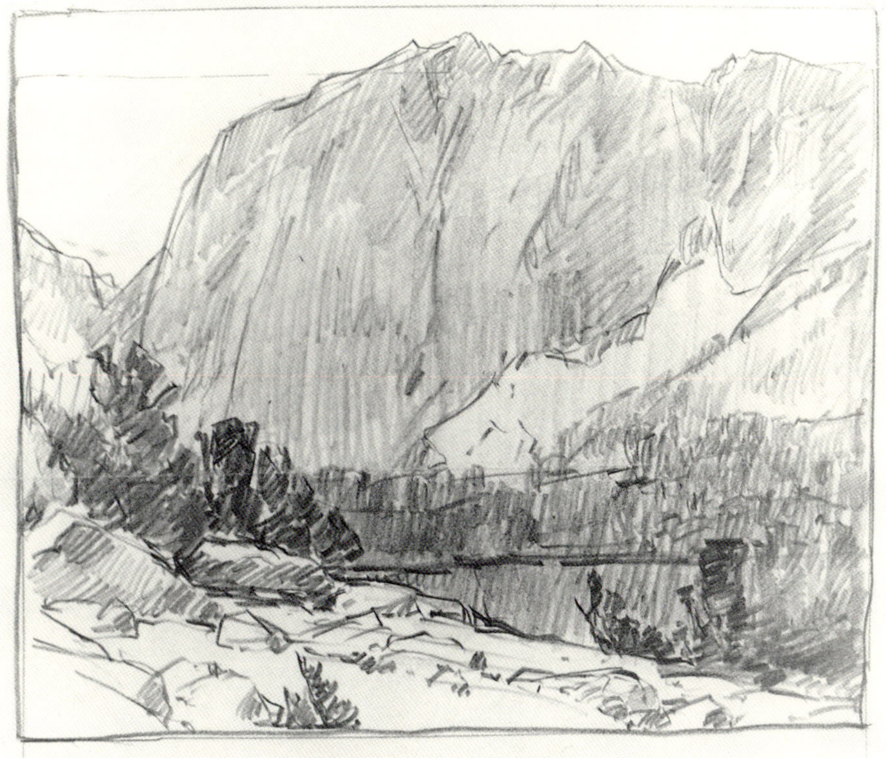

(S-16) High Sierra Lake 6" × 7½"

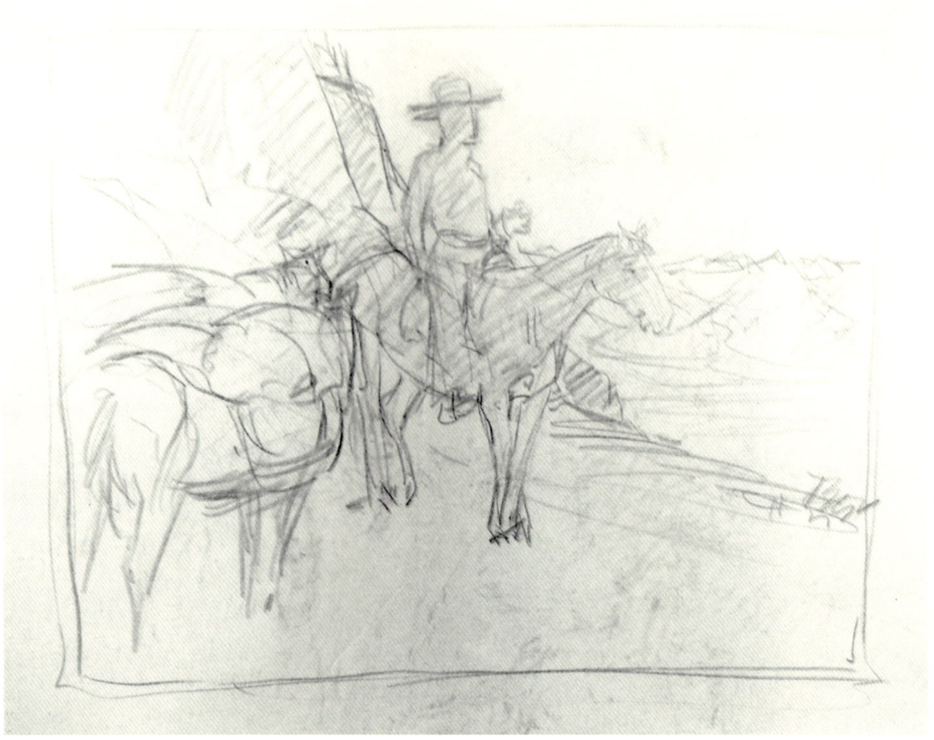

(S-34) Packer Overlooking the Valley 8" × 11"

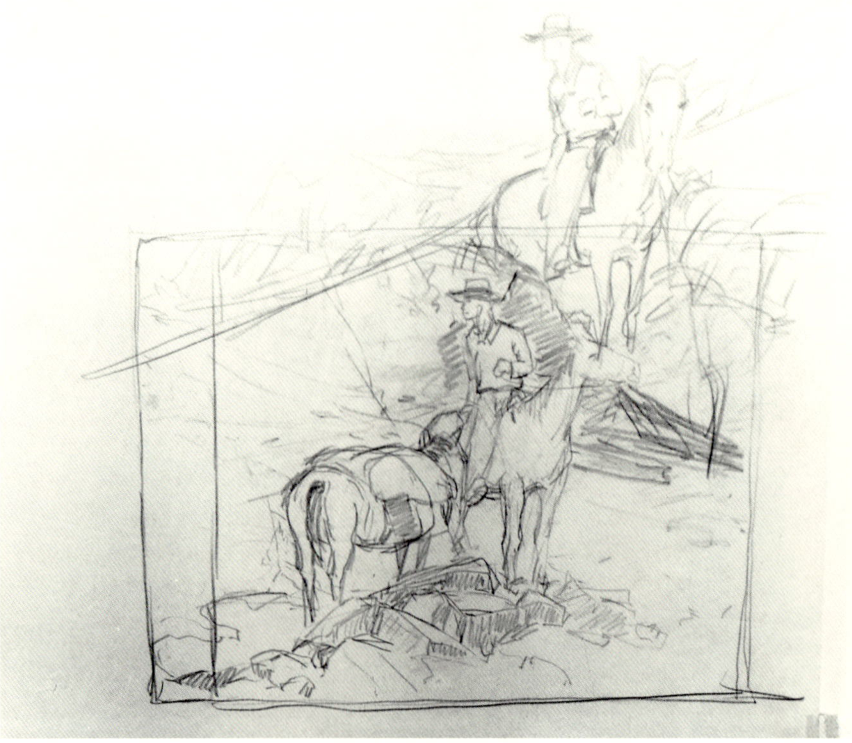

(S-33b) Back of S-33 Studies of Packers 8" × 11"

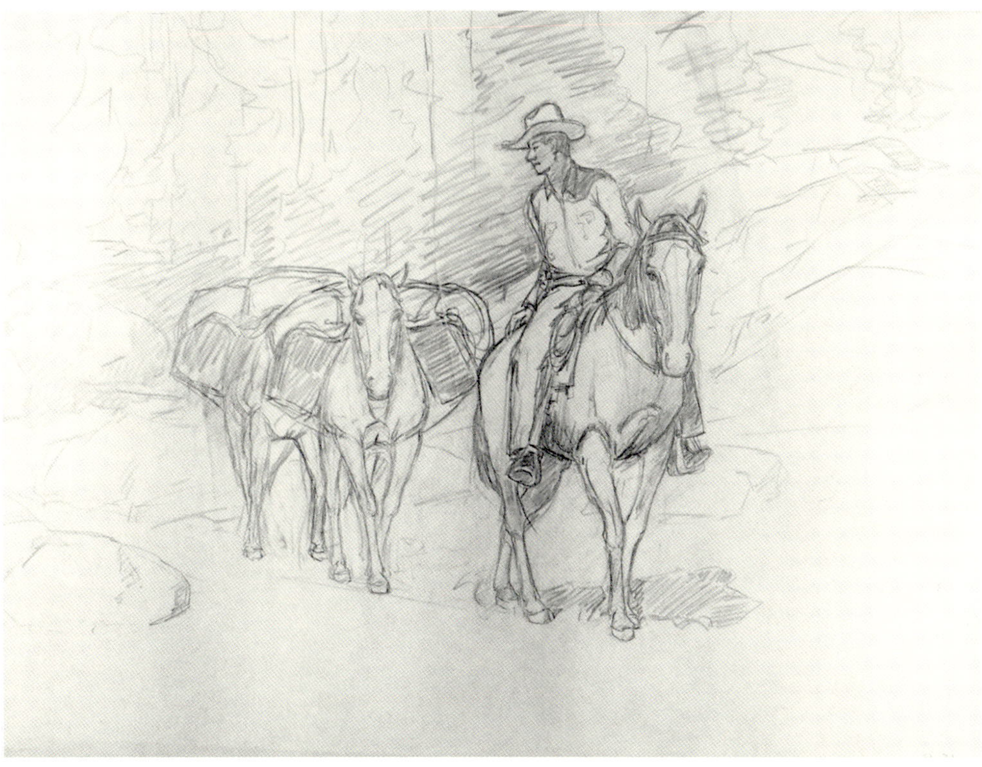

(S-31) On the Trail 15" × 22"

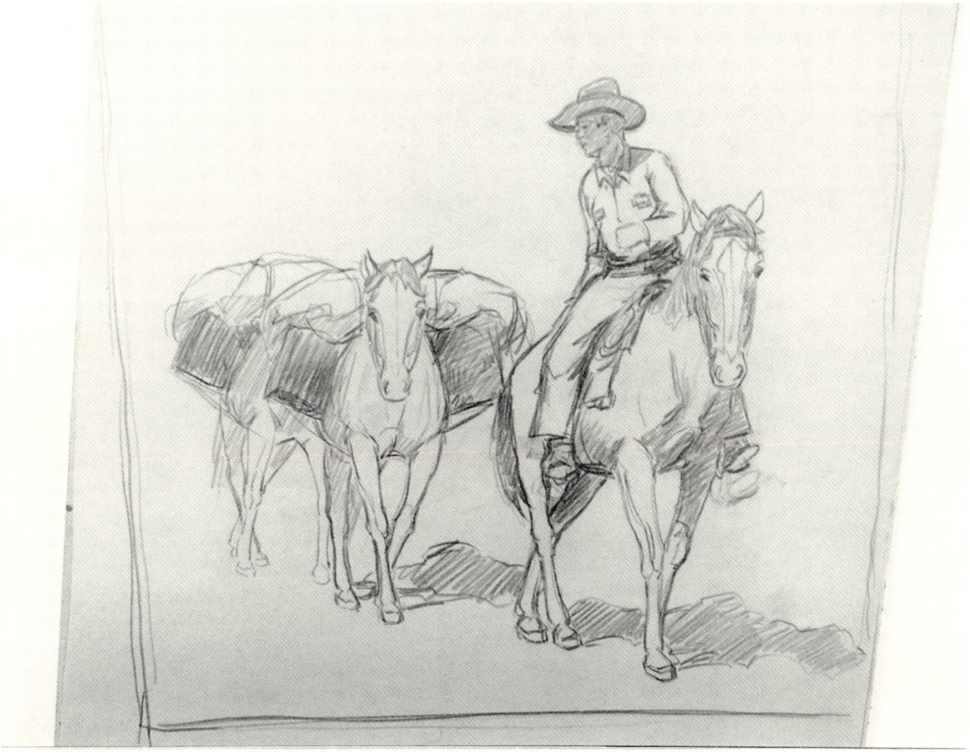

(S-33) Packer and Horses 13" × 14"

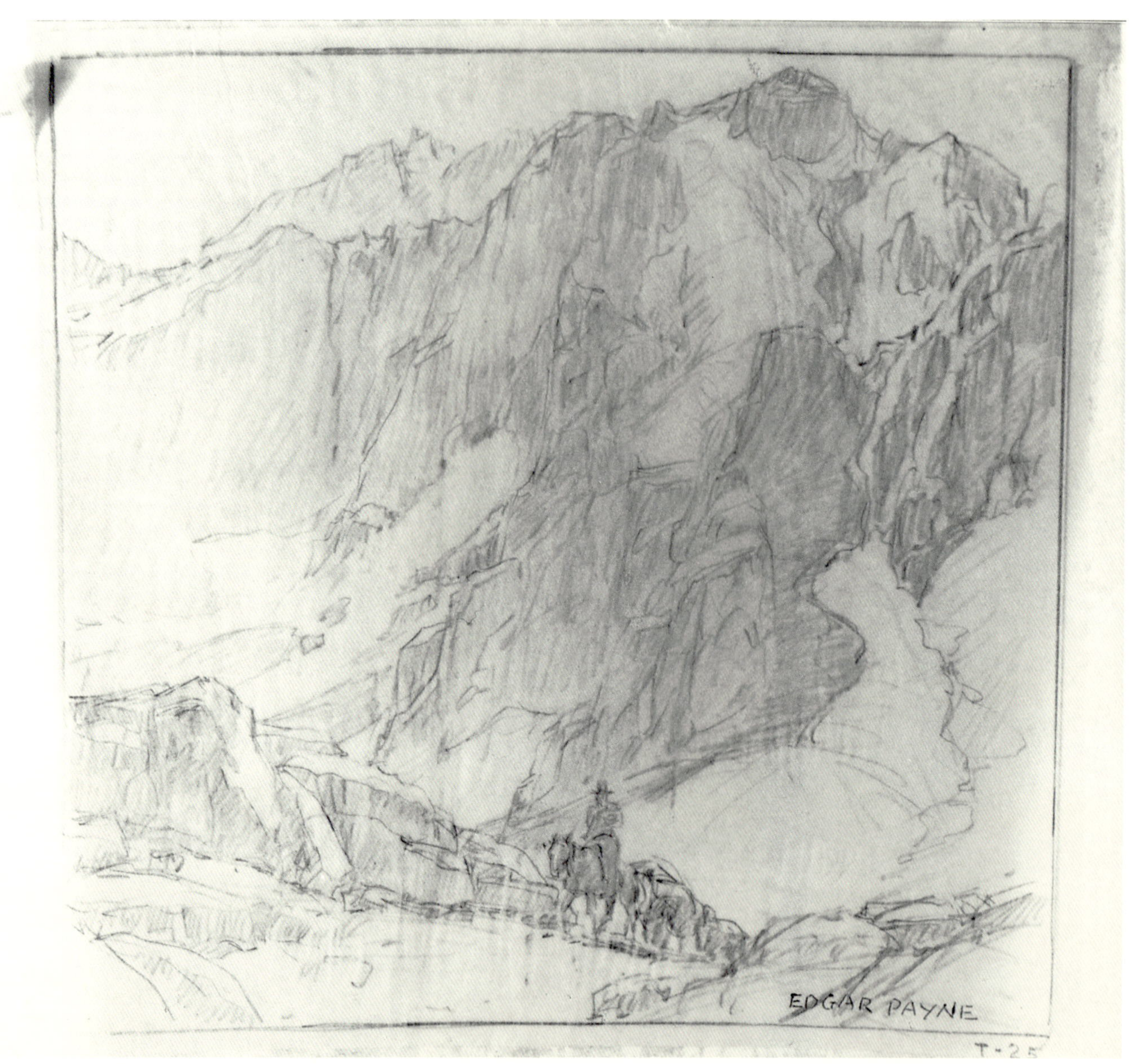

(T-25) Pack Train Climbing 10" × 10½"

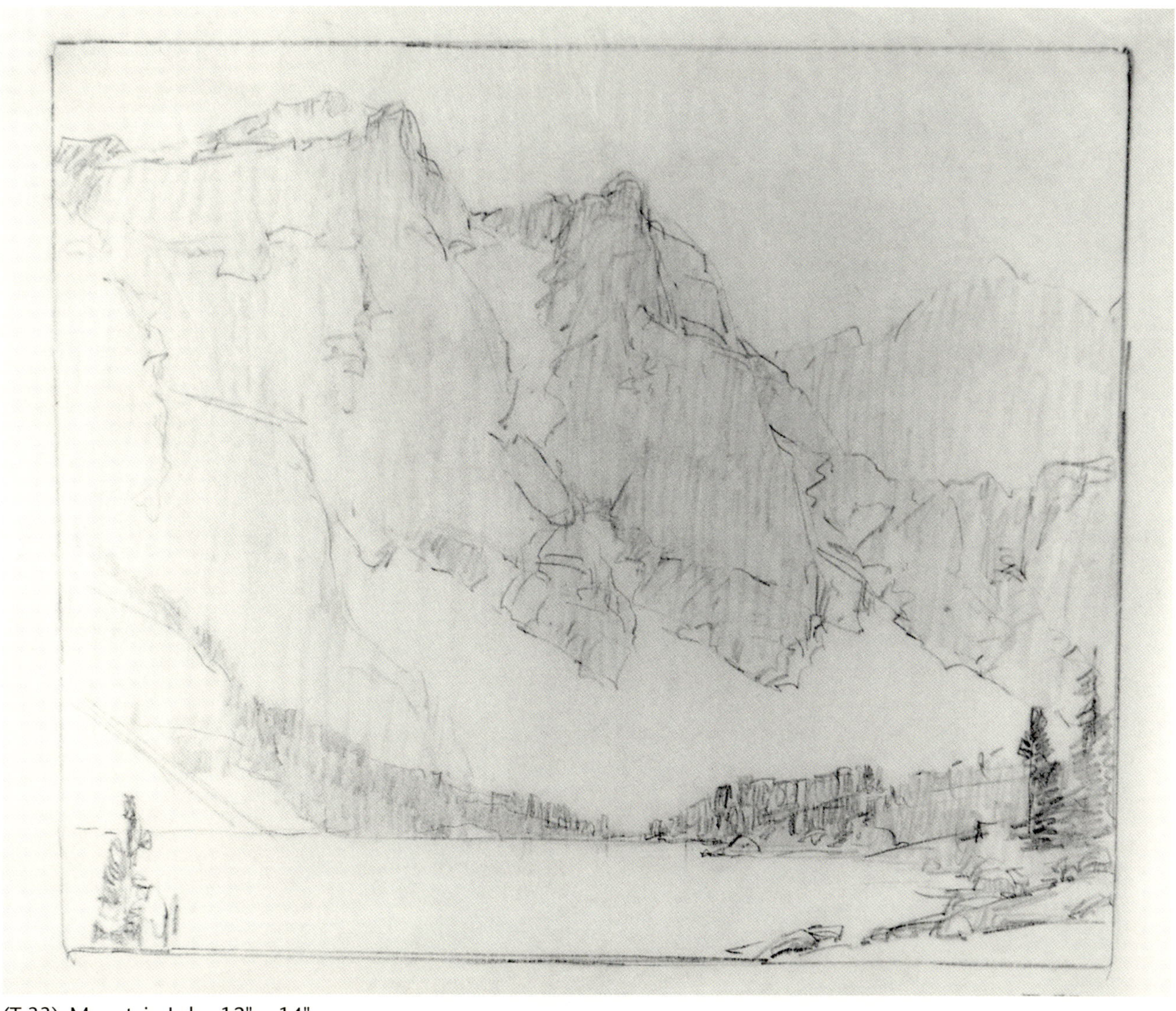

(T-33) Mountain Lake 12" × 14"

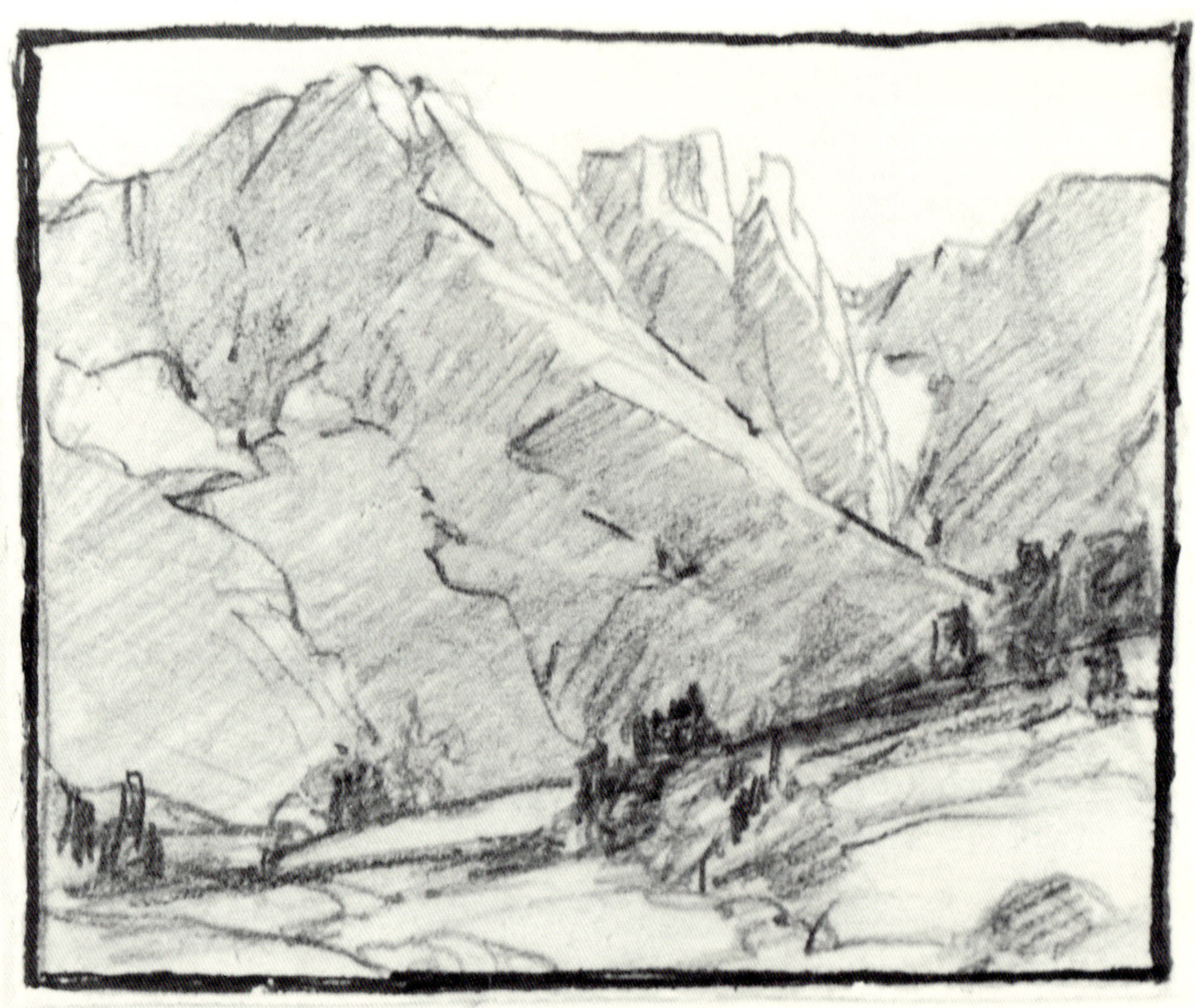

(M-28) Mountain Composition 2" × 3"

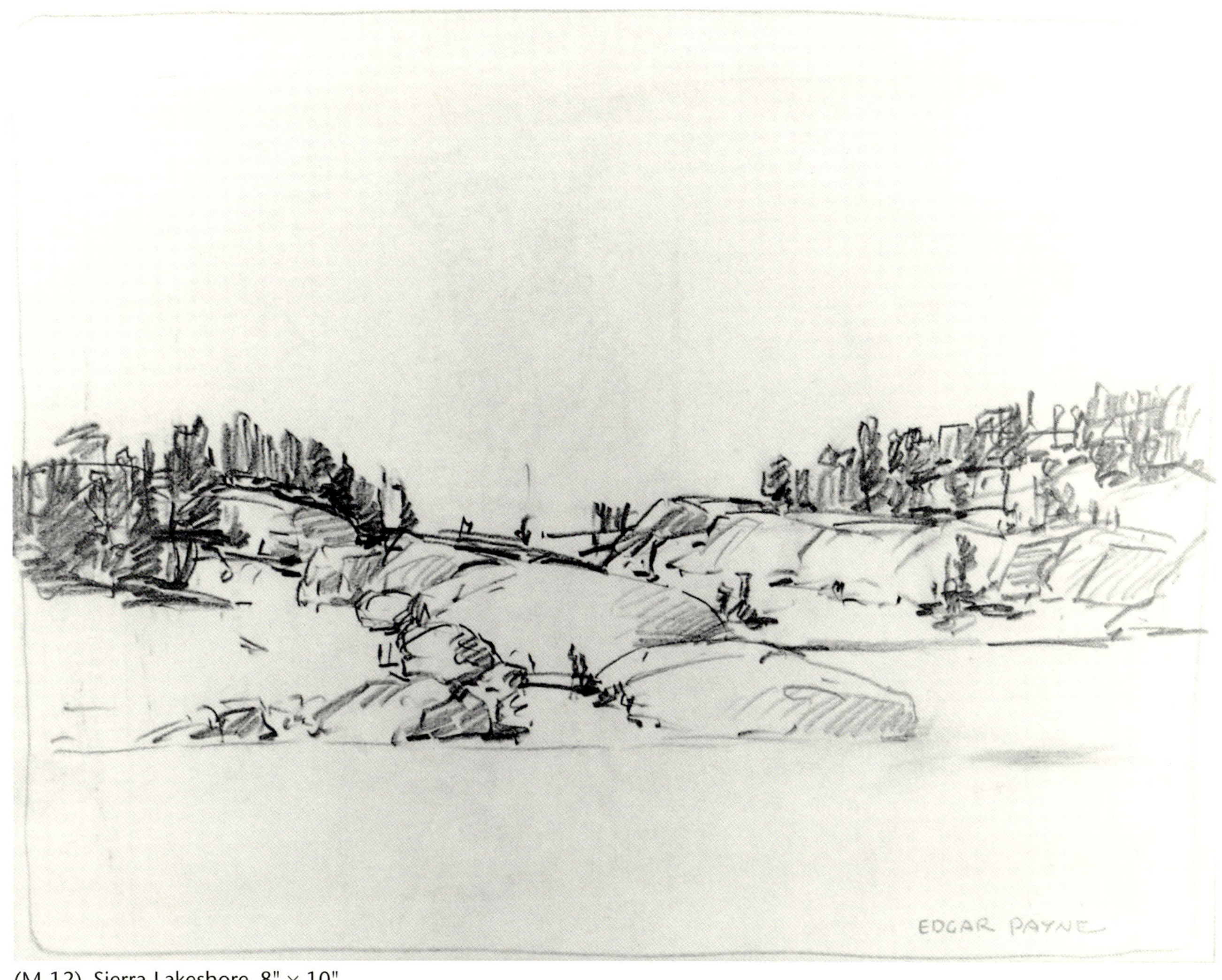

(M-12) Sierra Lakeshore 8" × 10"

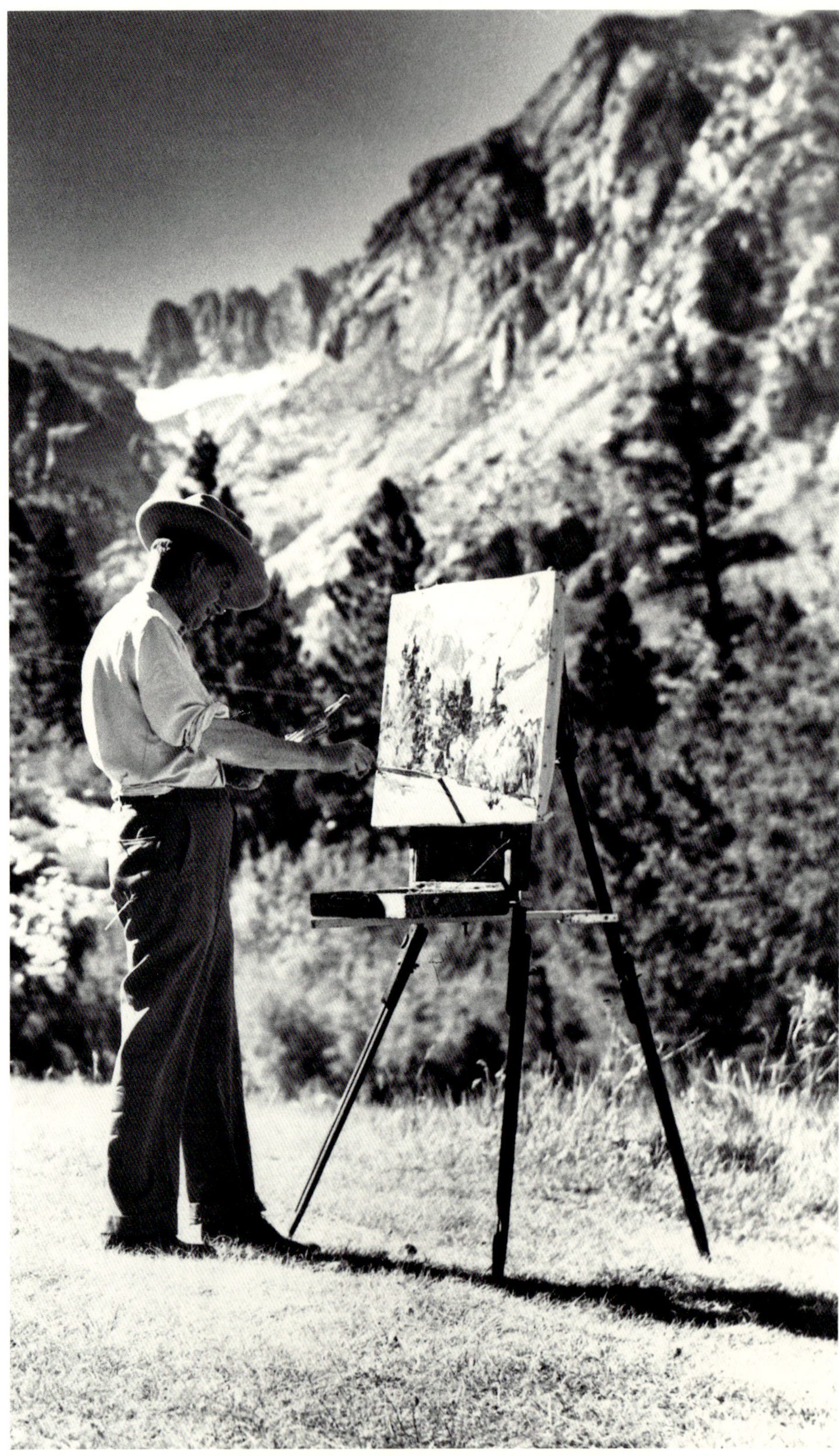

Photograph of Payne sketching on one of the last trips to the Sierras

Chapter V

Versatility

These odd bits were plans of things to make, except for the little cartoons. The frame designs were actually carved, as my dad made his own frames when we lived in Laguna Beach. I enjoyed watching, and especially enjoyed the application of gold leaf.

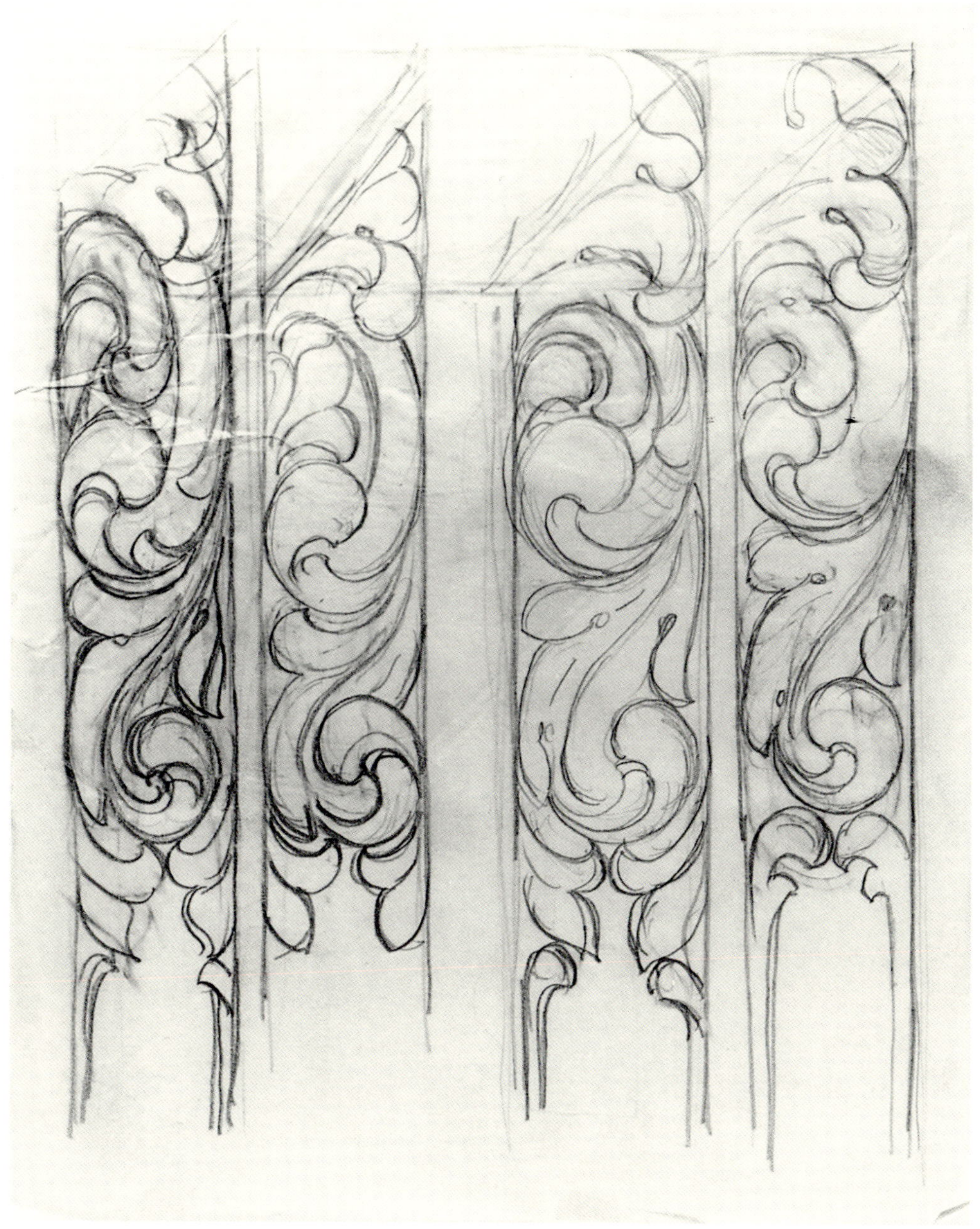

(T-44) Designs for Frame Carving 11" × 8"

These scraps make more sense when one realizes that they were intended to be one half of a corner carving. So I have reversed some of them and put them together with a copy of the original to show the complete design.

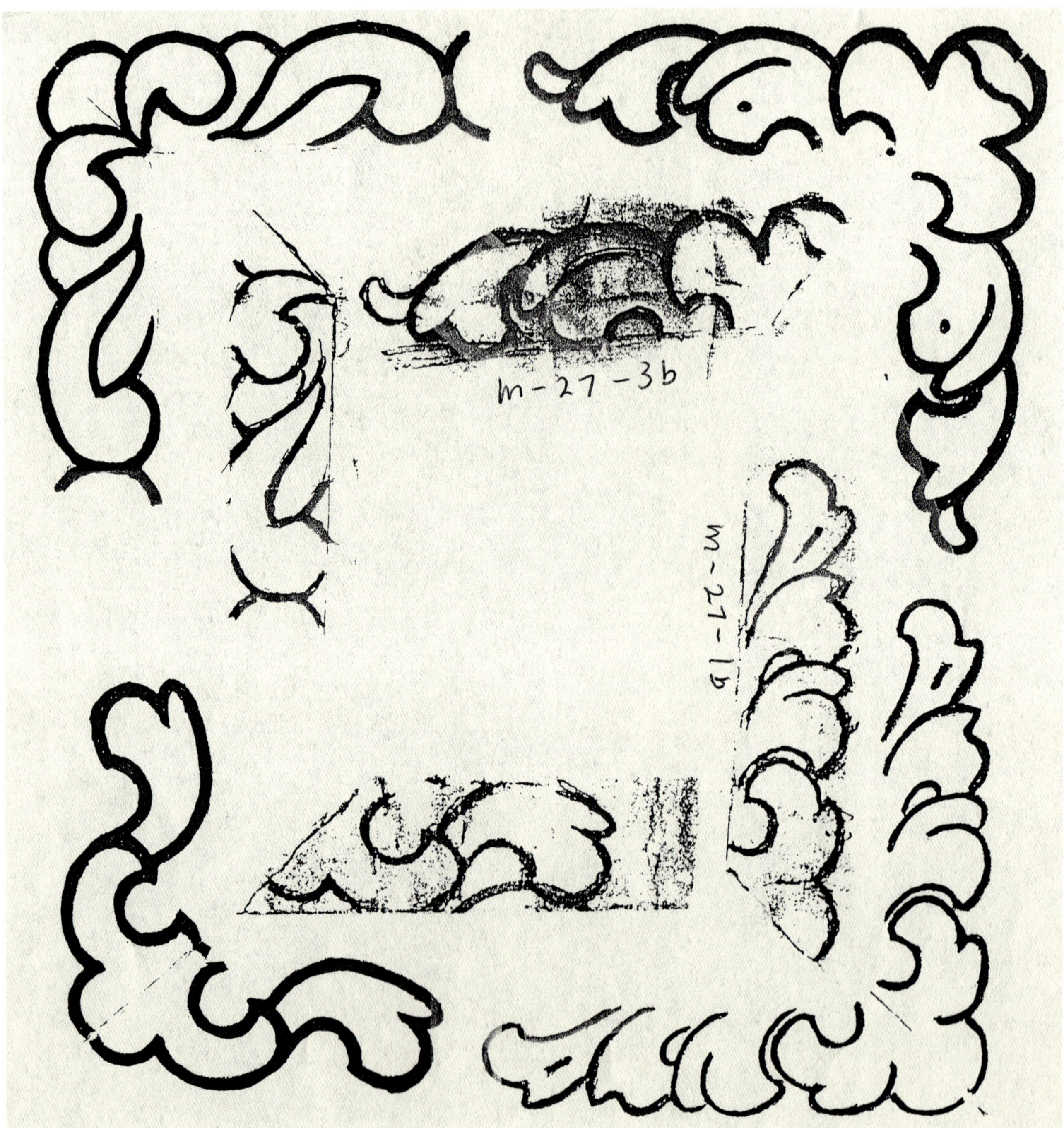

Small Designs for Frame Corners 1" × 3" each

It was surprising to me to find the bits of tracing paper with designs to be carved on frames, as I do not remember his carving his own frames after 1920, as he had taught Buck Weaver the craft and had turned over the shop to him. But it is possible that he made his own frames again in his studio in the Depression years.

When Dad carved, he did so very rapidly, because he had the pattern so firmly in mind, he was able to use quick sure strokes of his carving tools. In recent times frame makers have sought to copy his work in order to frame his paintings appropriately, but copying never gets the same effect.

While I have no frames left, I do have examples of his carving in the form of a table and two chests which were long in his or Mother's studio.

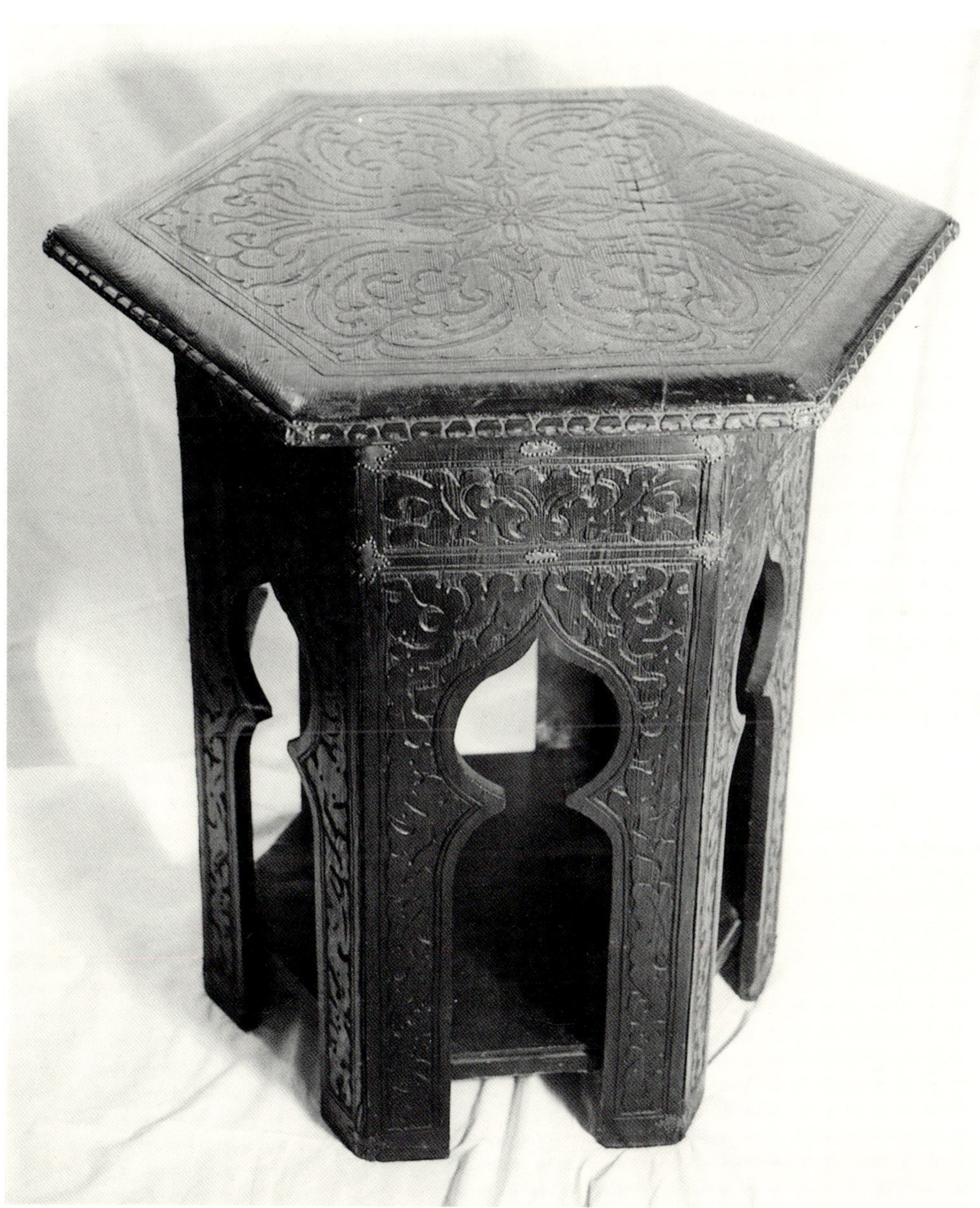

Table Carved in "Moorish" Style (photograph)

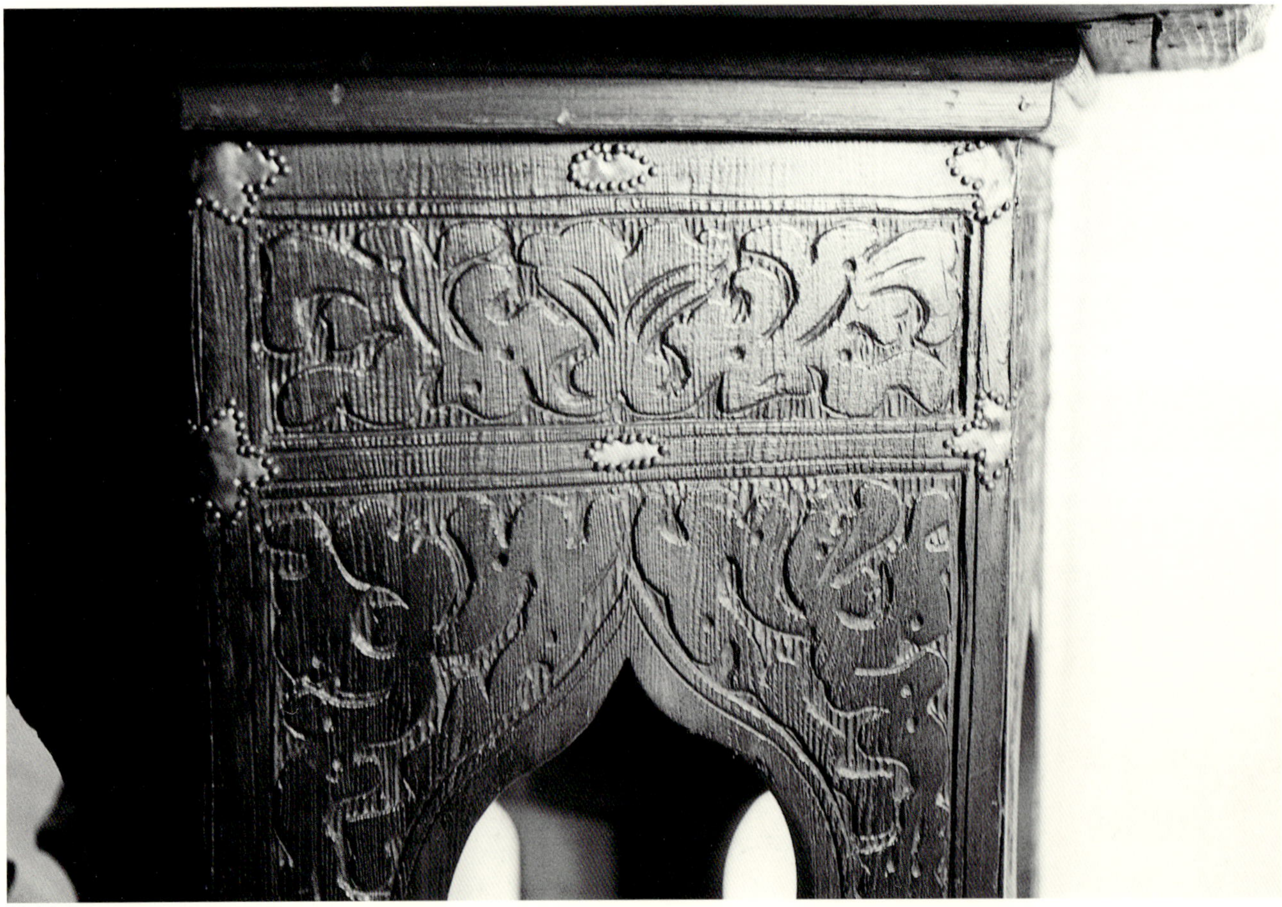

Detailed Views of Table (photographs)

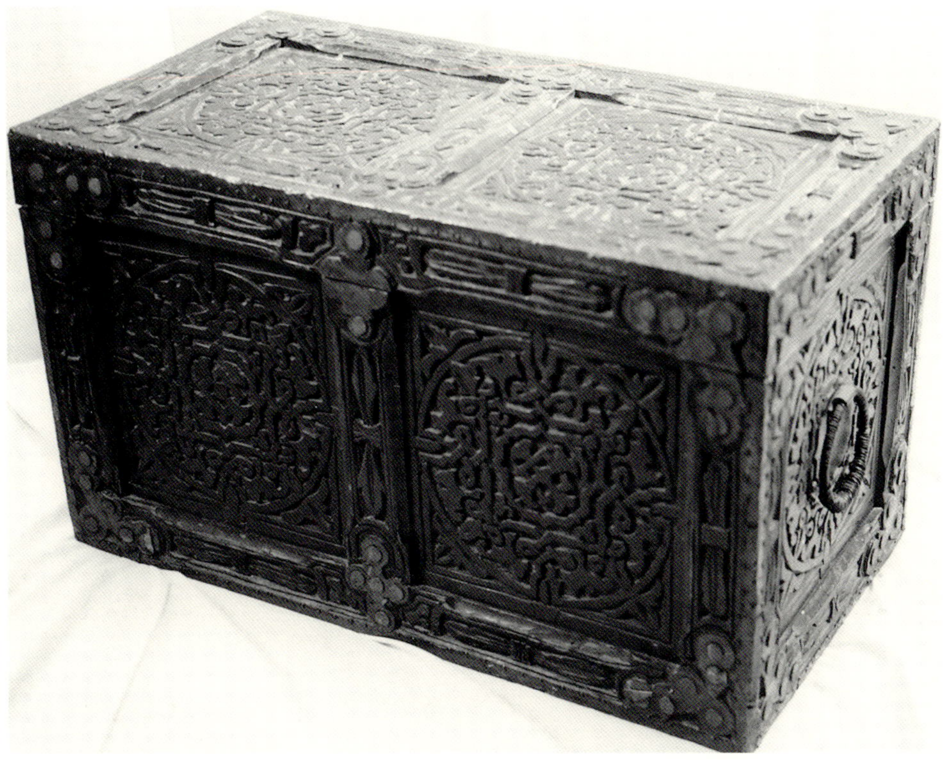

Chest Carved in Style Similar to Table (photograph)

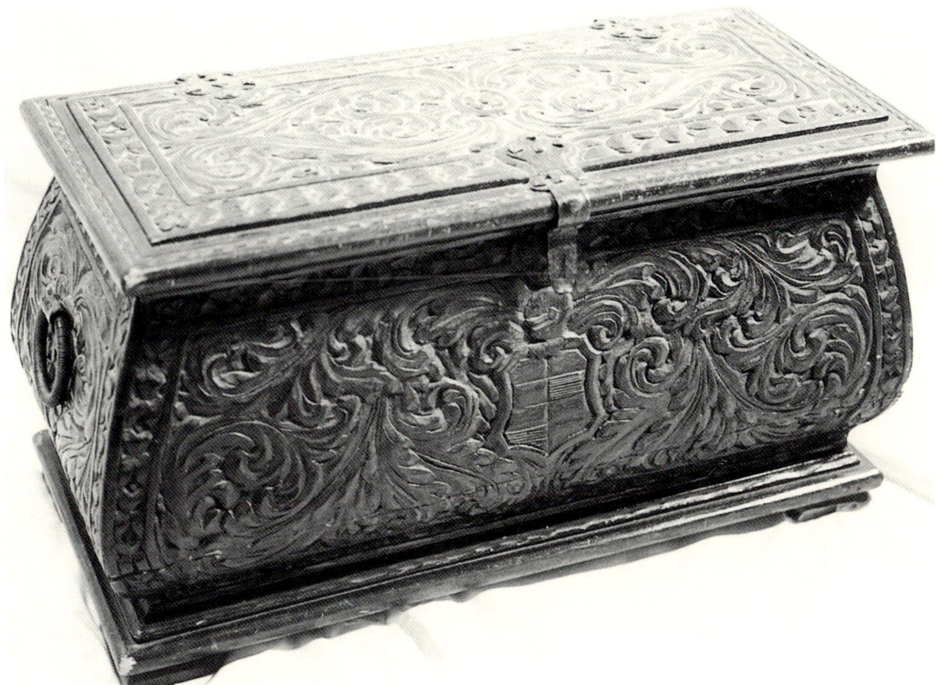

Chest Carved in Renaissance Style (photograph)

The house was to go on the lot my parents bought in Spuyten Duyvil in New York City, but then came the stock market crash and the Depression, and so it was never built.

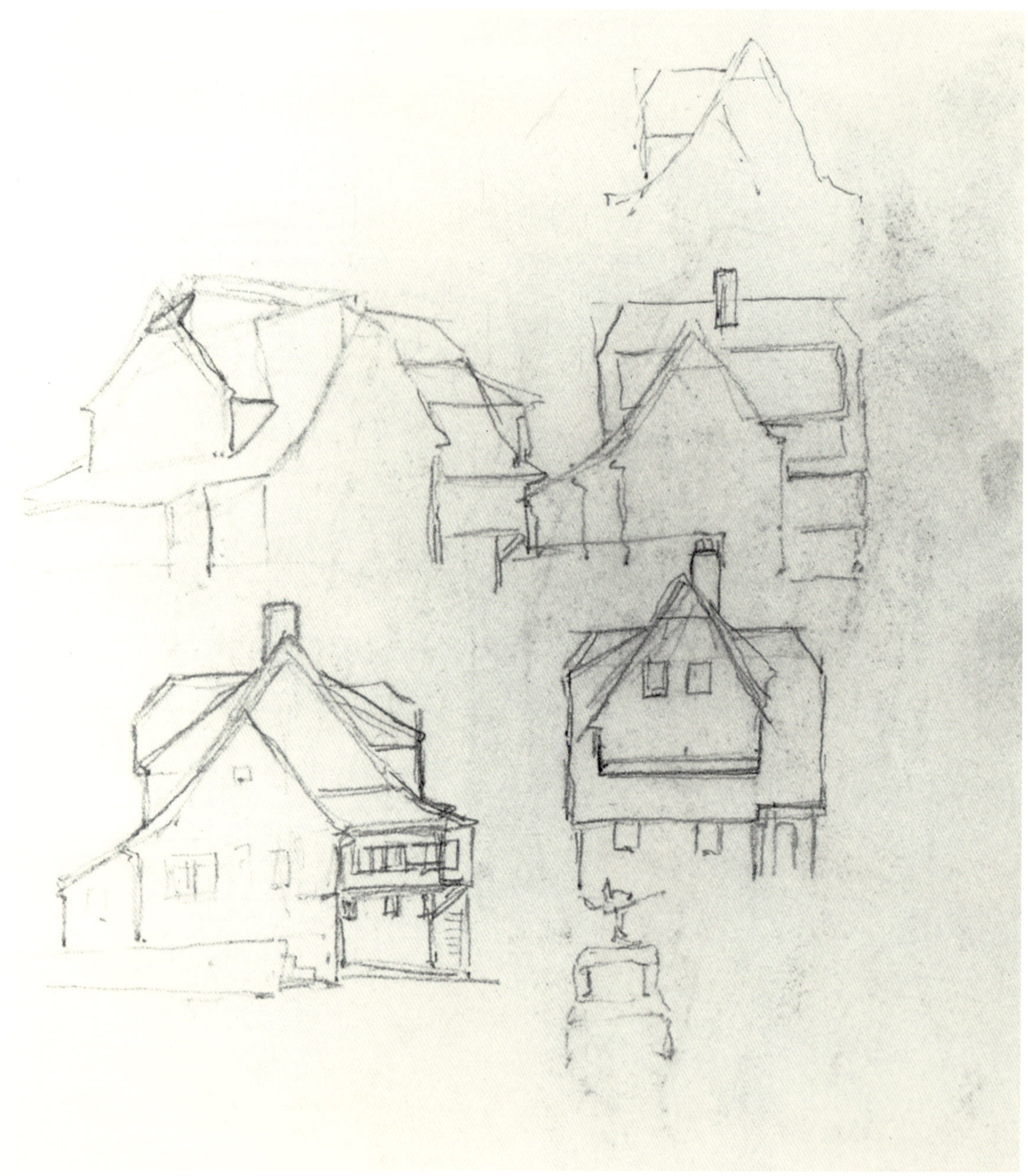

(SL-13) Sketches for the Dream House 10" × 8"

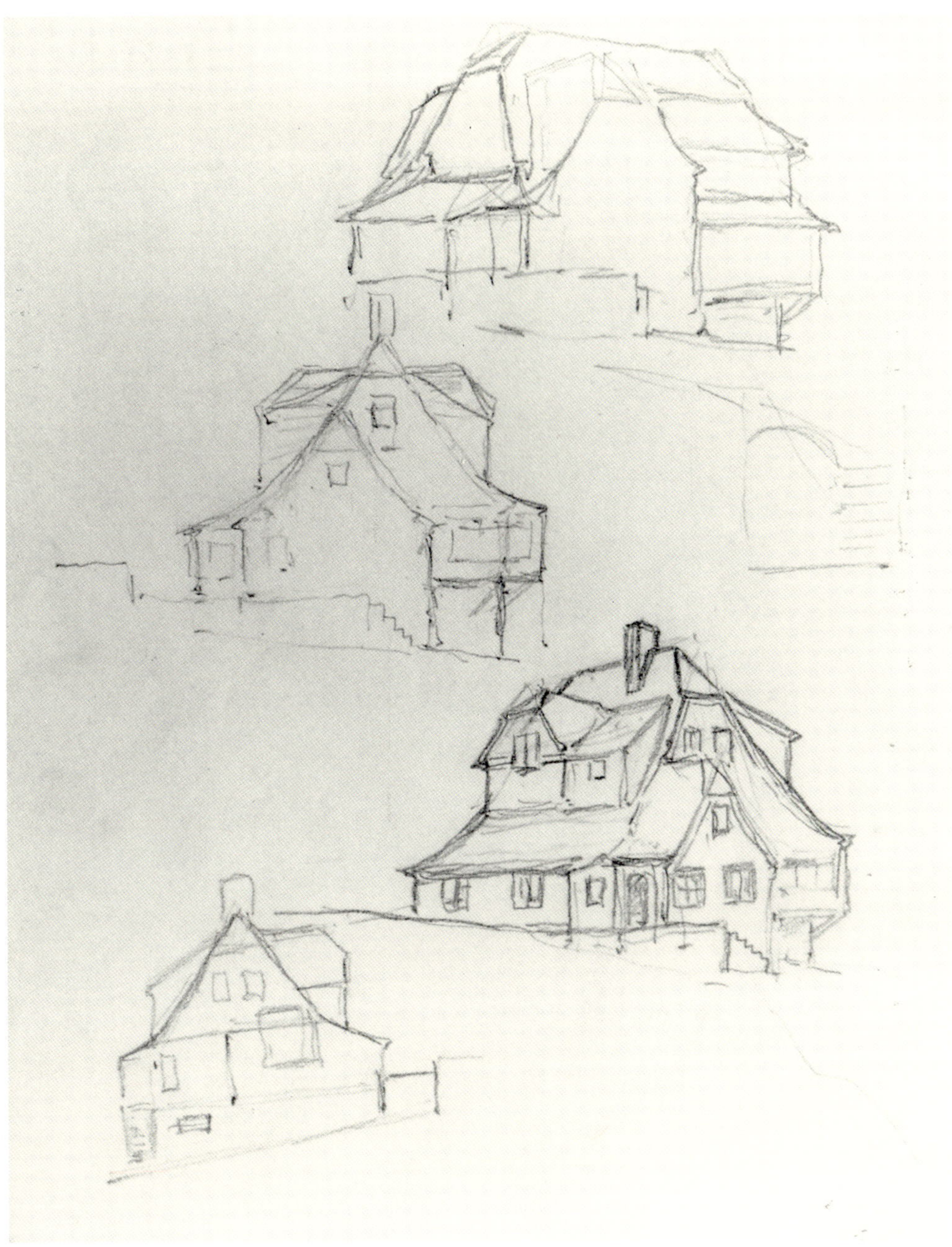

(SL-11) House Sketches 10" × 8"

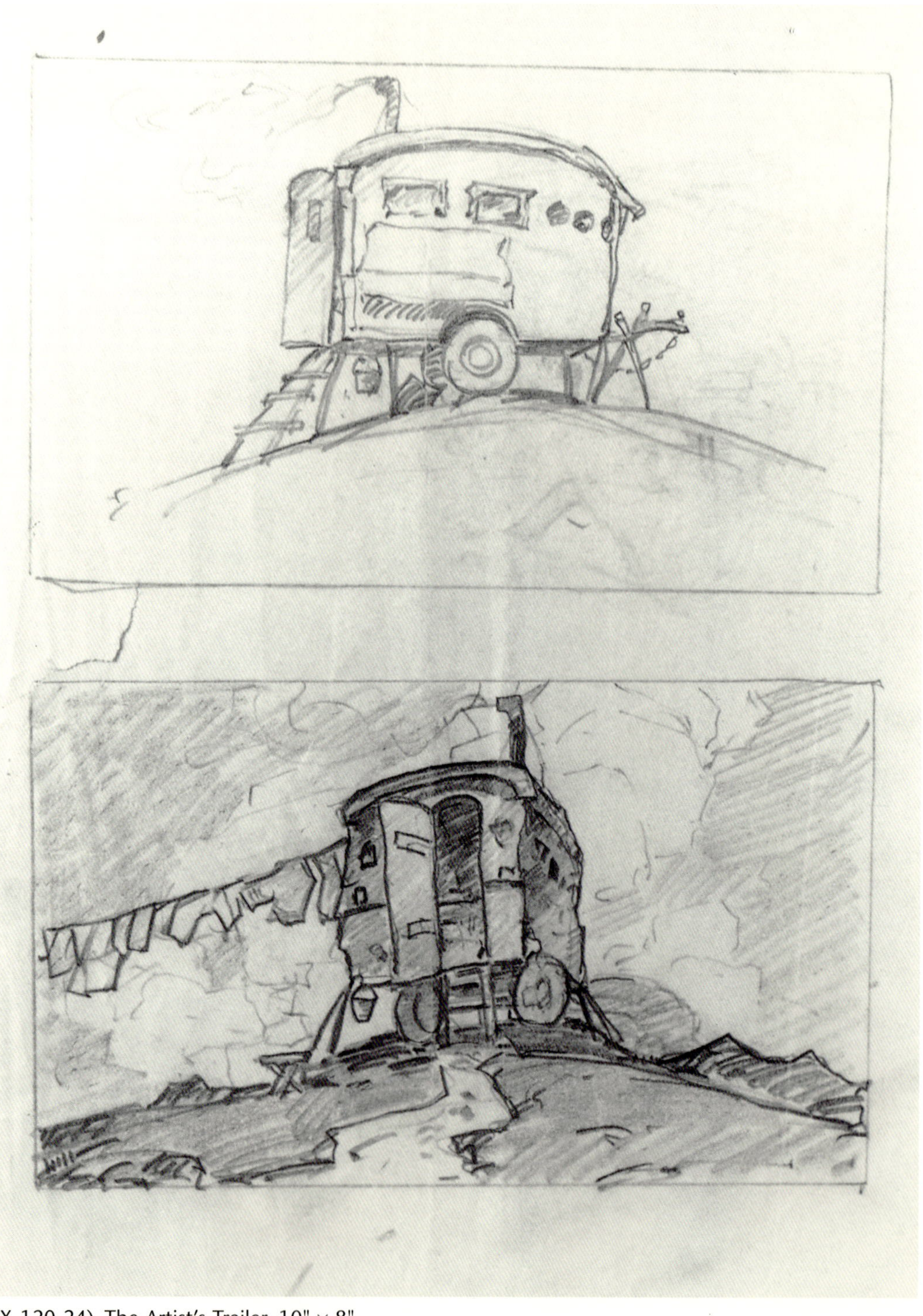

(X-120-24) The Artist's Trailer 10" × 8"

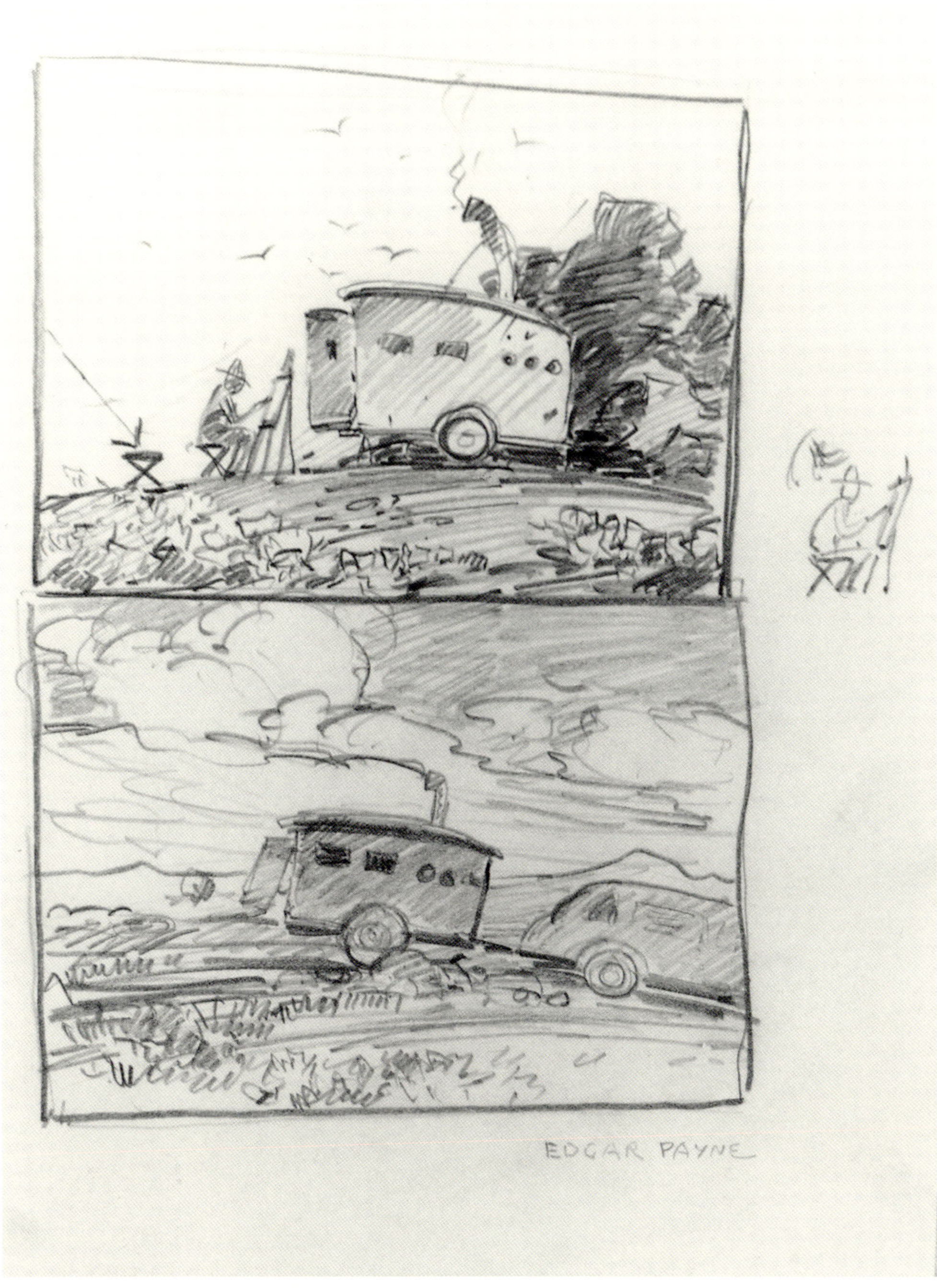

(S-22) Sketching and Leaving 10" × 6½"

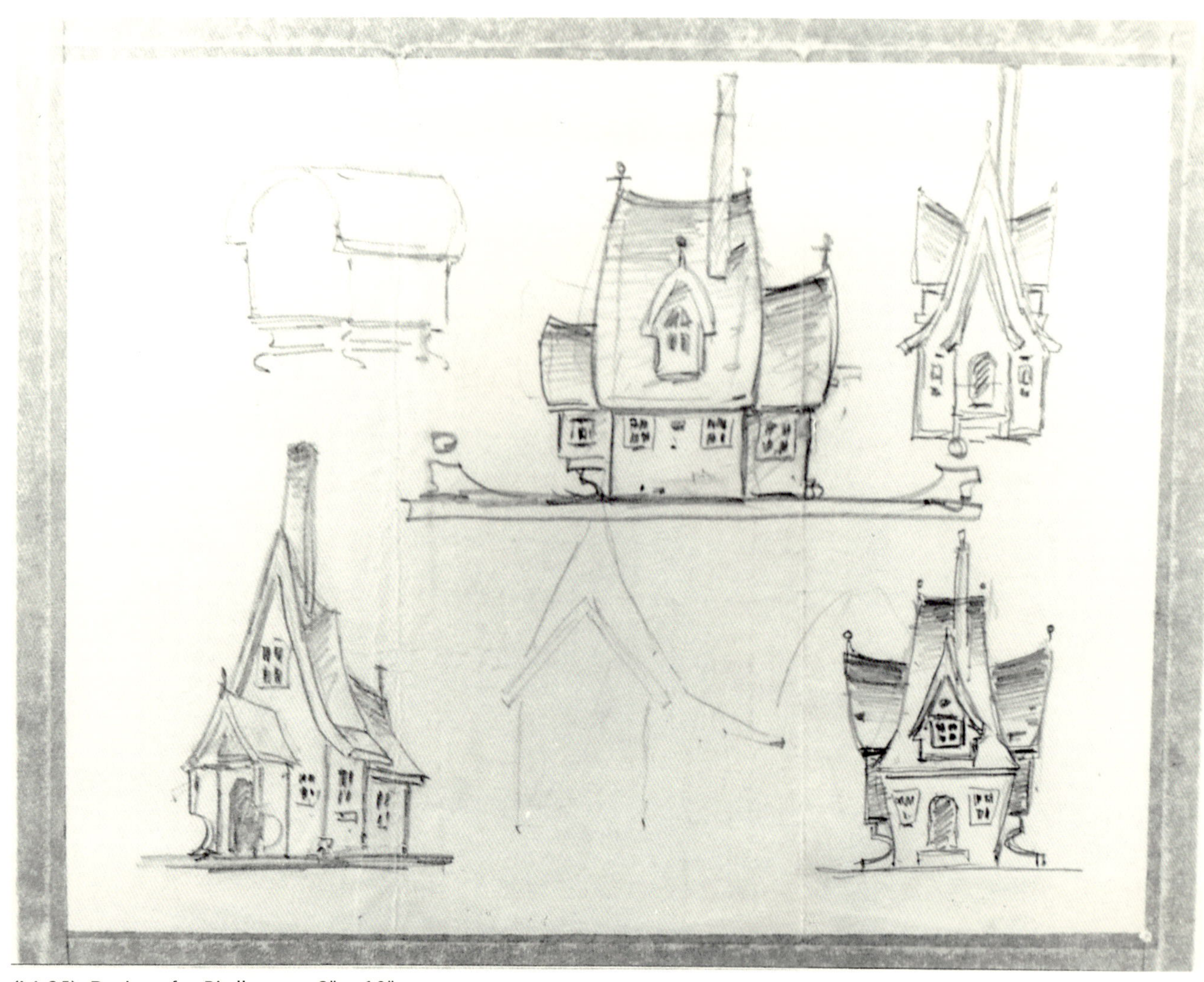

(M-25) Designs for Birdhouses 8" × 10"

A full-sized model of the "birdhouse" was made, but it was never made as a real birdhouse, as it has no openings. As I understand it, the plan to import purple martins to California fell through. But he built the large version and it is now considered a form of wooden sculpture. It is interesting to see by the sketches how the idea grew in his mind, and from this it seems fairly clear that his interest was more in the art form than in the birds, and he enjoyed it as fun.

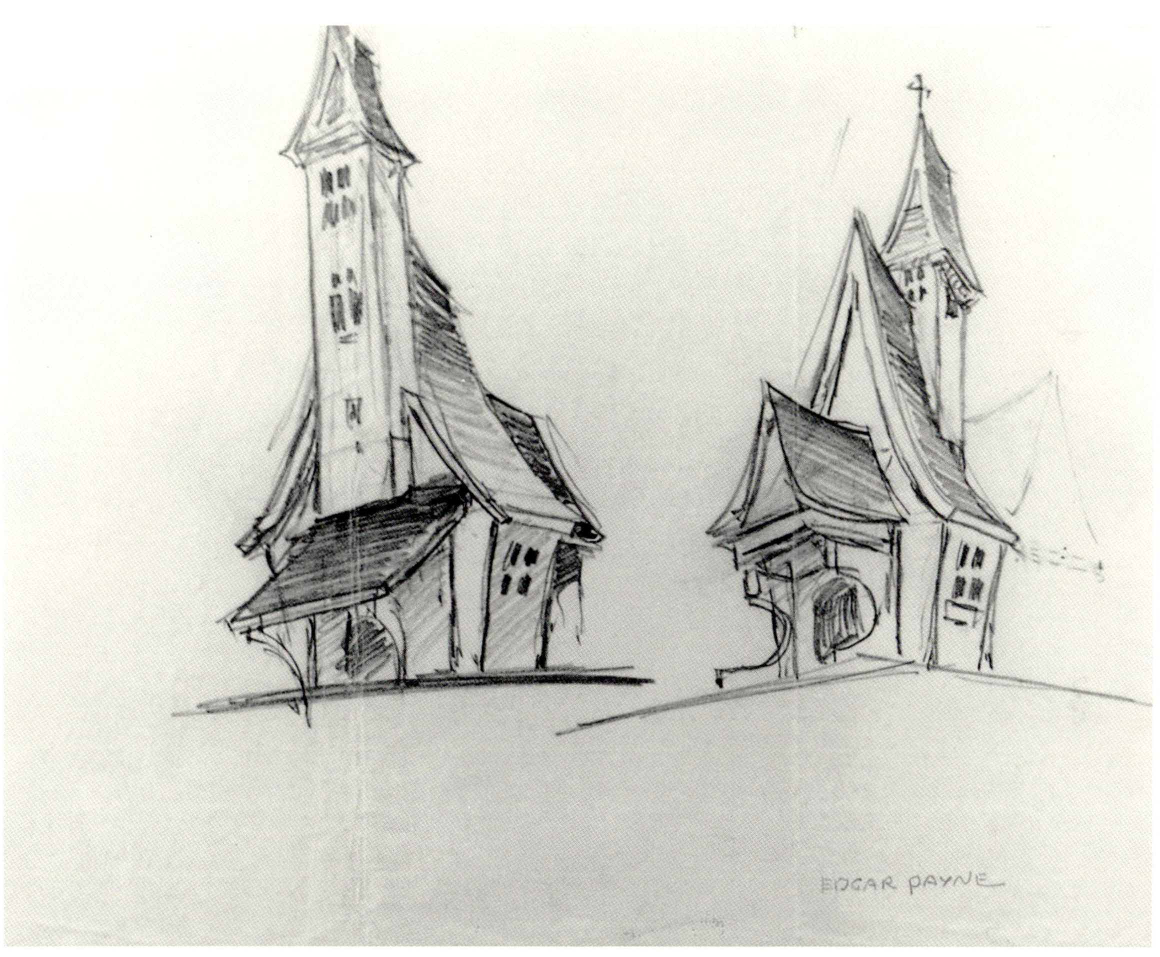

(M-24) Birdhouses with Towers 8" × 10"

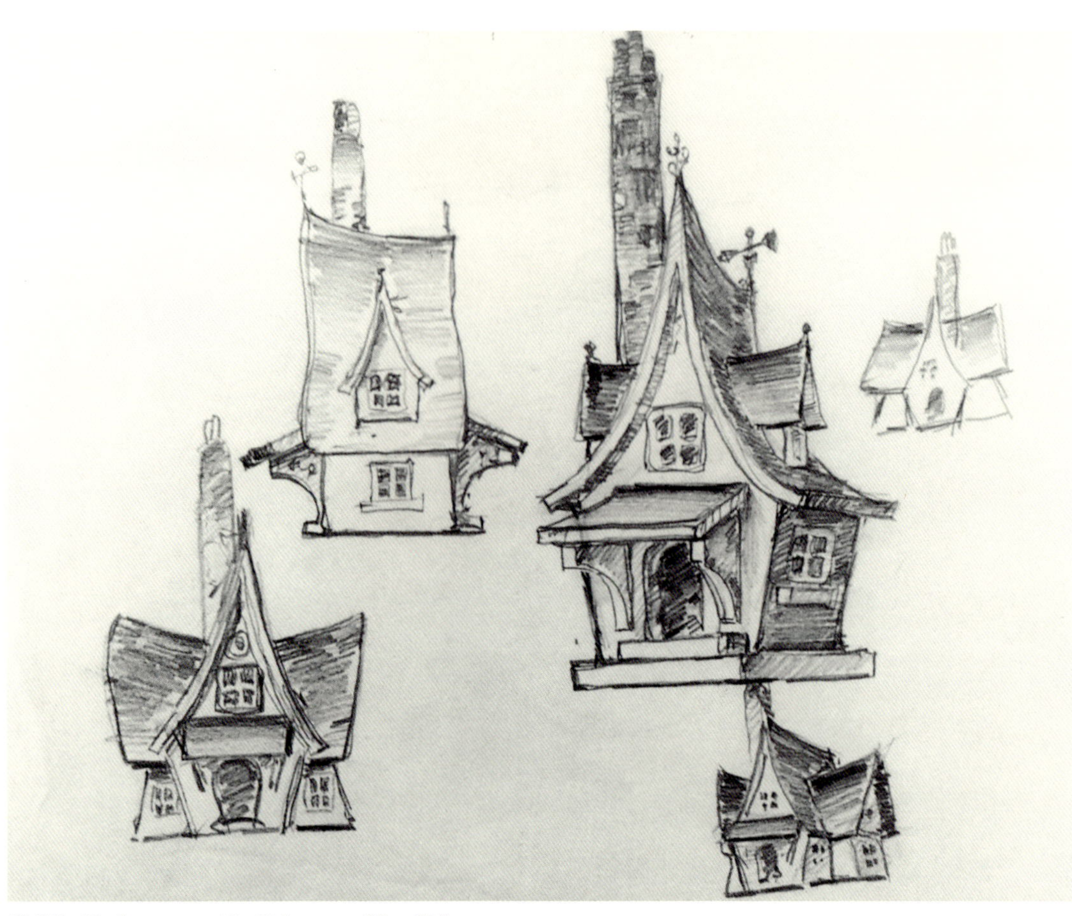

(S-25) Birdhouses with Chimneys 9" × 11"

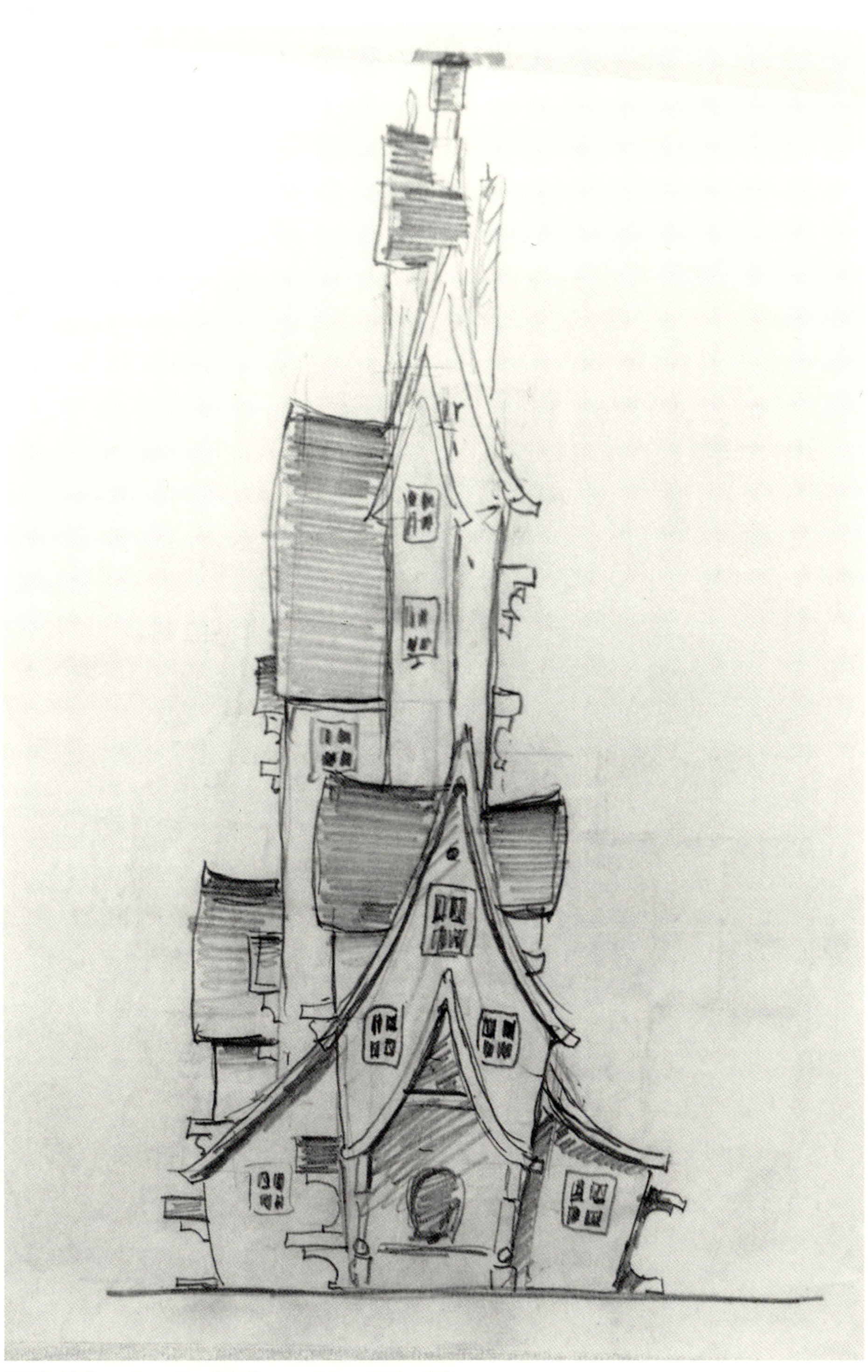

(T-5) Elaborating the Birdhouse Idea 11" × 9"

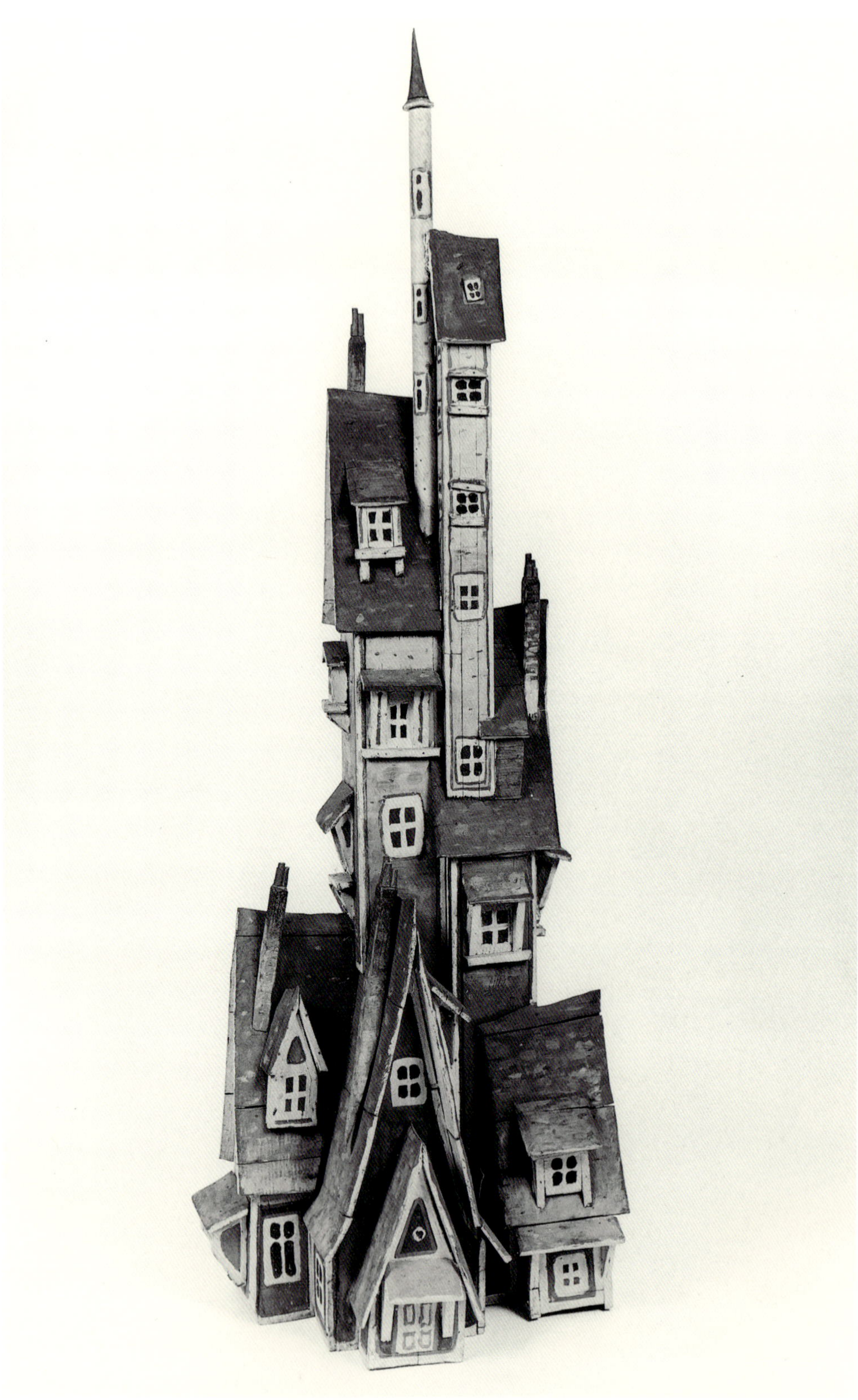

Photograph of the Wooden Sculpture

Chapter VI

Arizona and New Mexico

There were many visits to the Southwest. The first one was in 1916. Mother and I went along, but I don't remember it.The Santa Fe Railroad sent my Dad, but he didn't rent a place in Taos and paint Indians — he rented a wagon — I think a covered wagon — and we went all over, as far as the Hopi Reservations. But Mother and I did not go down into Canon de Chelly (pronounced *de shay*). That was just too rugged at that time.

During the early 1930s the trips were usually based at the trading post of Lloyd Ambrose at Thoreau in New Mexico, about forty miles from Gallup. I was there with my parents in 1930. At that time it was a tiny settlement, and I infer that this was the time he made most of the field notes on horses. It was not until a few years ago that I learned from a Tony Hillerman mystery story why Thoreau is pronounced *thru* — because it was named after an engineer who drove the train that ran through the area and that was how he pronounced it.

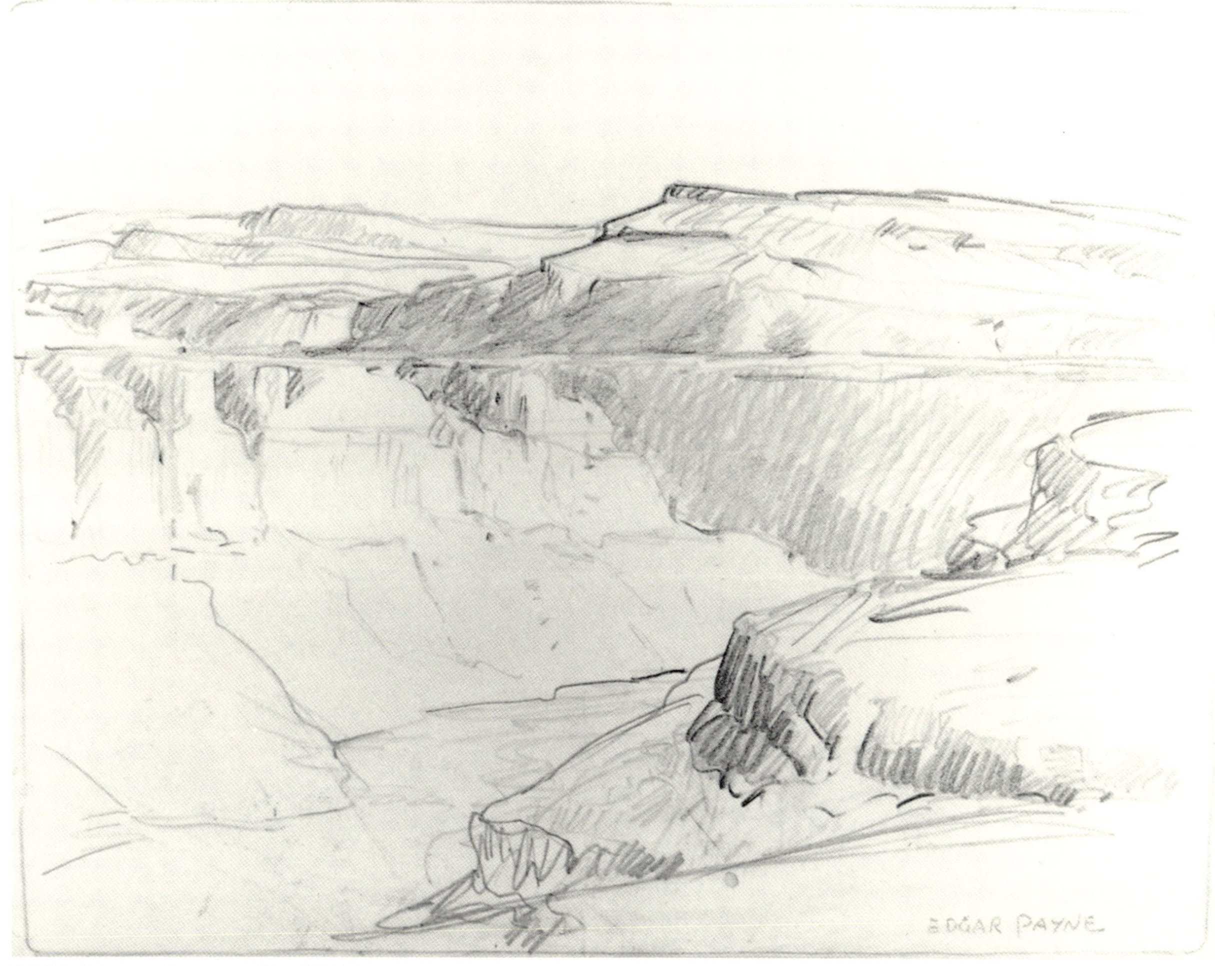

(M-5) Arizona Canyon 8" × 10½"

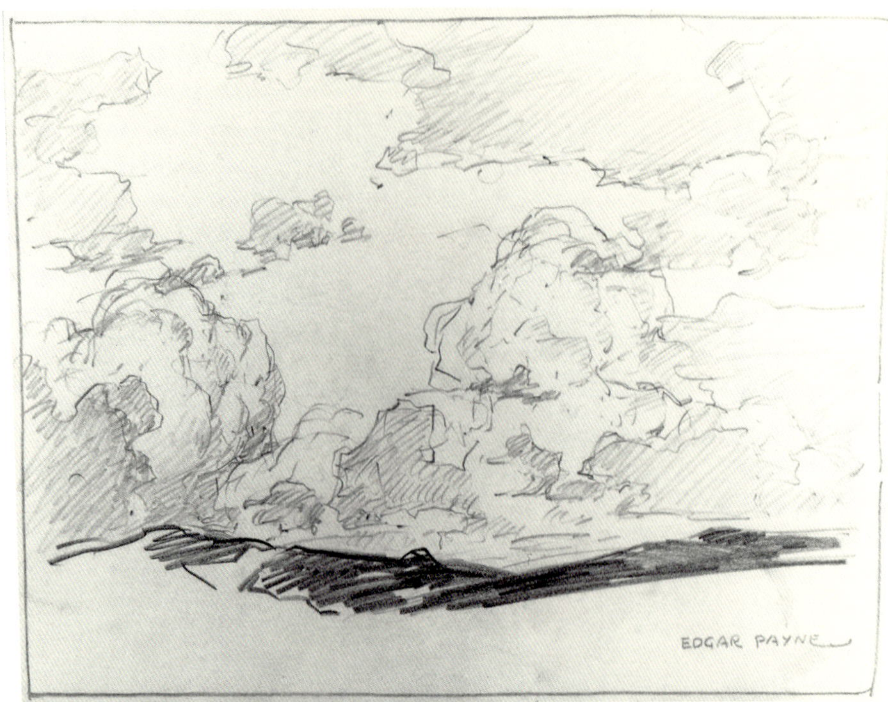

(M-11) Cloud Study 8" × 10"

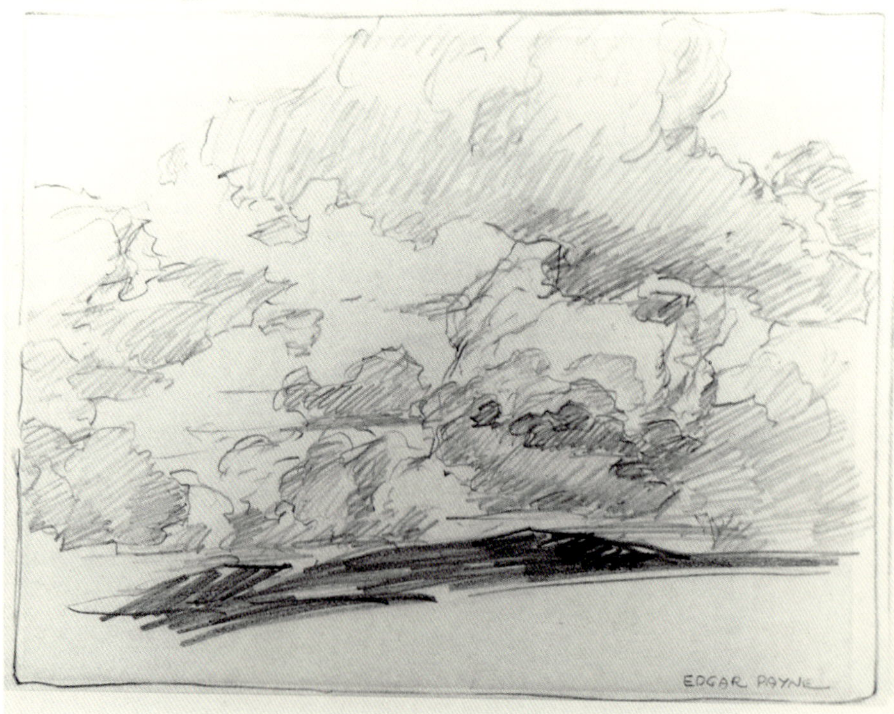

(UN-1) Desert Cloud Study 8" × 10"

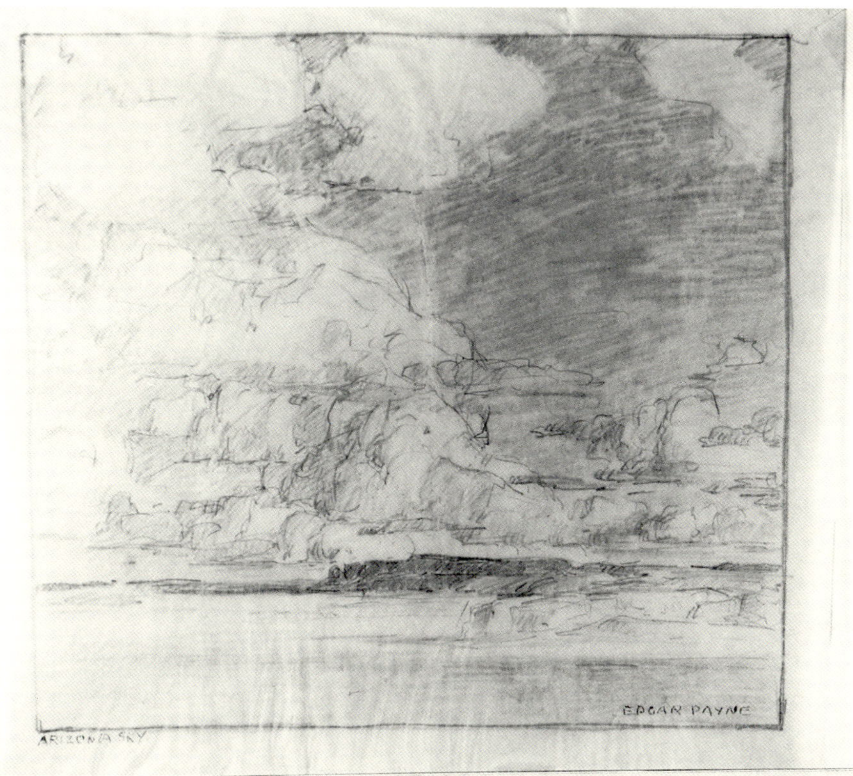

(T-23) Arizona Sky 10" × 11"

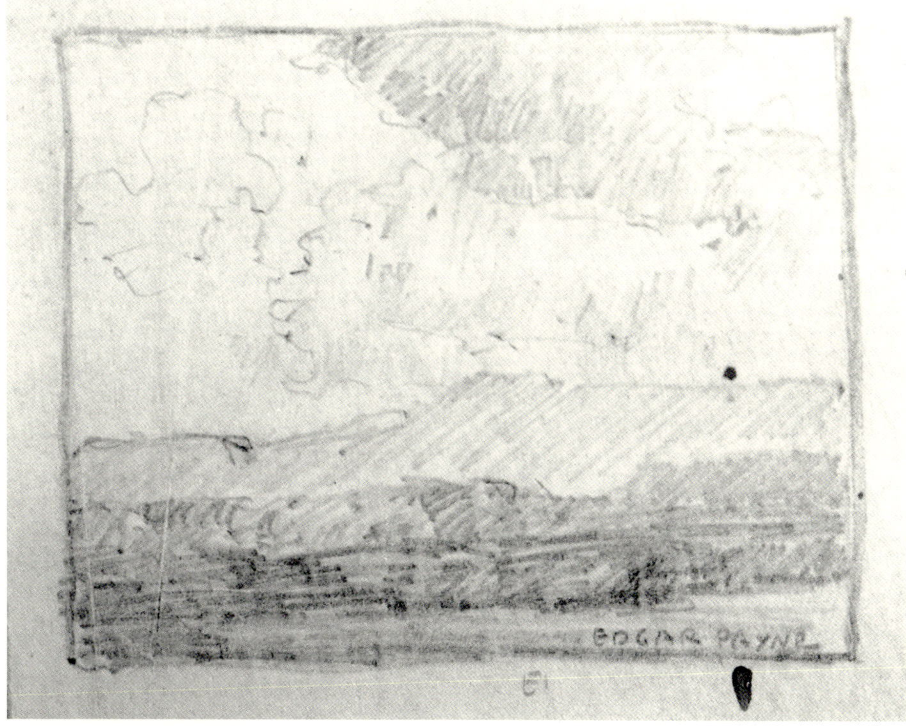

(M-19) Valley Scene 5" × 6"

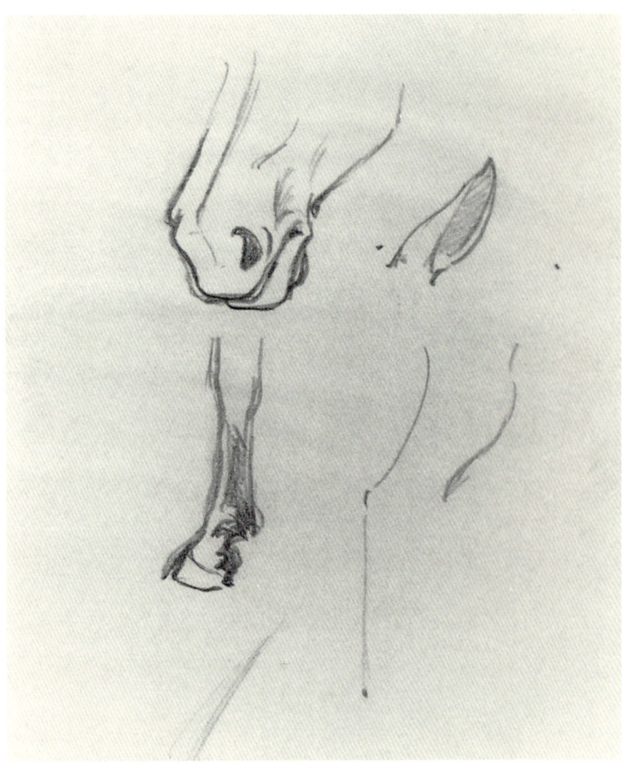
(X-120-20) Study of Horses 10" × 8"

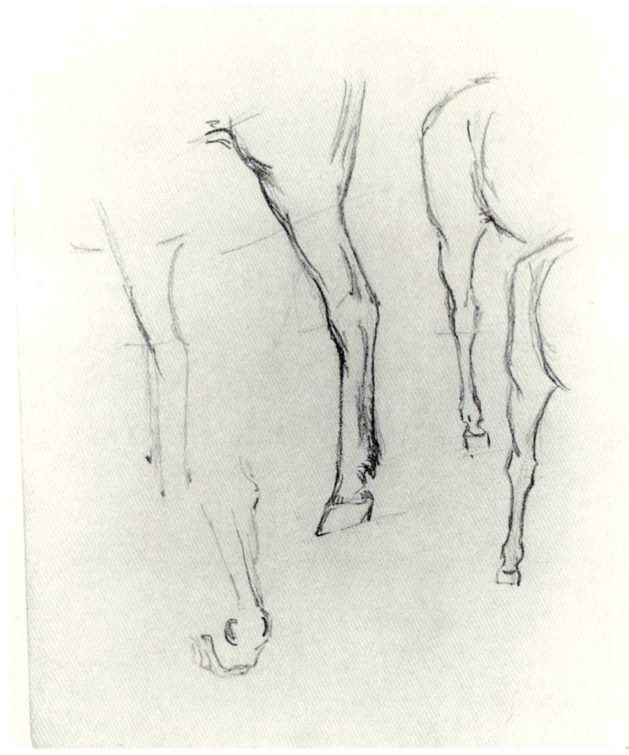
(SL-13A) Horse Studies 10" × 8"

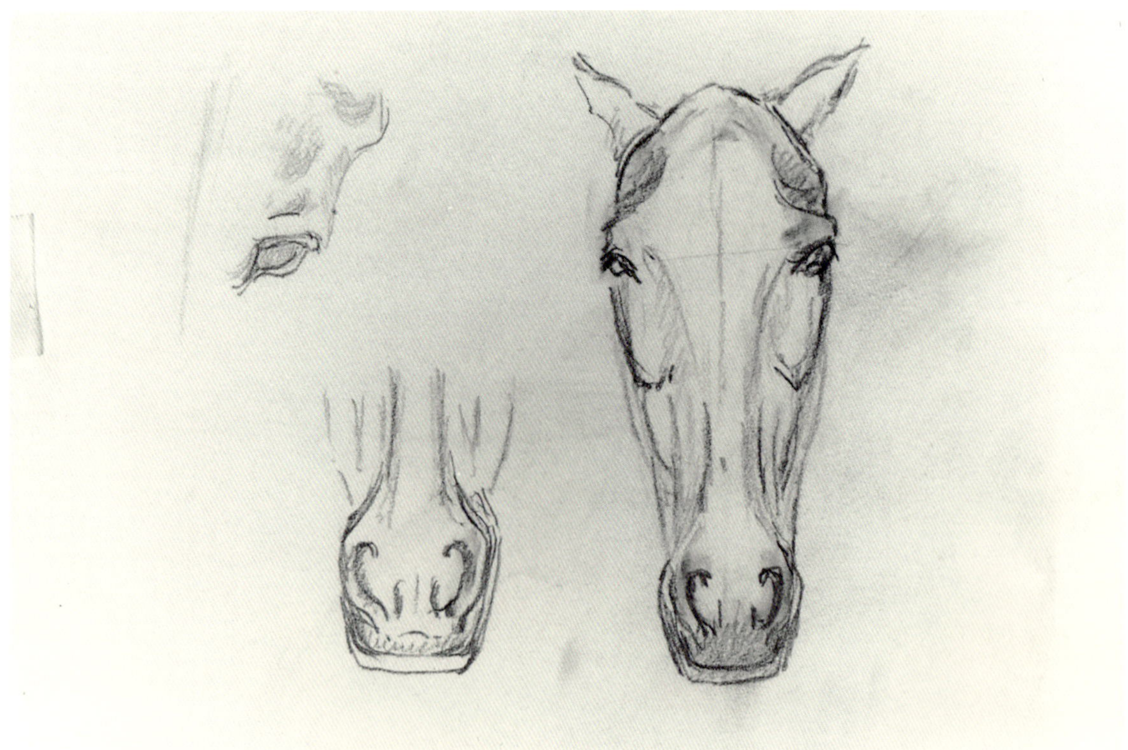
(SL-5a) Notes on Navajo Horses 10" × 8"

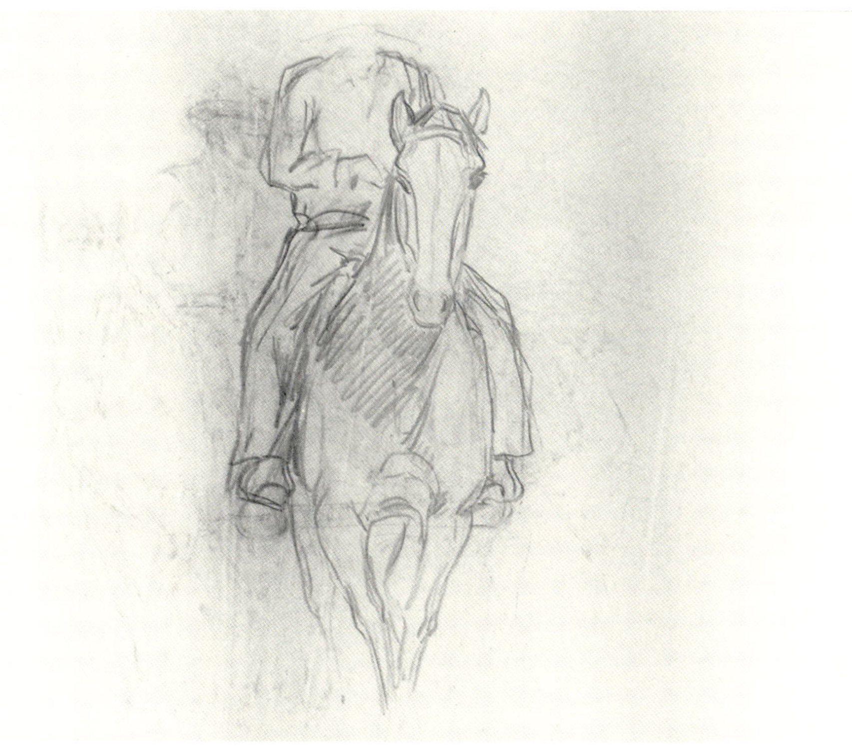

Back of S-34 9" × 12"

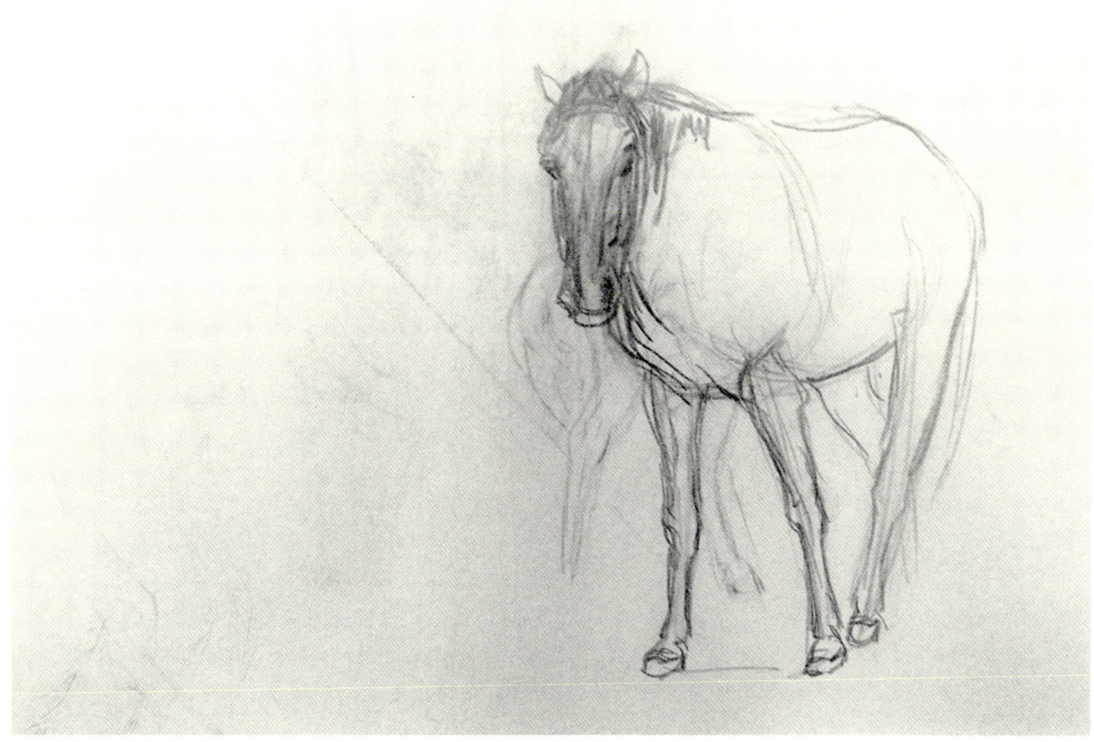

Back of S-31 15" × 22"

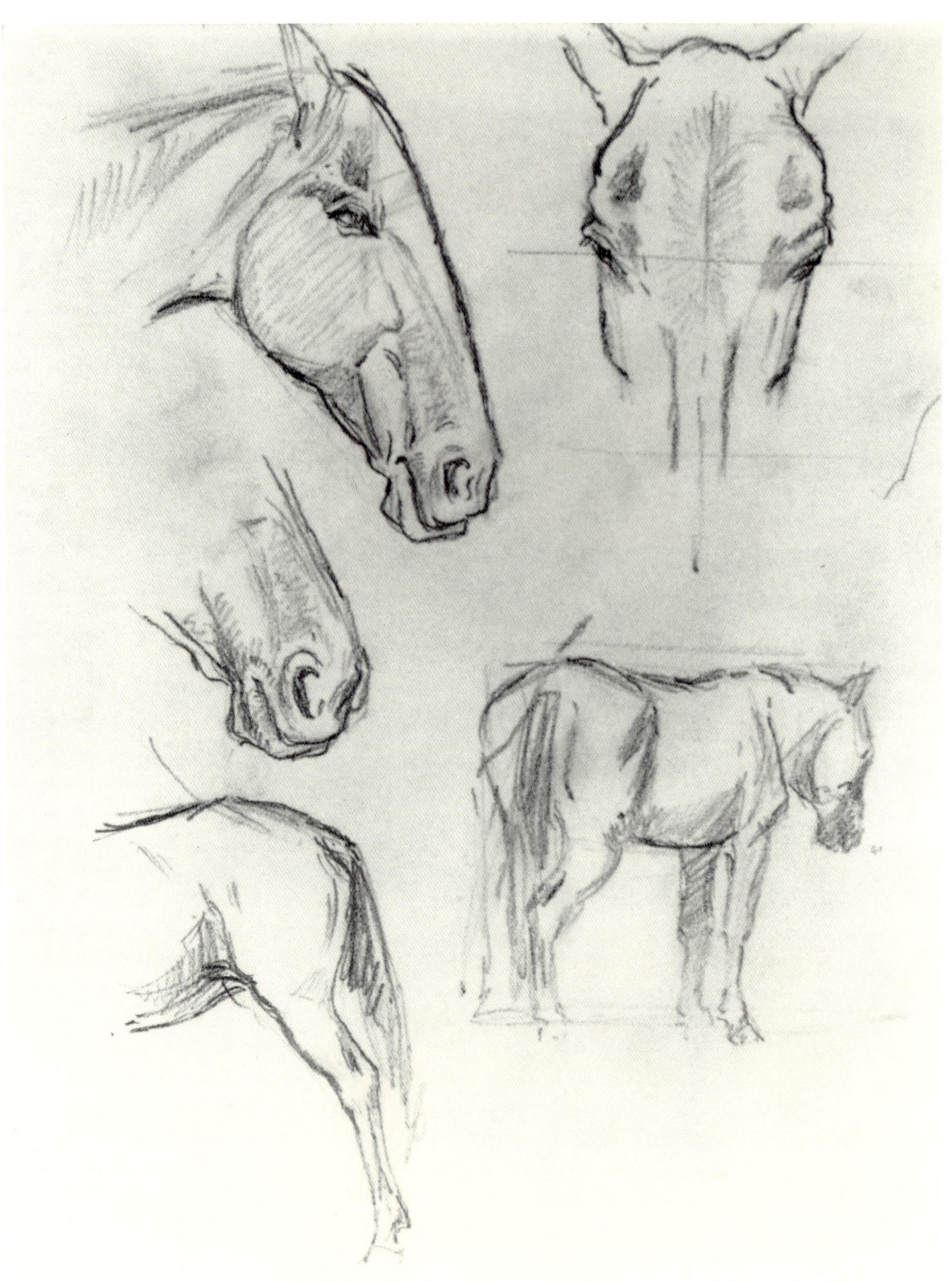

(SL-2a) Details of Horse Anatomy 10" × 8"

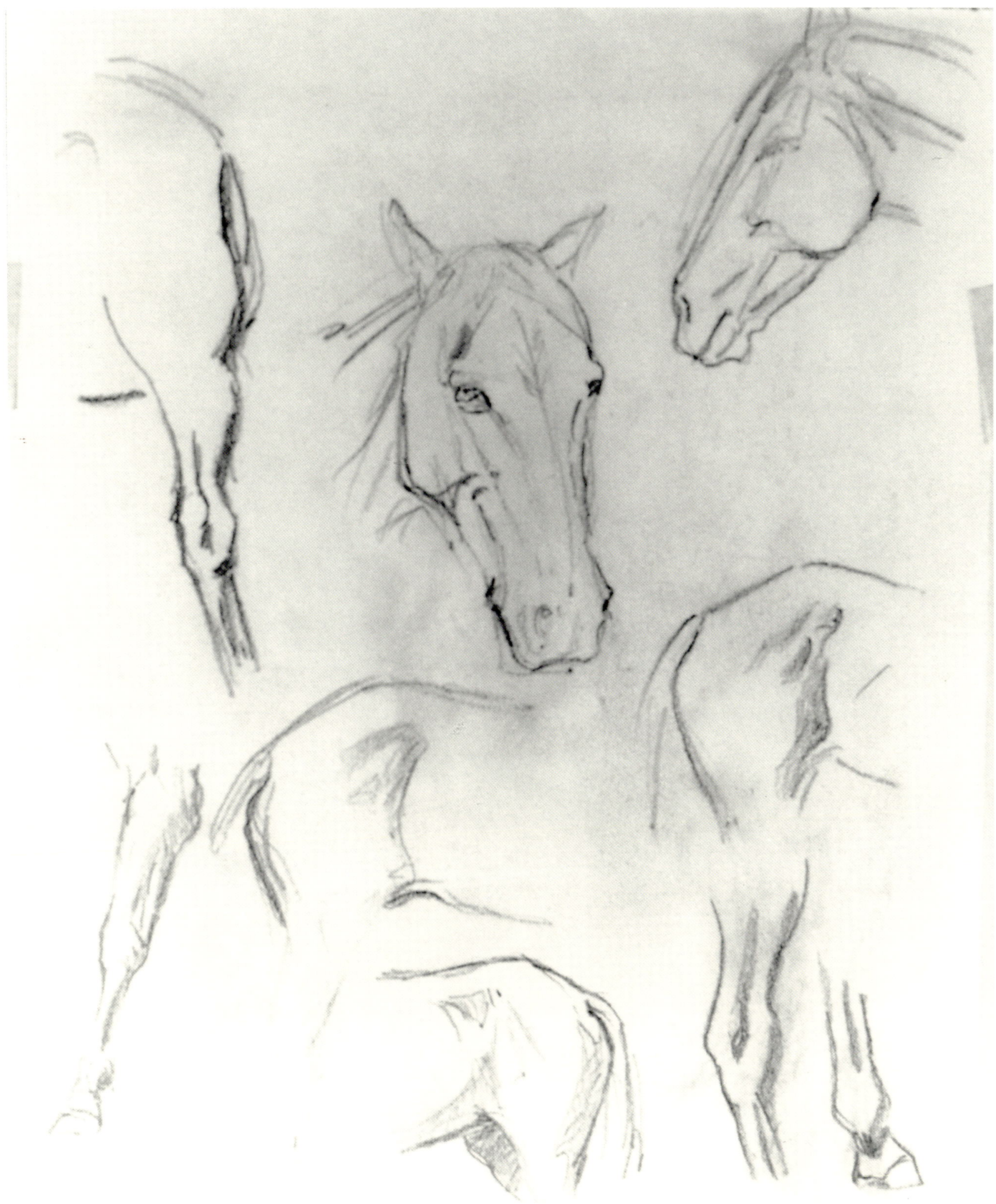

(SL-3a) Sketches of Horses 10" × 8"

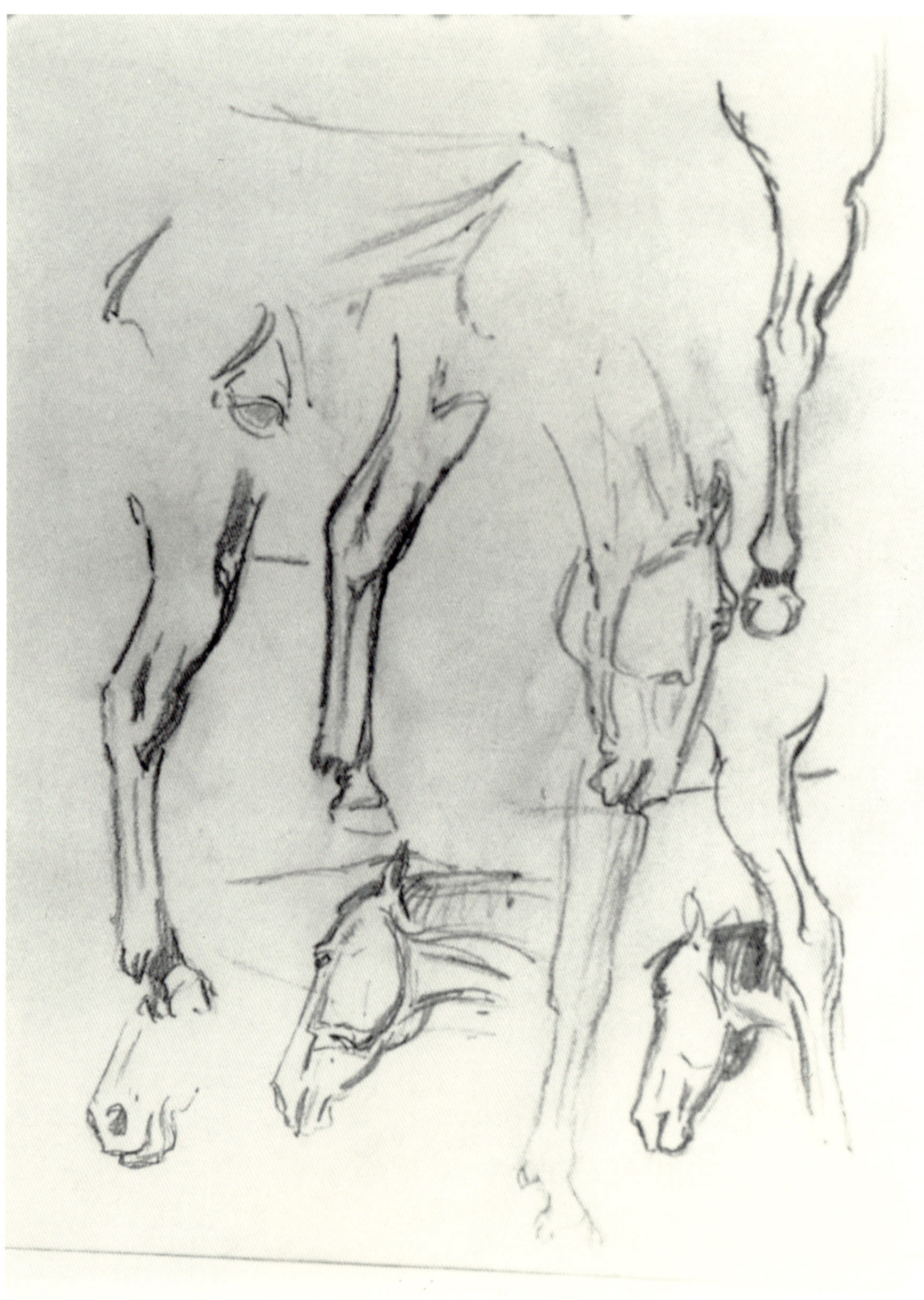

(SL-12a) Details of Horse Anatomy 10" × 8"

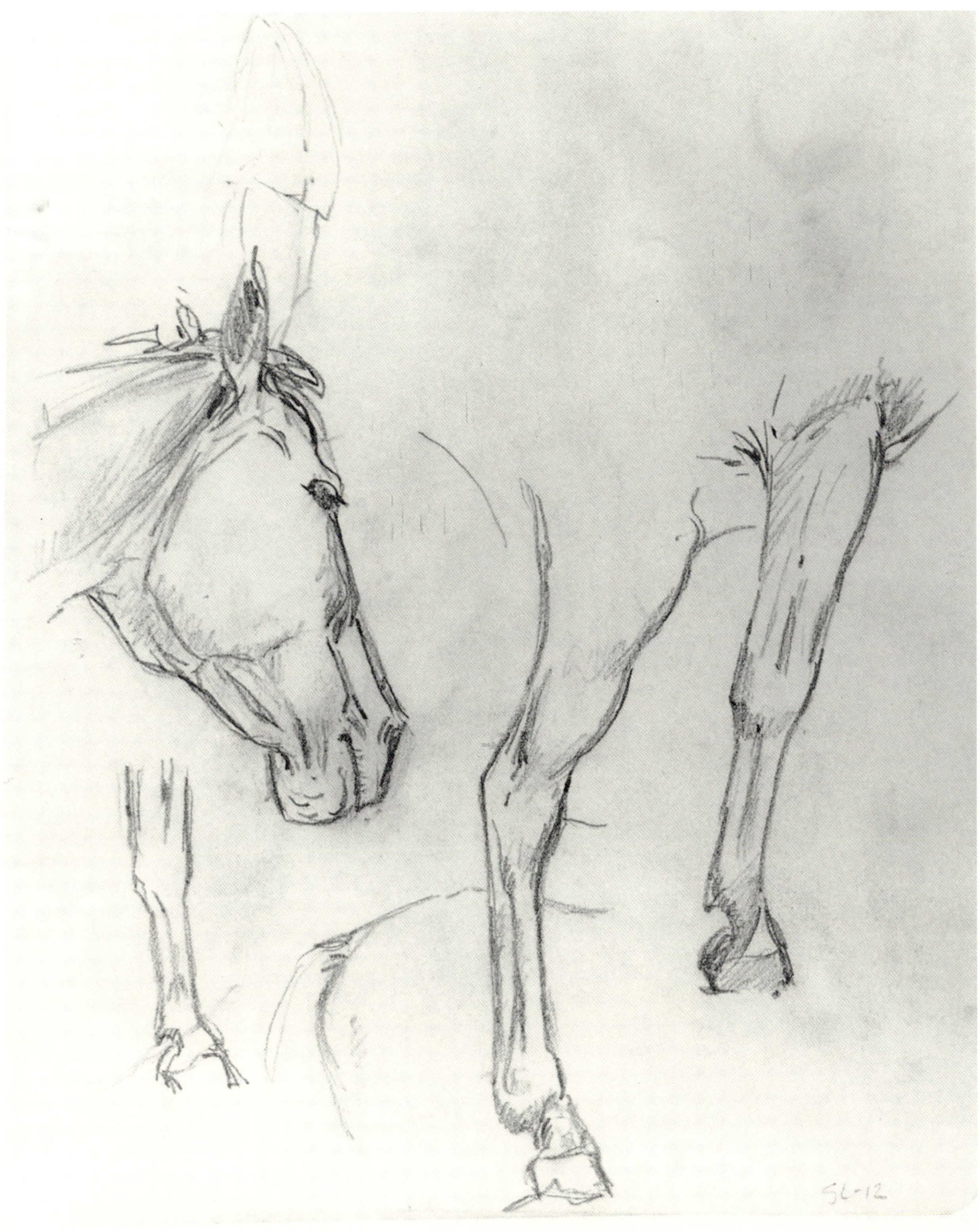

(SL-12) Studies of Horses at Rest 10" × 8"

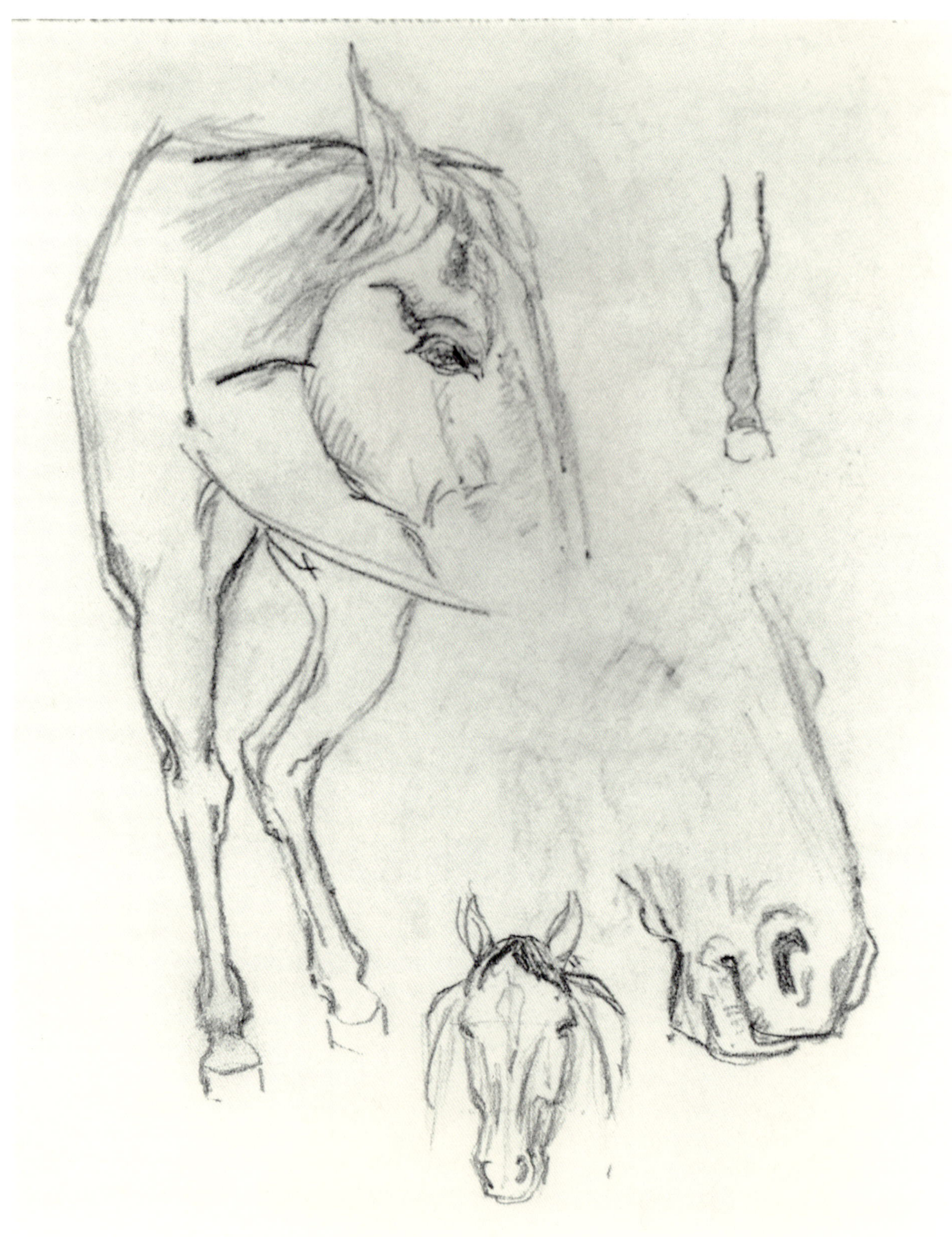

(SL-1 back) Quick Study of Horse Parts 10" × 8"

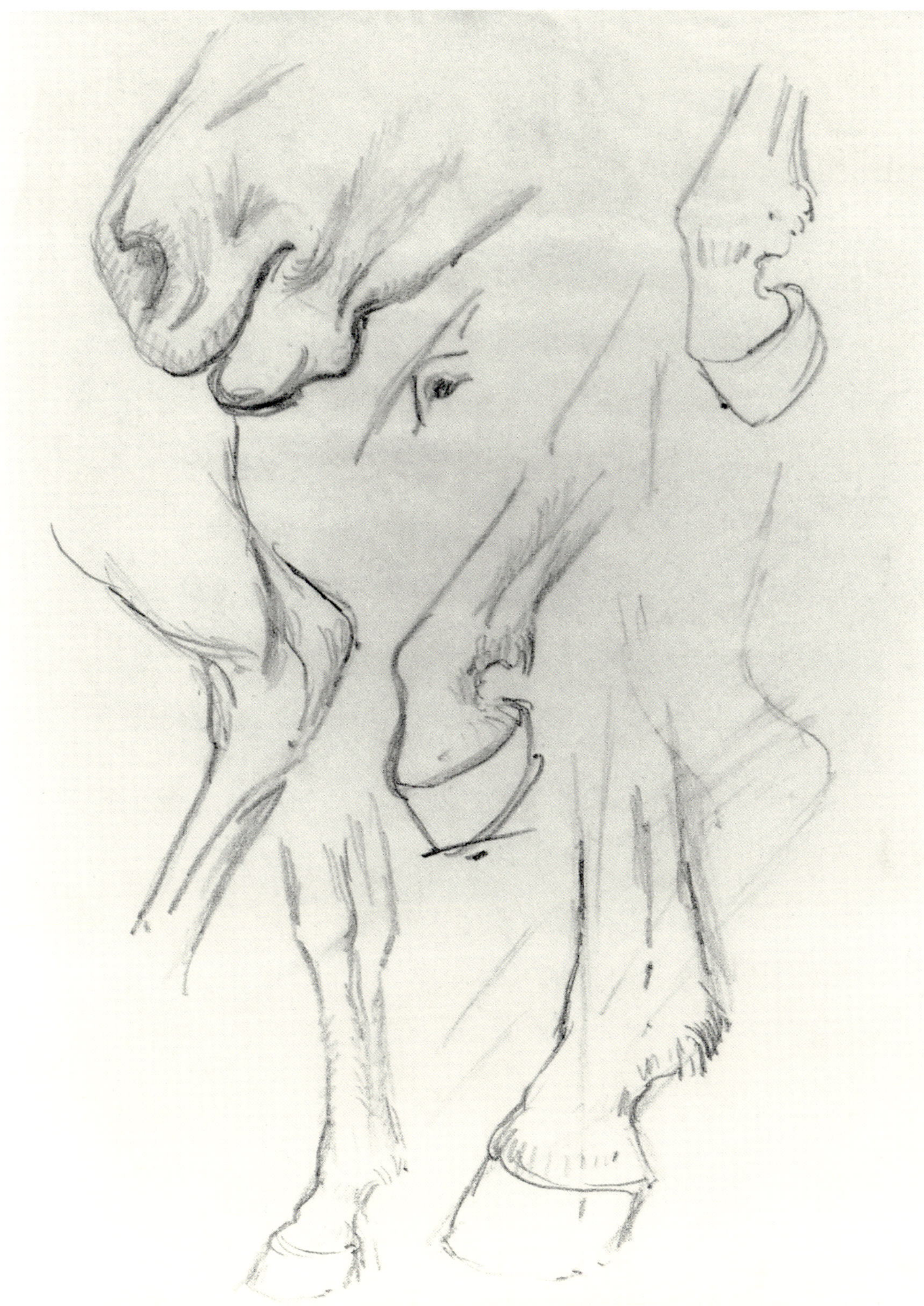

(T-11) Studies of Unshod Navajo Horses 10" × 8"

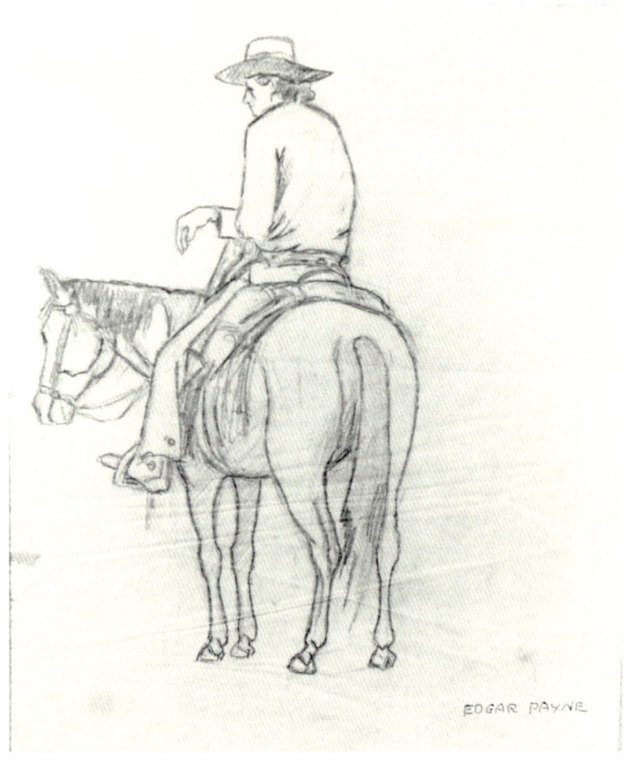

(T-29) Cowhand Resting 12" × 10"

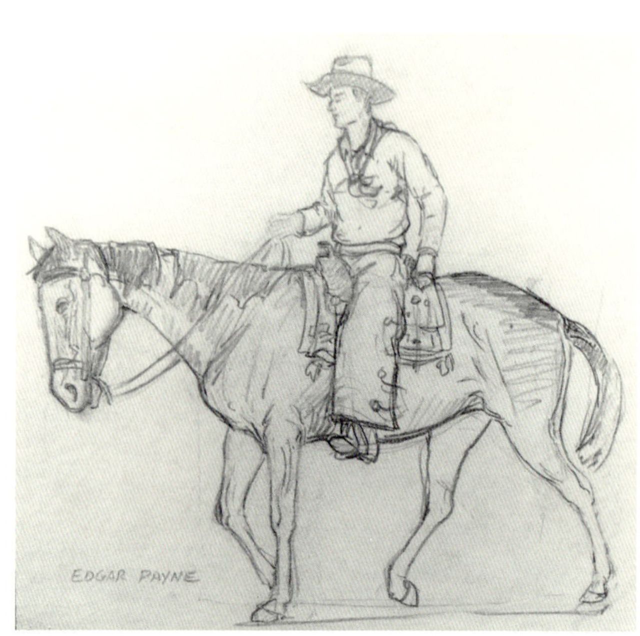

(T-39) Mounted Cowhand 12" × 13"

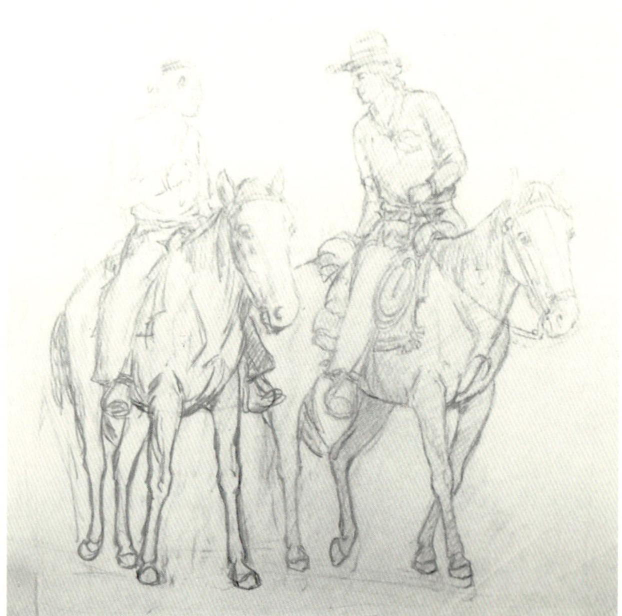
(T-18) Cowboy and Indian 15" × 16"

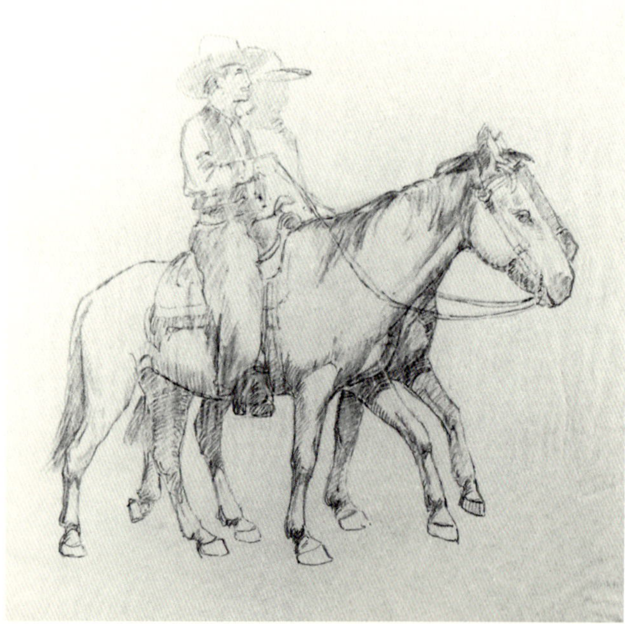
(T-31) Two Cowhands 12" × 12"

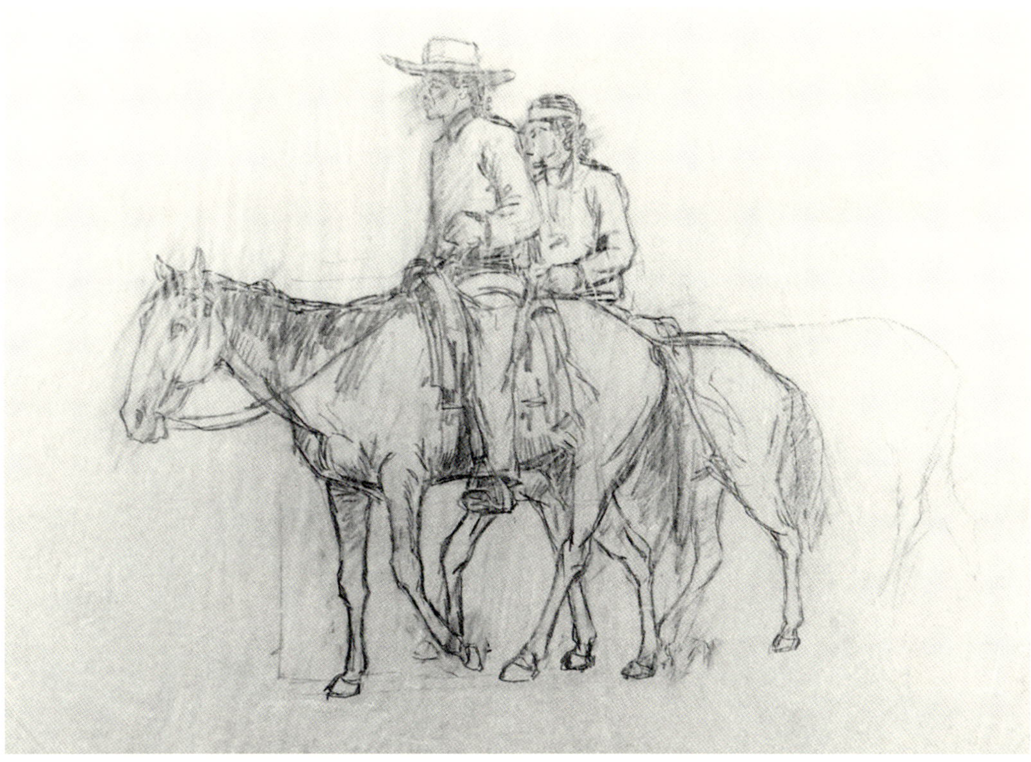

(T-32) Navajos on Horses 12" × 16"

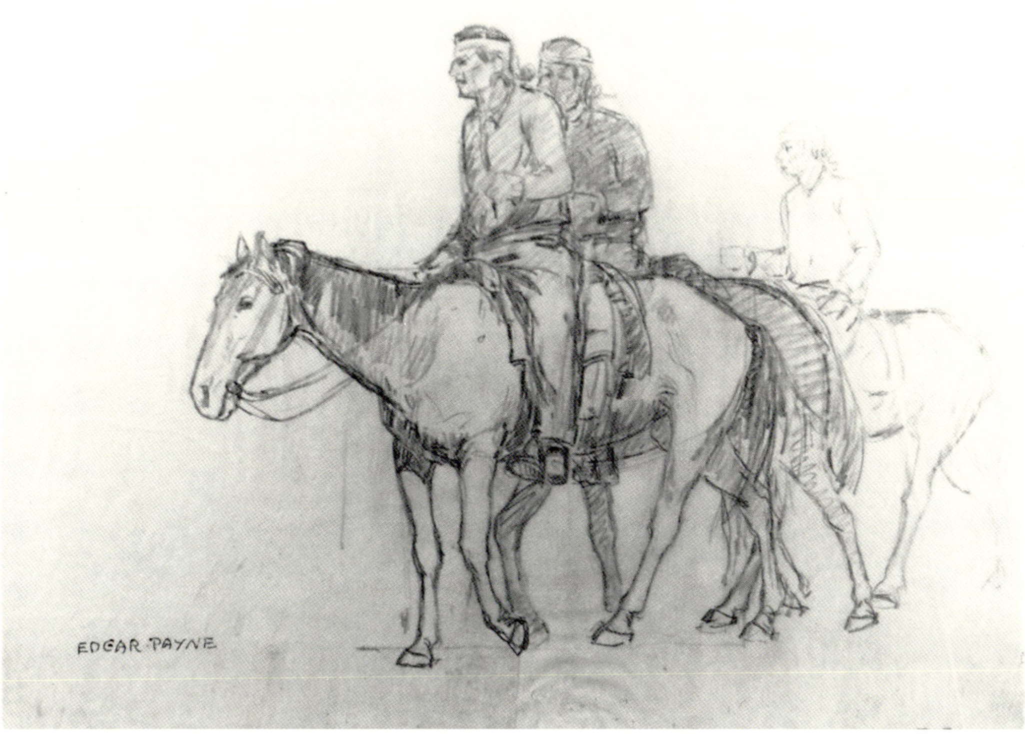

(T-30) Navajo Riders 11" × 14"

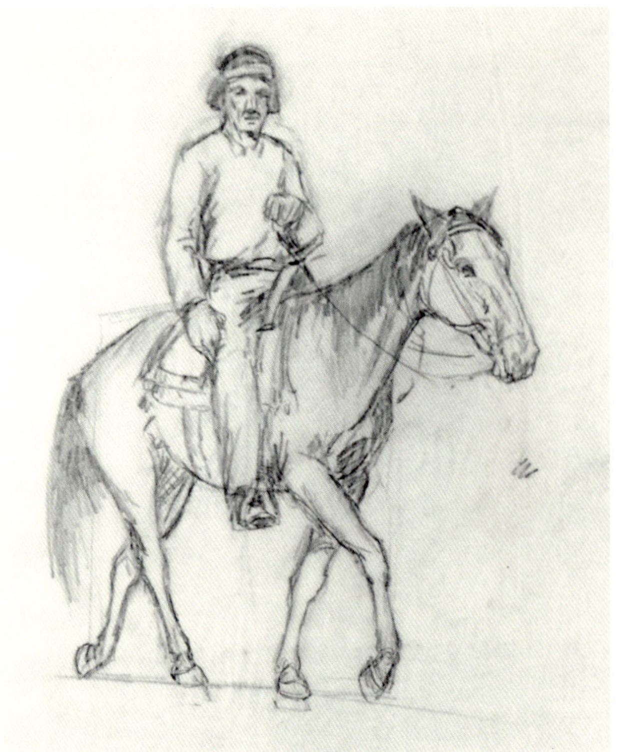

(T-47) Single Rider 13" × 16"

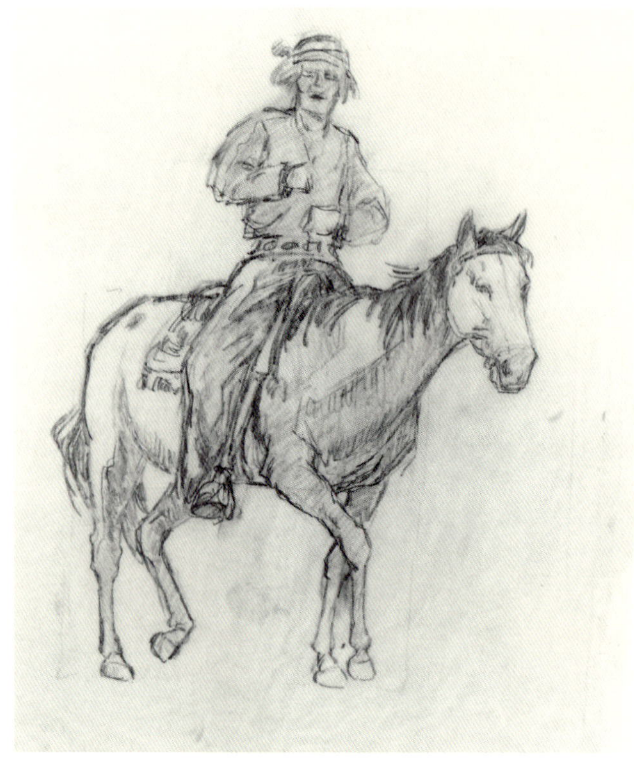

(S-23) Navajo on Horseback 12" × 10"

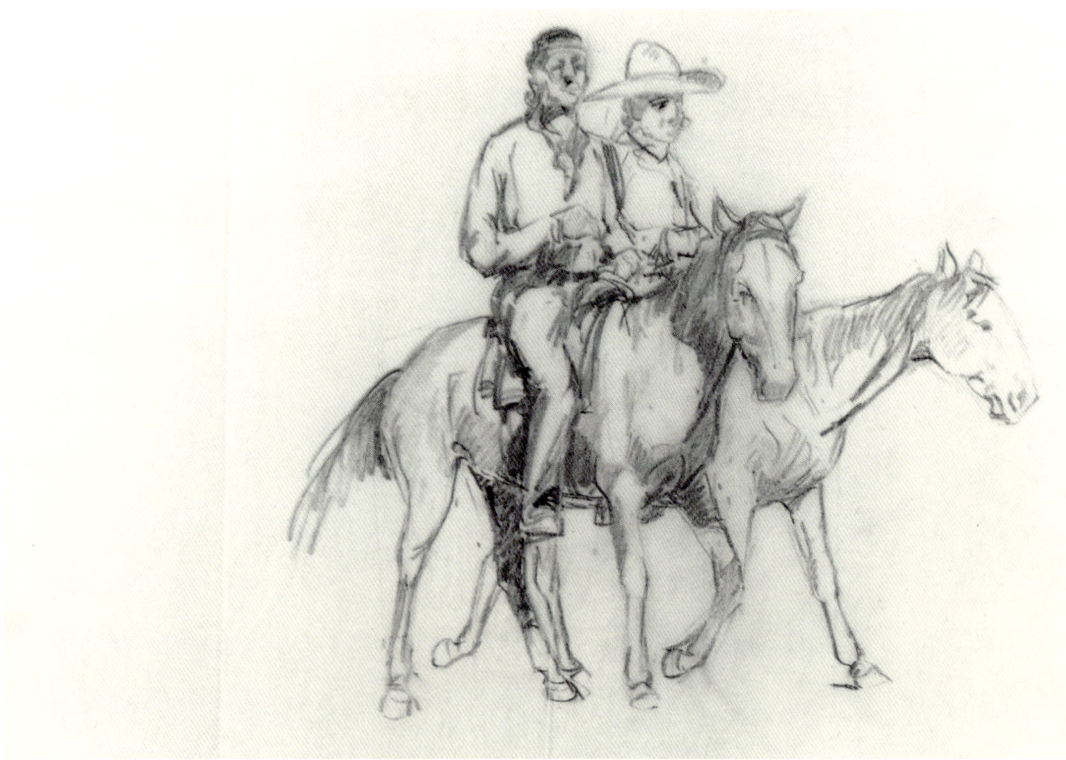

(T-46) Sketch of Two Riders 10" × 12"

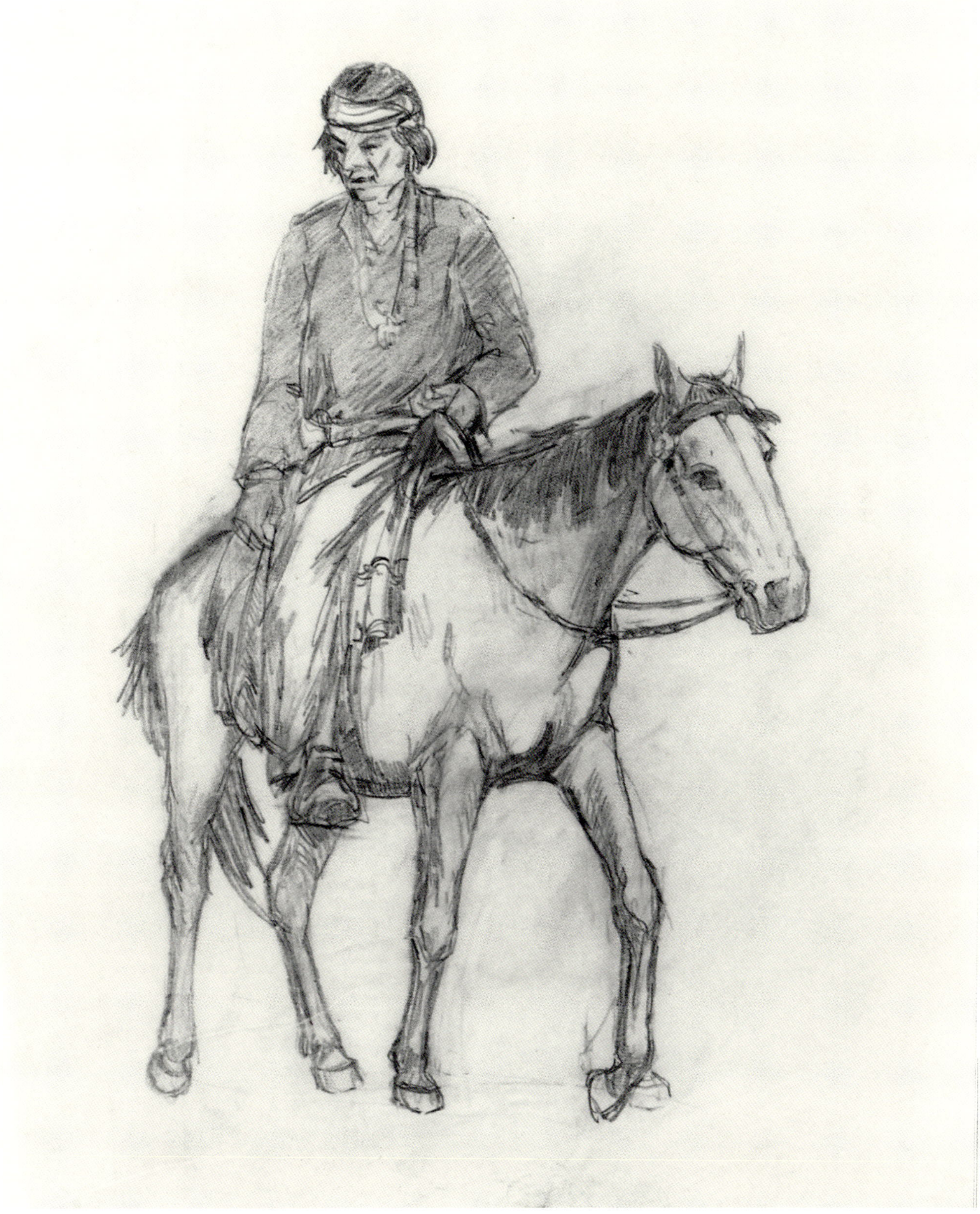

(T-50) Rider Studying the Ground 14" × 10"

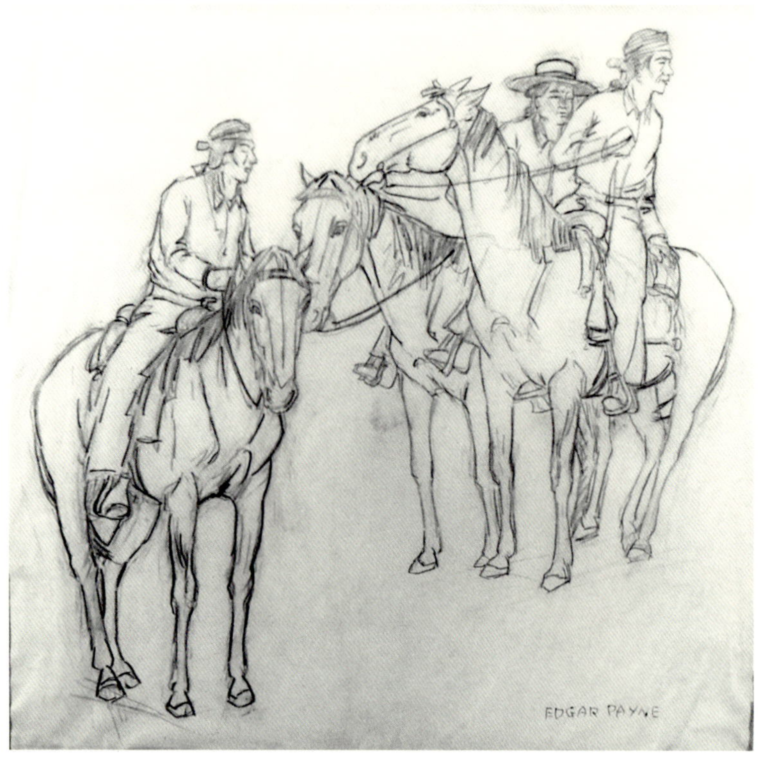

(T-17) Looking 13" × 13"

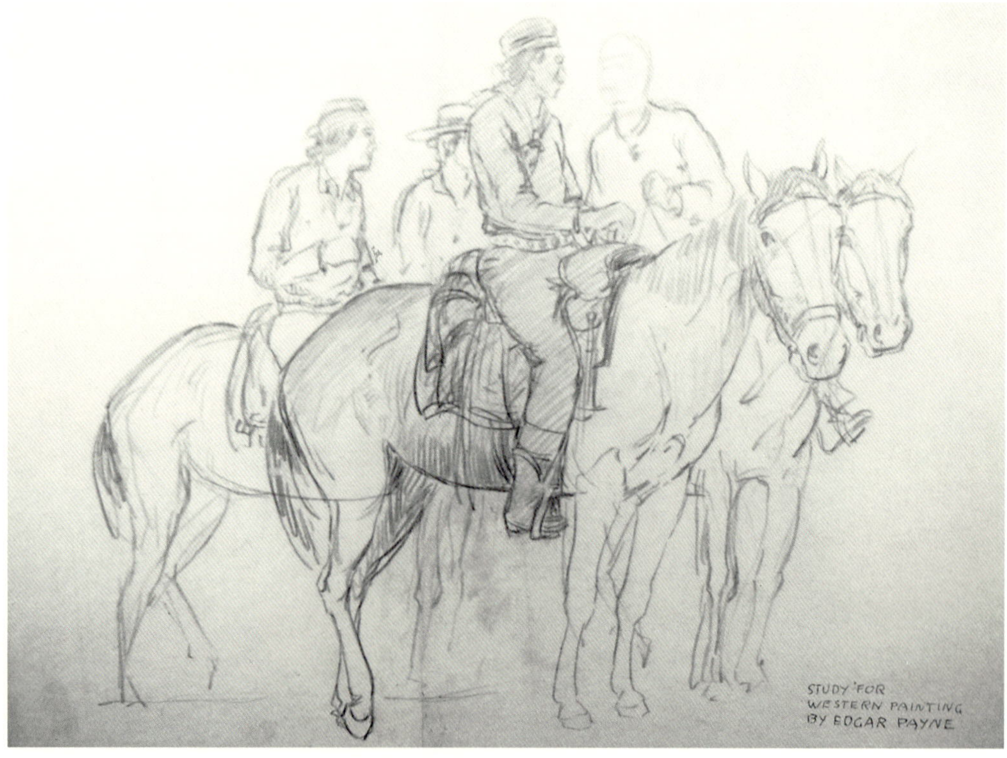

(T-36) Study for Western Painting 16" × 19"

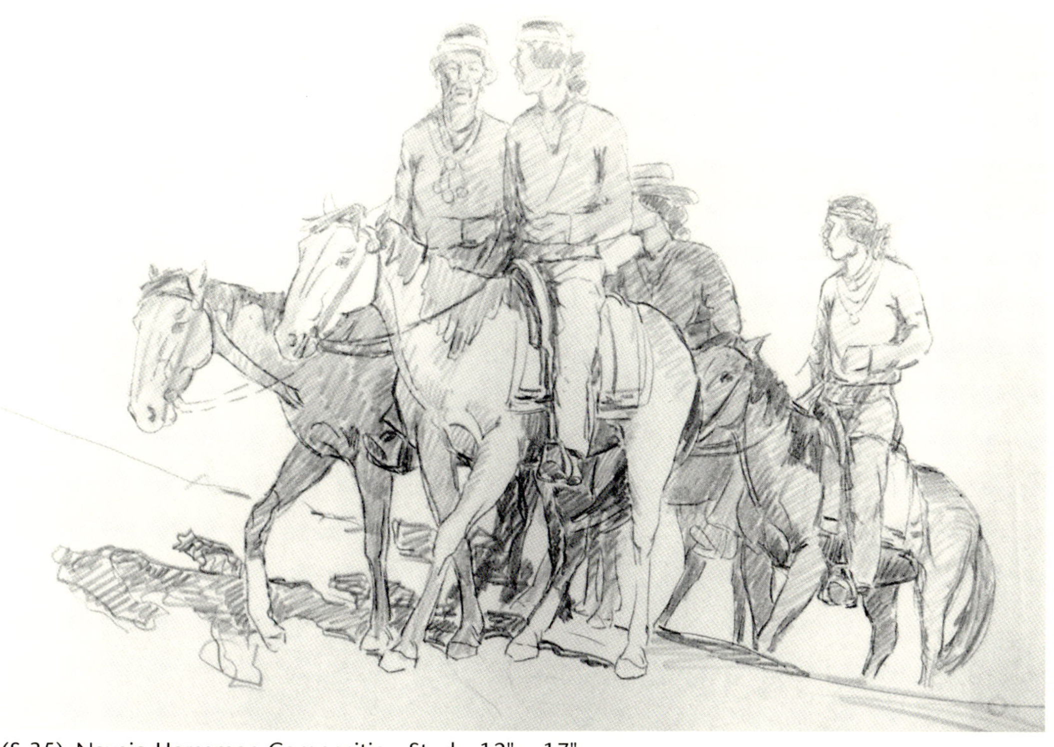

(S-35) Navajo Horsemen Composition Study 12" × 17"

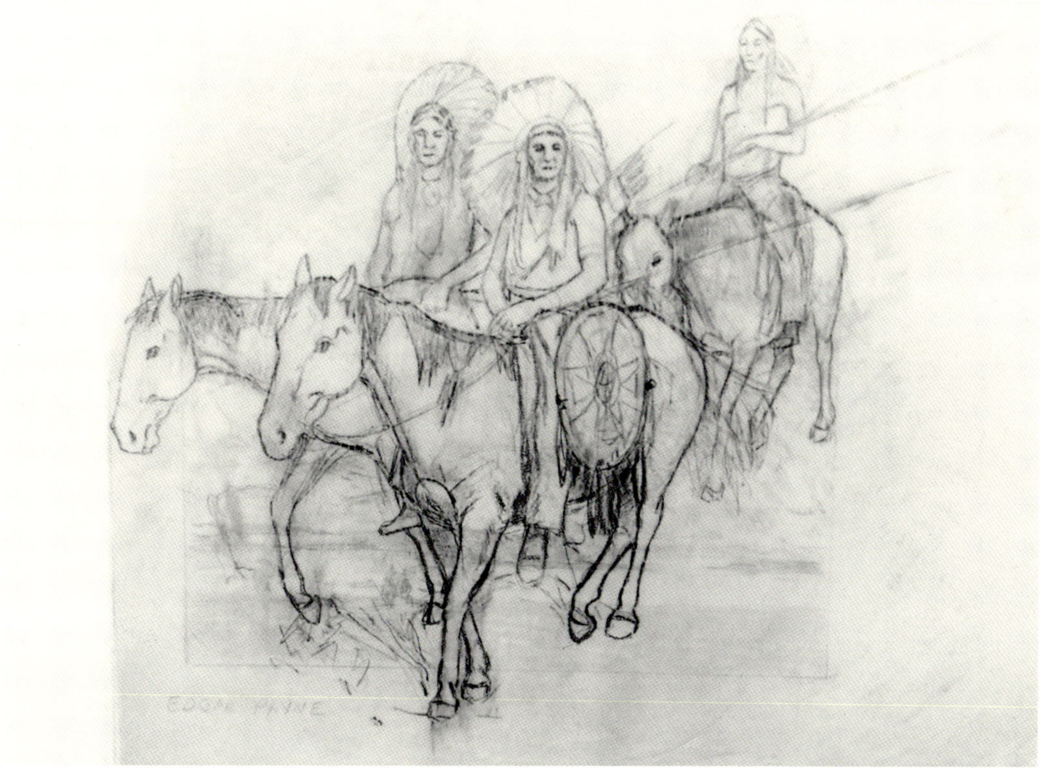

(X-203) Indians in Plains Attire 13" × 15"

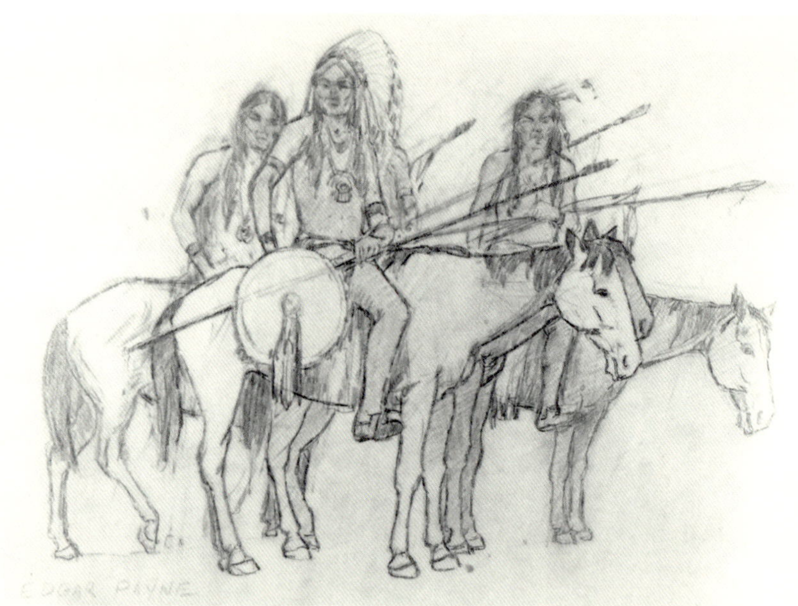

(X-202) Mounted Indians with Spears 11" × 15"

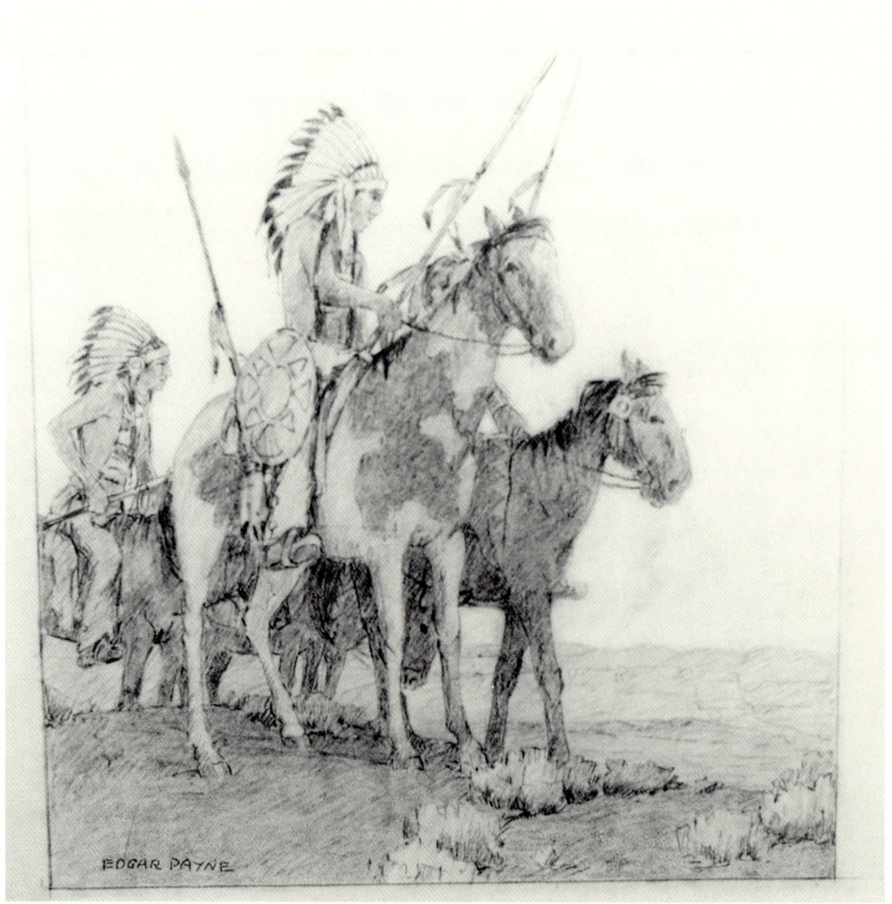

(T-3-6) Plains Warriors Composition 12" × 12"

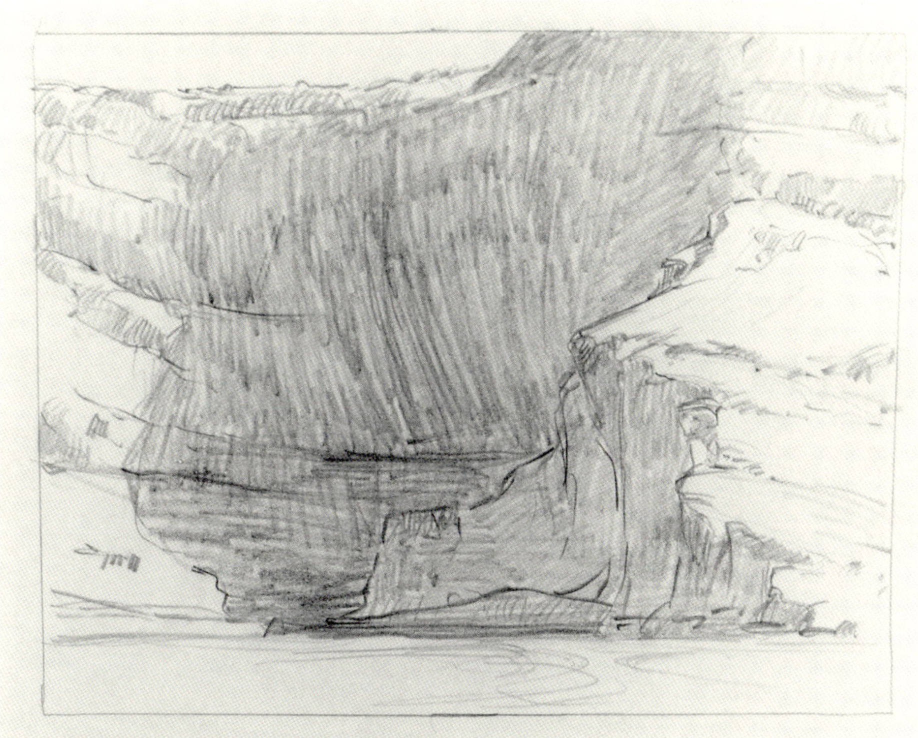

(M-20) Shadowed Canyon Wall 8" × 10"

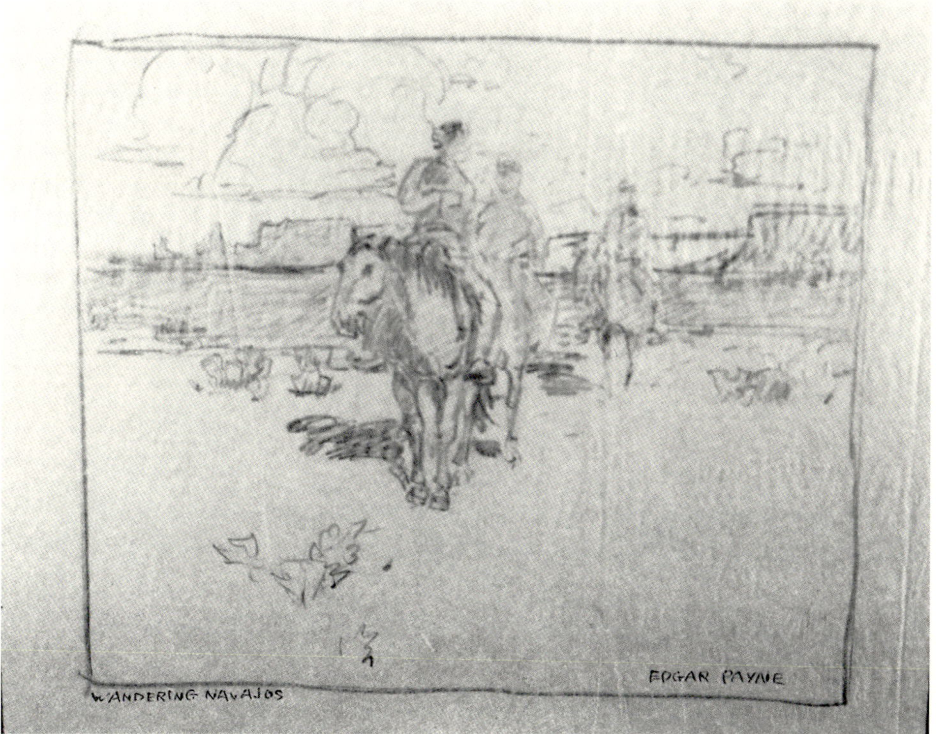

(T-22) Wandering Navajos 9" × 12"

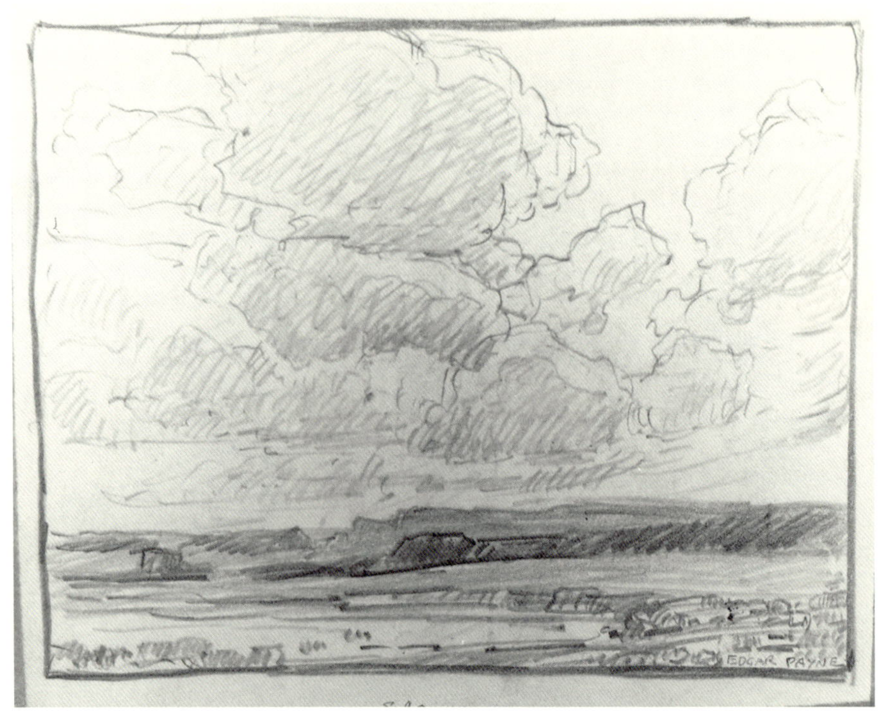

(S-40) Arizona Sky 6" × 8"

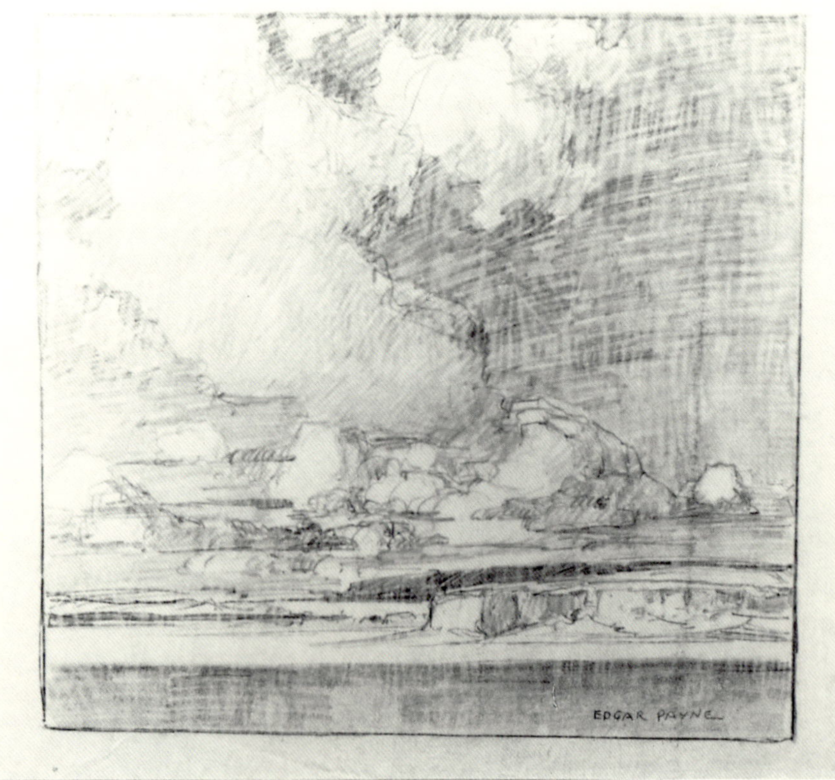

(T-15) Cloud Study 12" × 13"

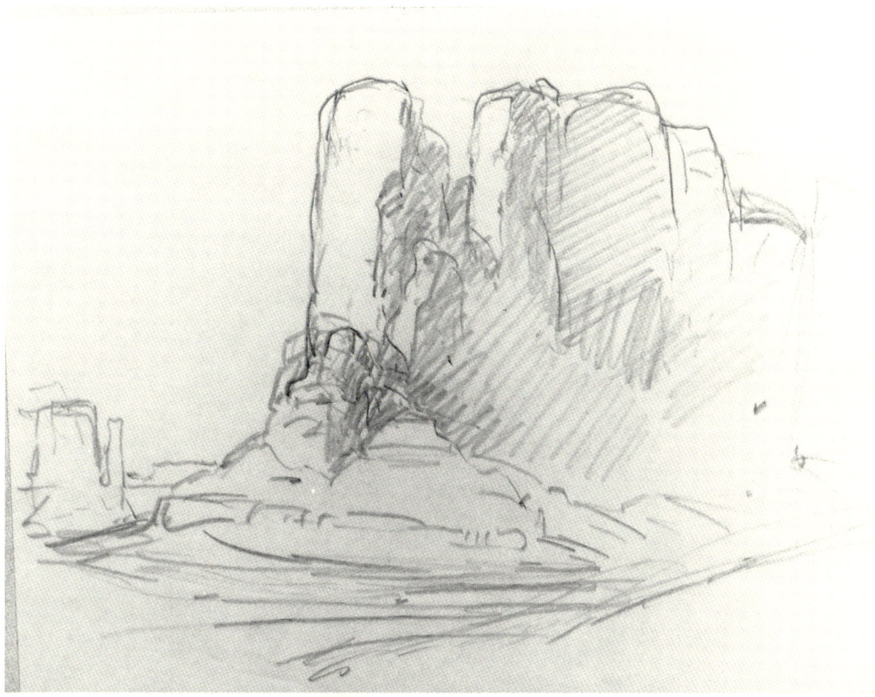

(M-3) Monument Valley 8" × 10½"

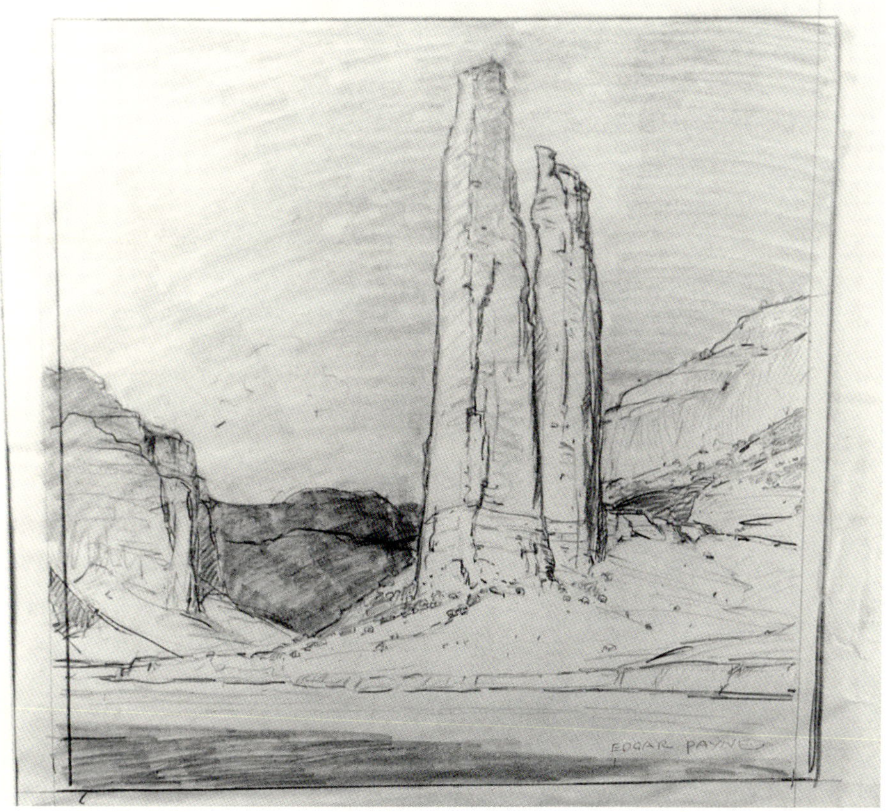

(T-9) Natural Monuments 12" × 12"

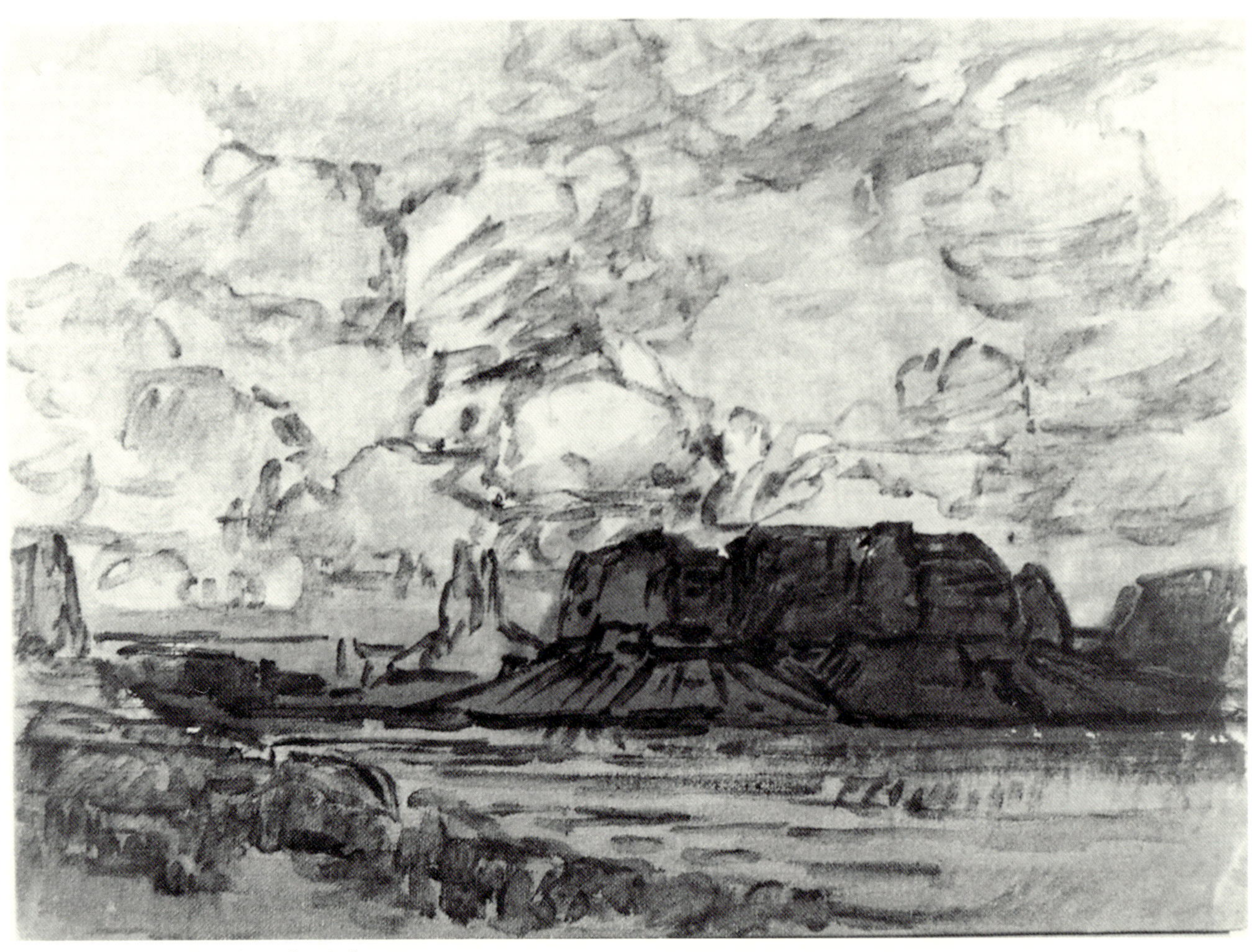

(U-2) Mesas and Clouds 10" × 14"

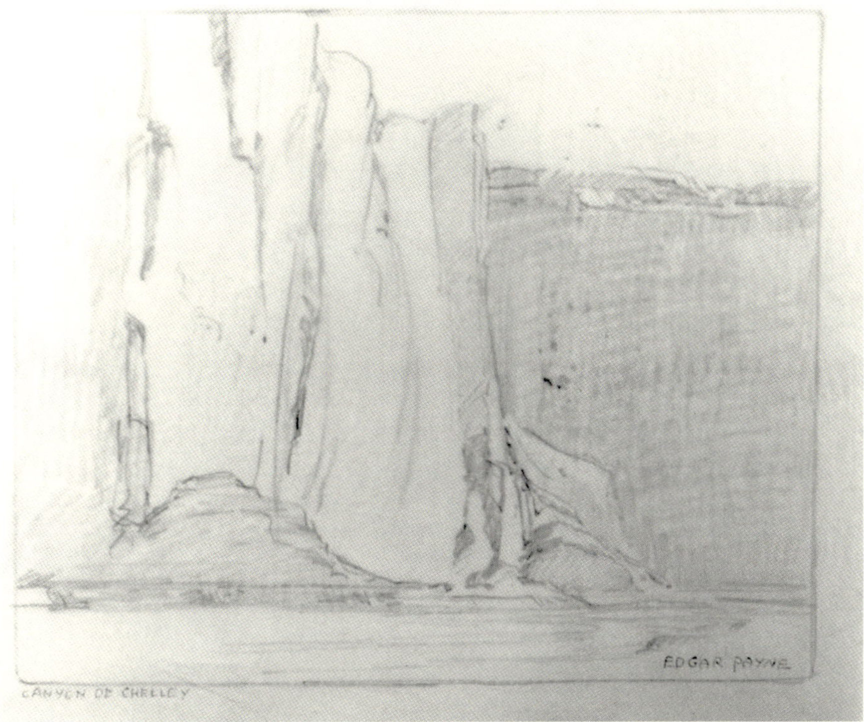

(T-24B) Canyon de Chelly 10" × 13"

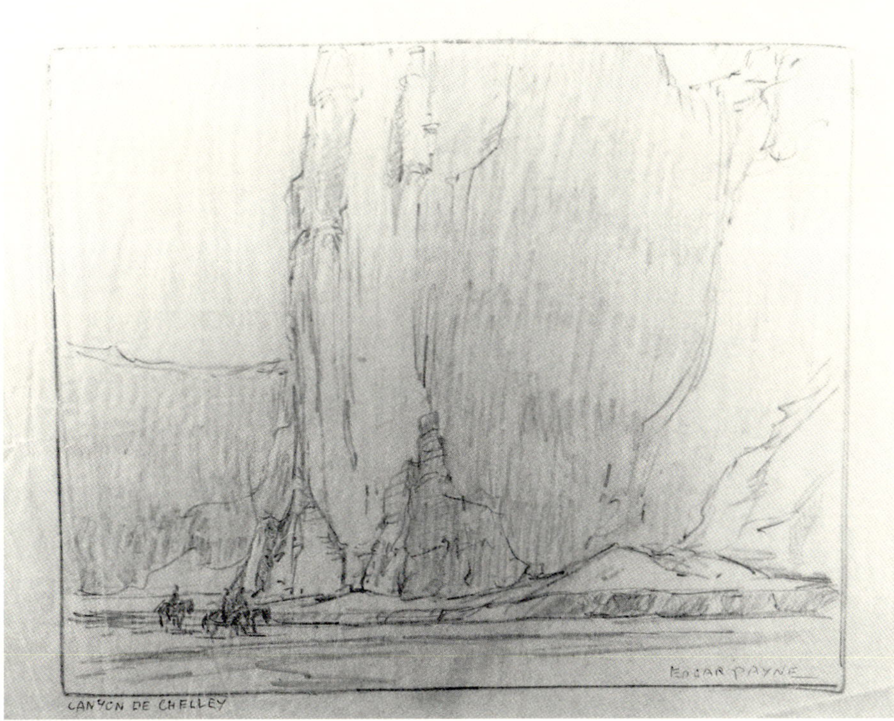

(T-24A) Riders in Canyon de Chelly 12" × 15"

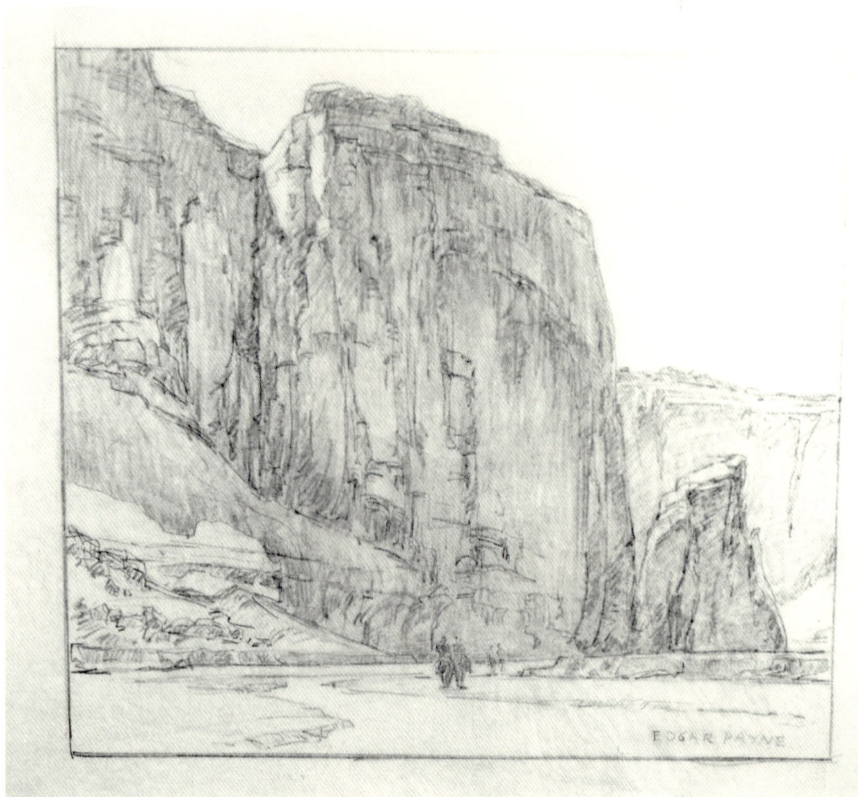

(T-48) Canyon Composition 10" × 12"

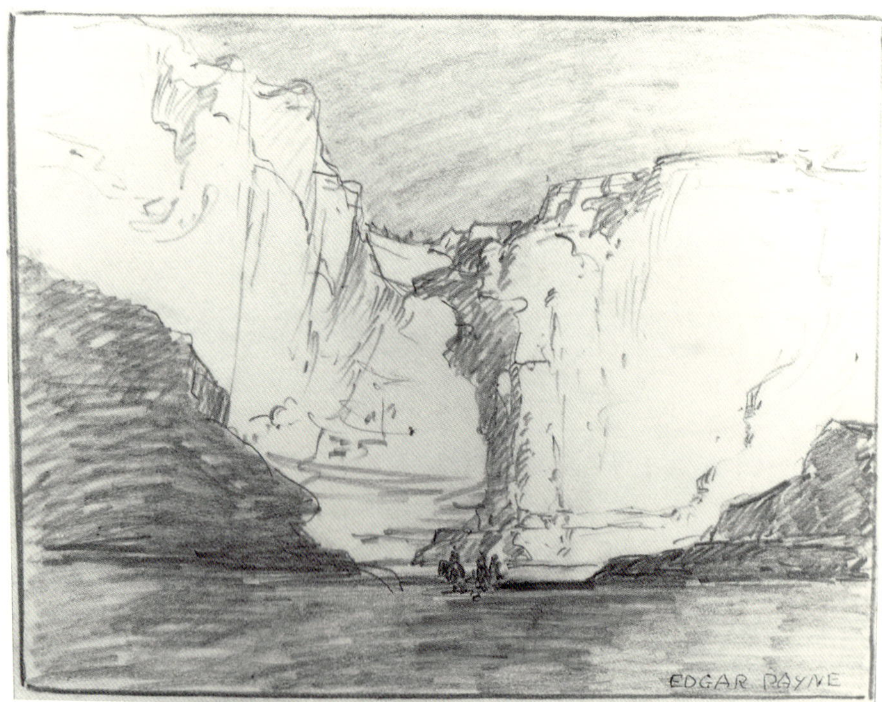

(M-4) Canyon de Chelly Study 8" × 10½"

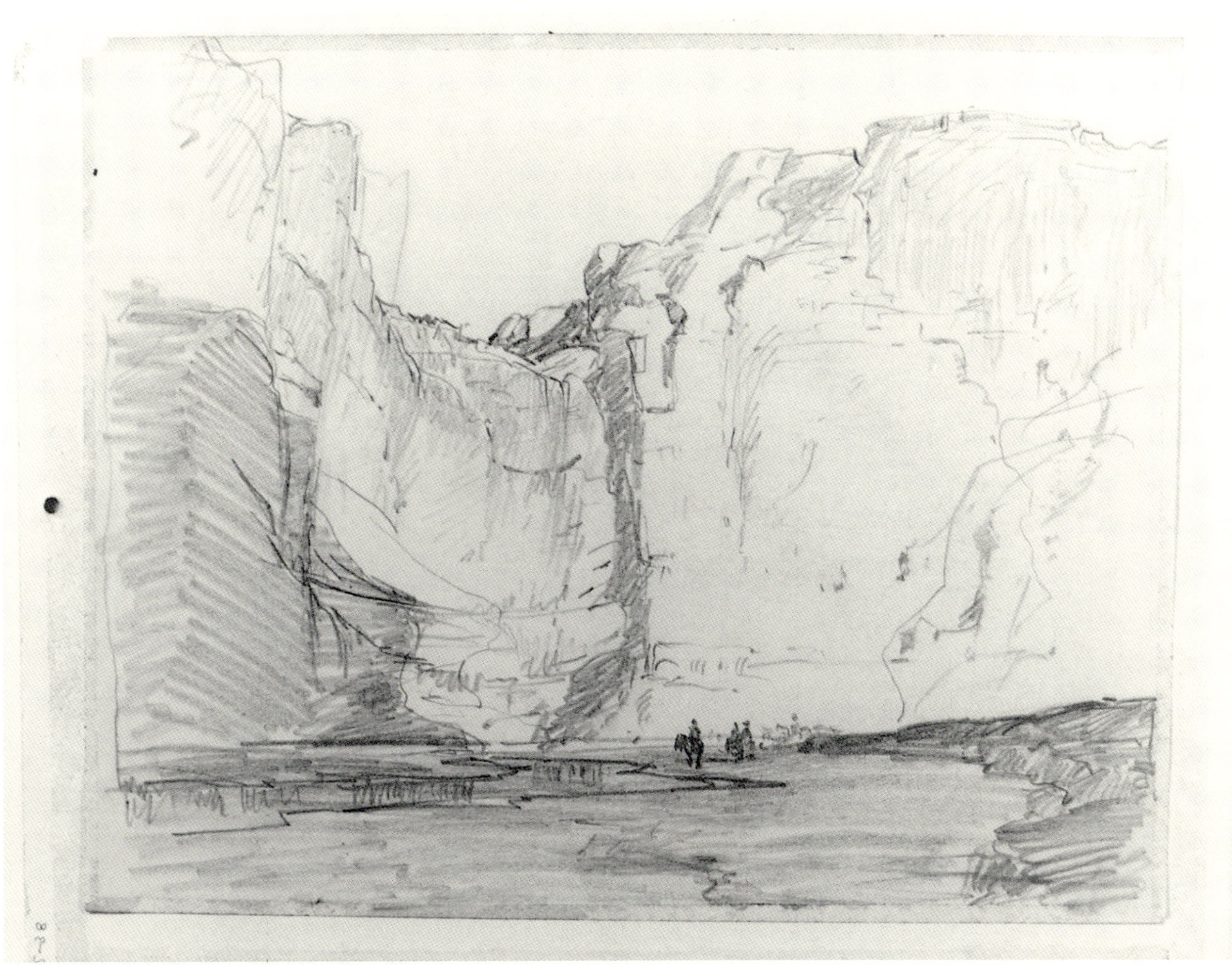

(S-38) Stream in the Canyon 8" × 10½"

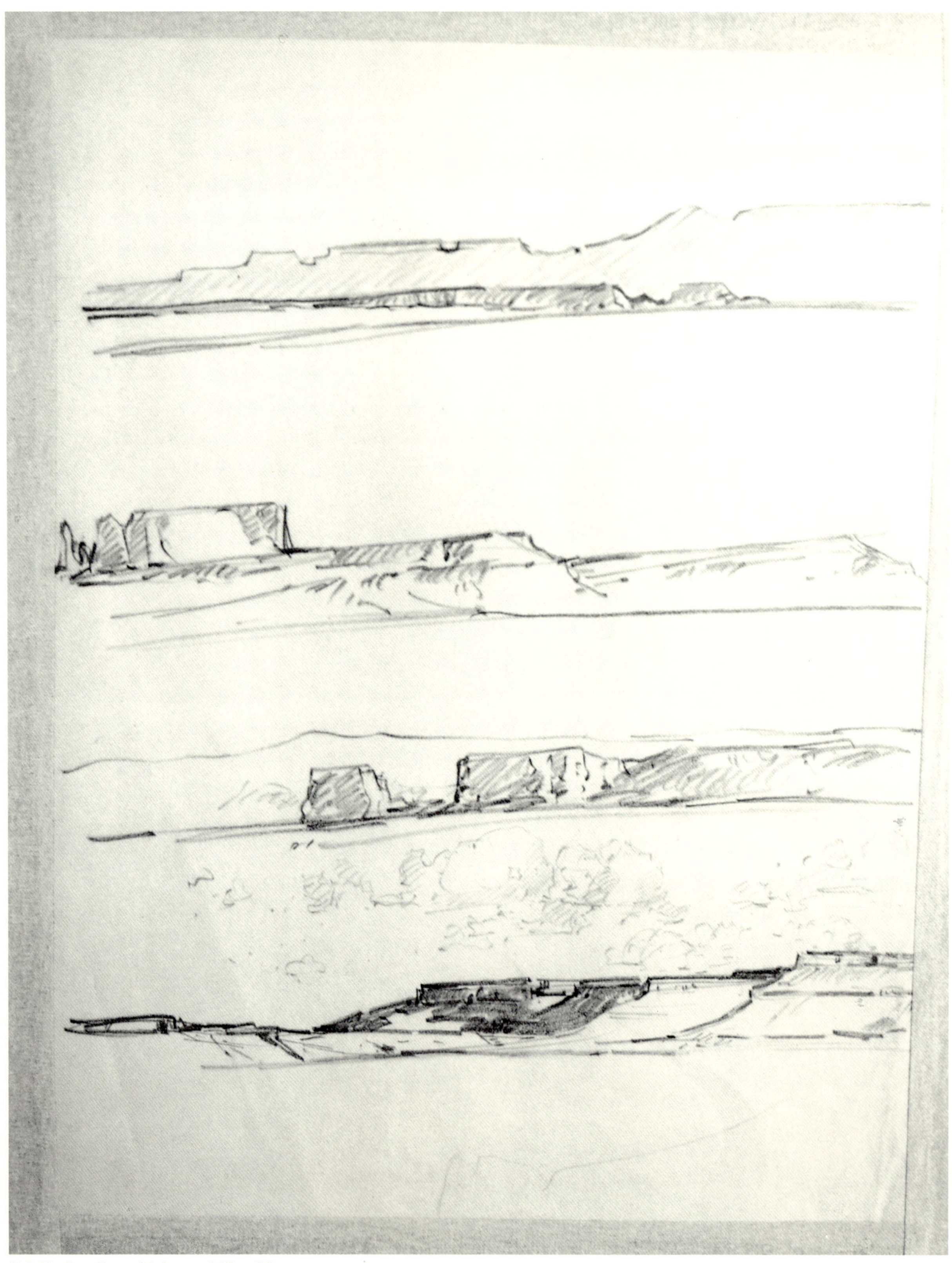

(M-2) Studies of Mesas 10" × 8"

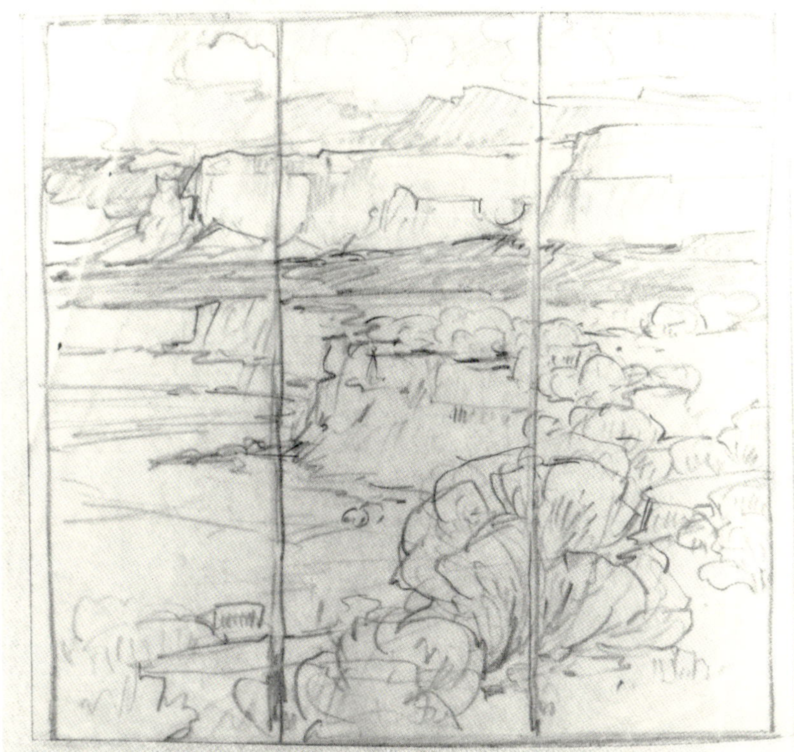

(X120-4) Mesas, Design for a Triptych 7" × 7"

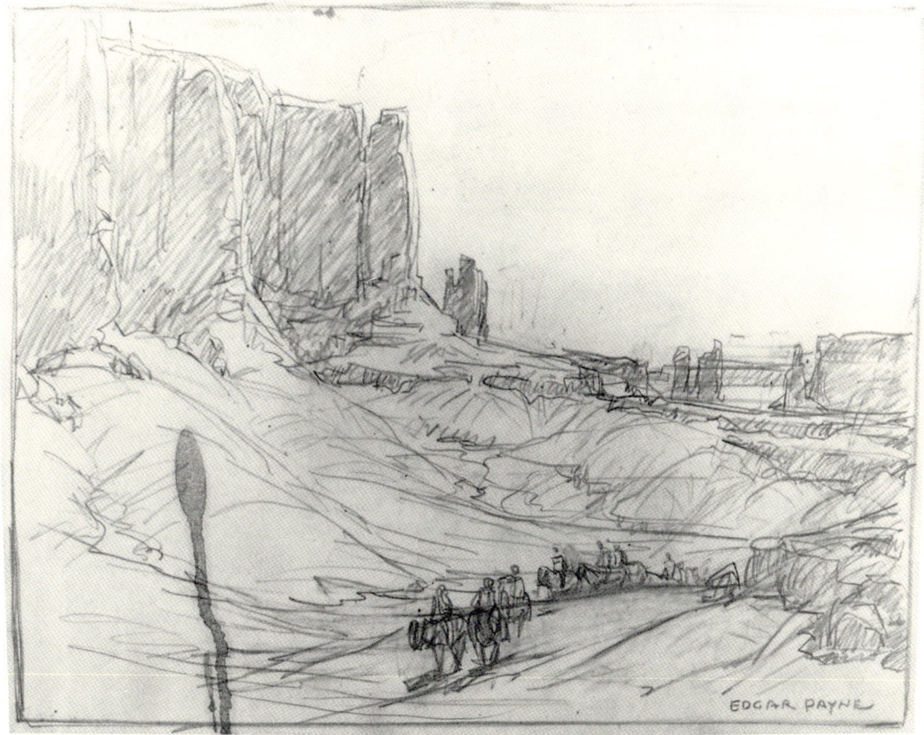

(S-39) Monument Valley 12" × 13"

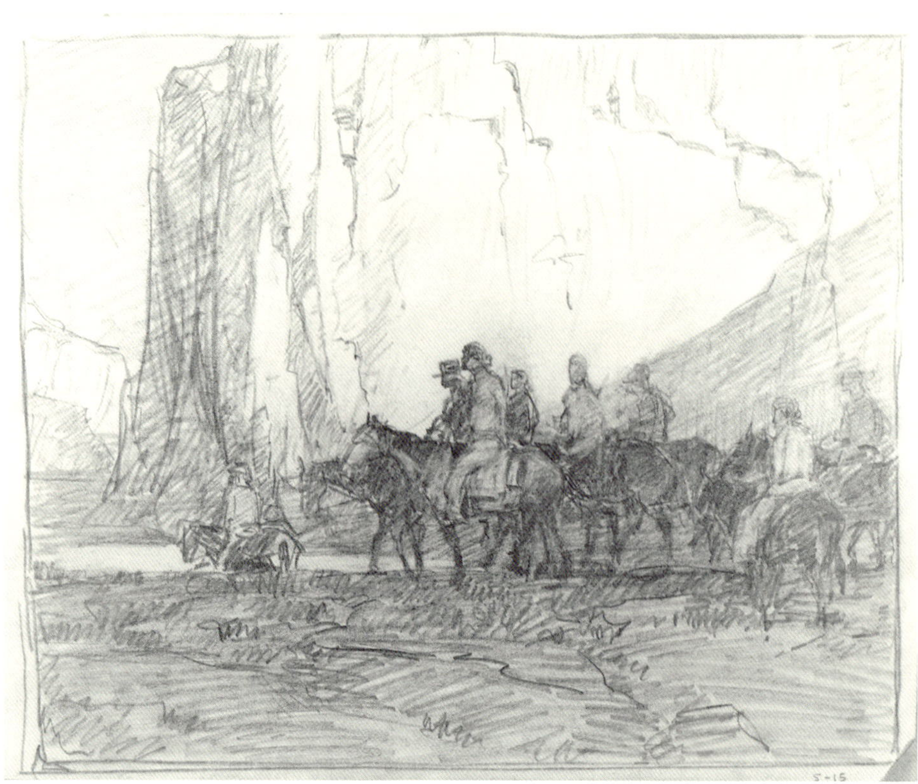

(S-15) Indians in Canyon 8" × 10"

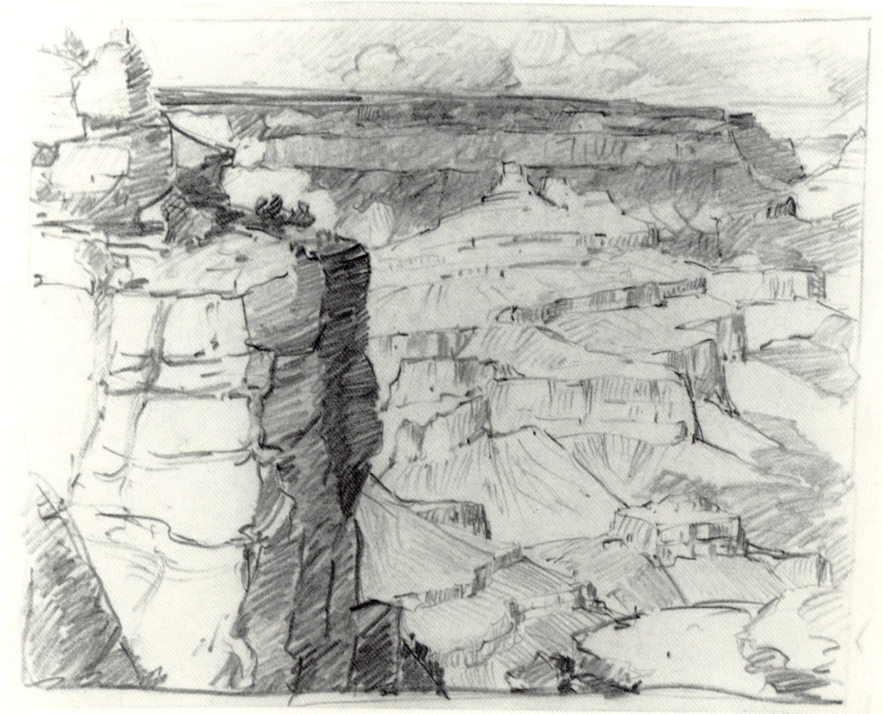

(M-6) The Grand Canyon 8" × 10"

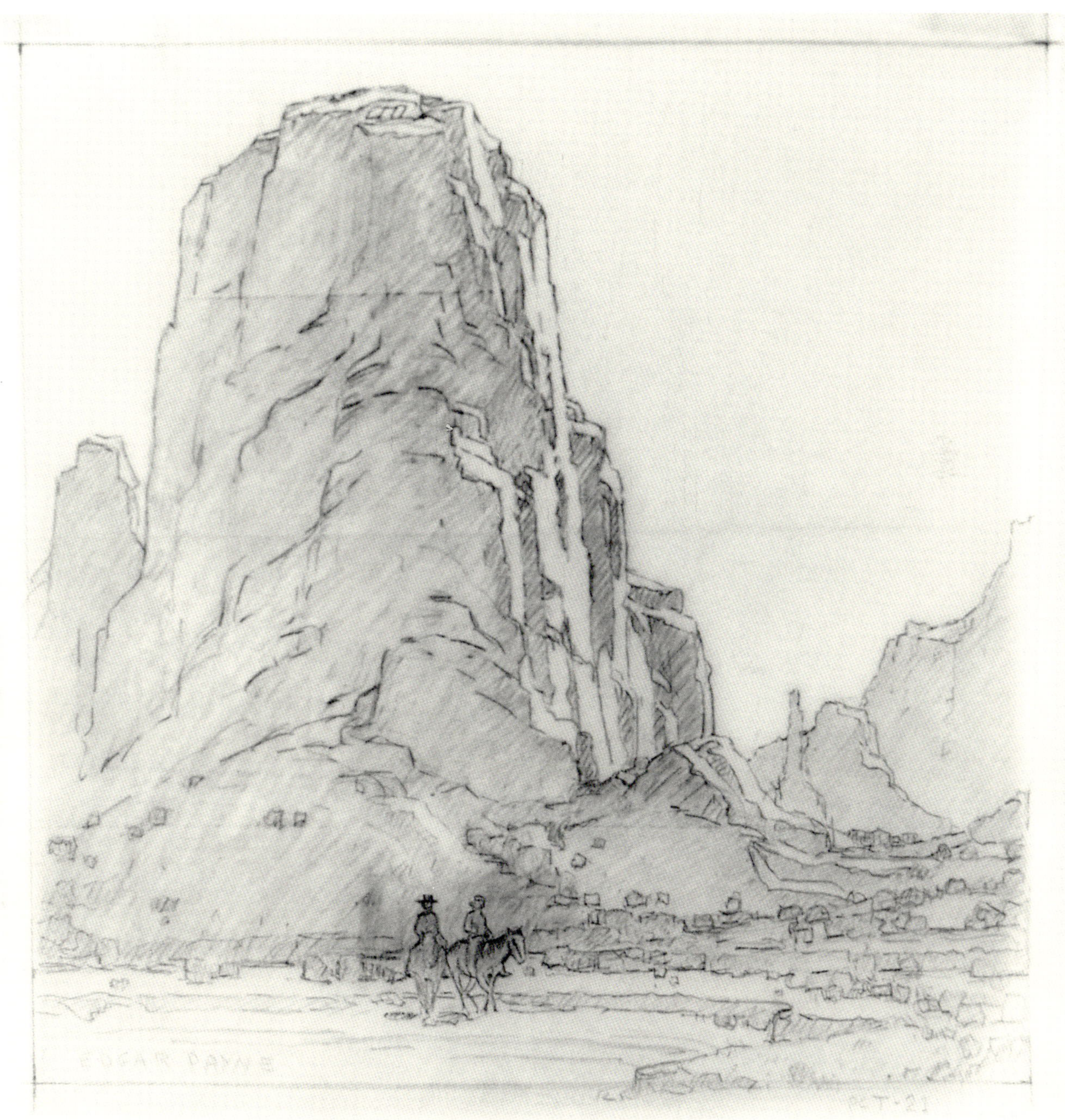

(PCT-21) Shadowed Butte 11" × 11"

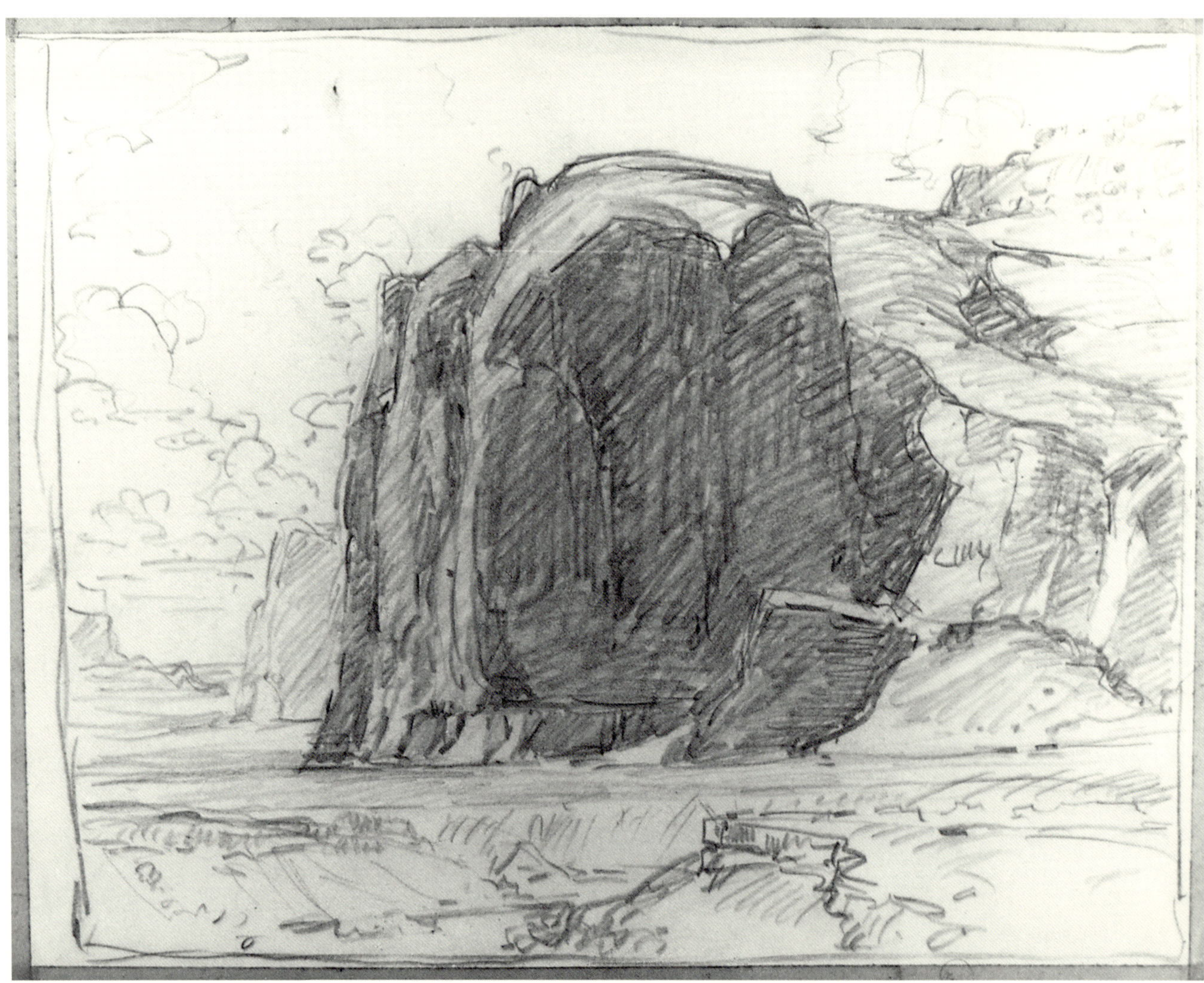

(X-120-2) Arizona Canyon 8" × 10"

Chapter VII

Planning Compositions

Nearly every evening after dinner, my father sat drawing. I remember this especially from the time we lived in New York and I was in high school. Mother would go to the kitchen to wash the dishes and she thought it was a good time for me and my dad to be together. We didn't know how to talk to each other very well, and so sat listening to the radio, and I sometimes did some schoolwork, while he drew continuously, planning paintings to be painted in the studio. But a kind of companionship was there.

It is hard for people in these times to realize how available light dictated so much for artists. It was necessary to have a studio with a large window on the north for a good source of light. One did not paint at night by electricity because the color so affected the appearance of the painting, especially oil painting. So, in the long winter evenings my father sat drawing and planning.

The great importance of light to artists early in the 20th century comes out strongly in the story of the wedding day of Elsie Philippa Palmer to Edgar Alwin Payne in Chicago. They had planned to get married by a justice of the peace on Saturday morning, with two friends in attendance. But my father-to-be called my mother-to-be earlier that morning and said, "Could you call our friends and change the wedding to the afternoon? The *light is right*."

Elsie said, "Of course, dear." She was an artist, too, and so were the friends. But when her sisters in San Francisco heard about this, they were shocked.

He took the pencil sketches to the studio with him. He probably often used them to make the charcoal drawings on canvas before painting, probably altering them before laying in the dark area as washes. I remember him having photographs handy to refer to, but he never copied these photographs.

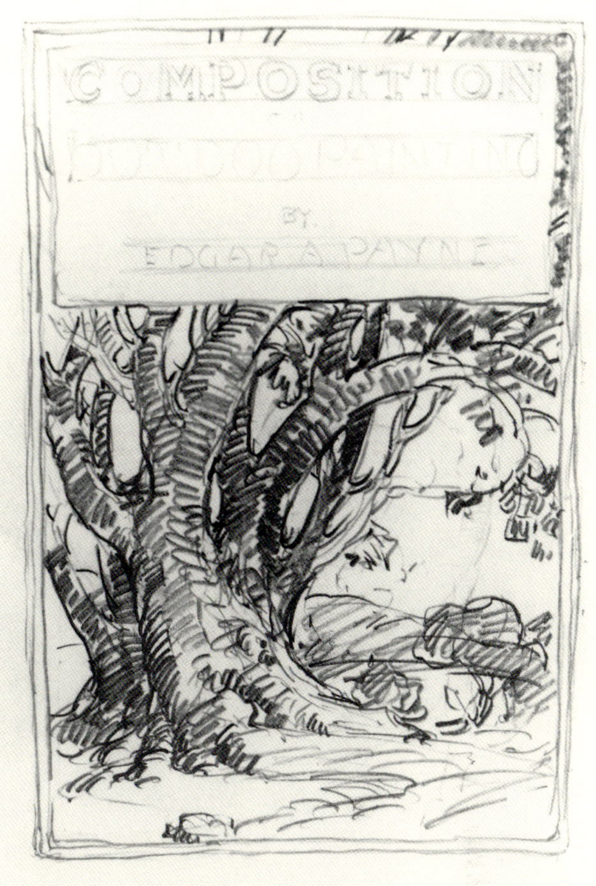

(X-120-26) Sketch for Title Page of Composition Book
6" × 8"

He considered the drawings as purely for his own use, as indeed he did even for the oil sketches made in the field. After he died, mother added his name, and sold some of the drawings and gave some as gifts. Often a long lower stroke on the last *E* on the signature shows the Elsie touch, but it marks the drawings as genuine.

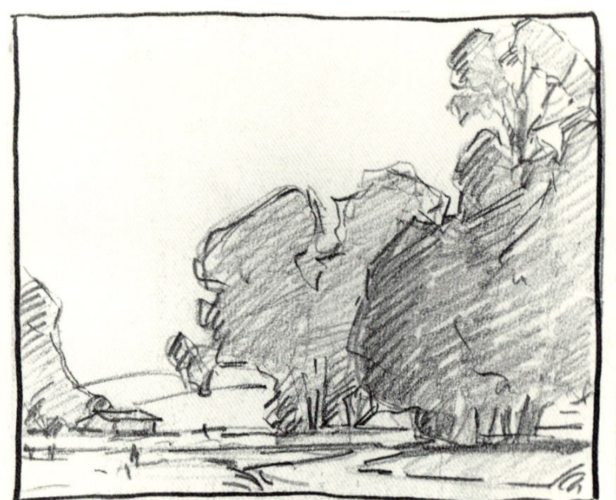

(UN-6) Trees with Building 3" × 4"

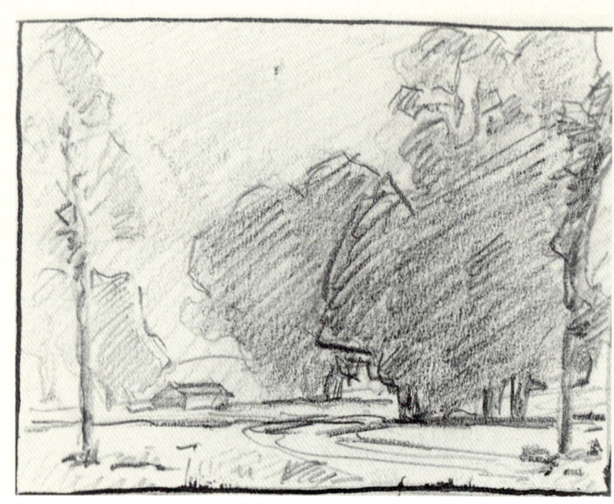

(UN-5) Trees with Building, Alternate Arrangement of UN-6 3" × 4"

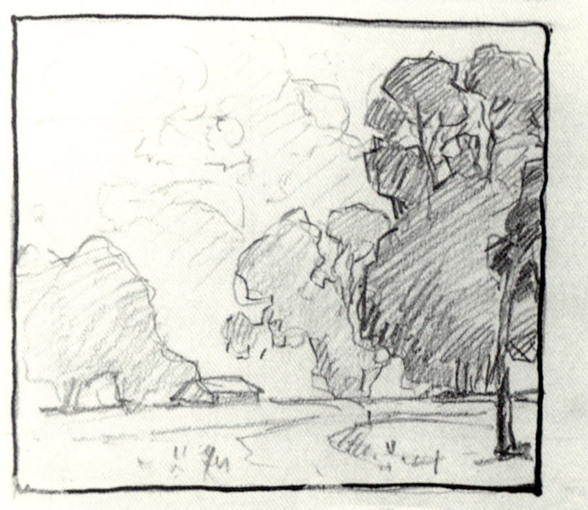

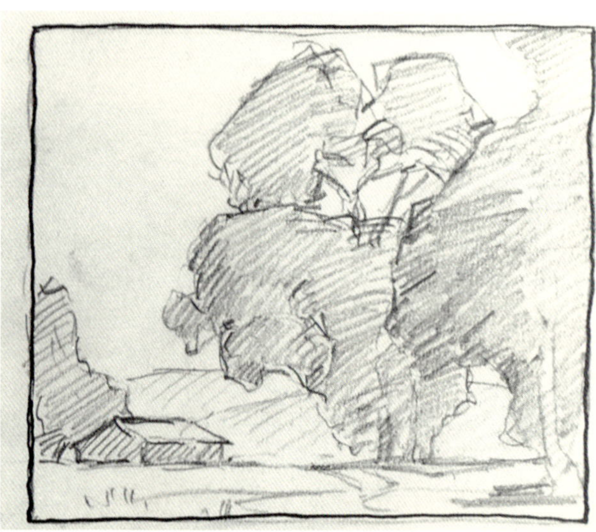

(UN-3) Trees with Building, Two More Variations of UN-6 3" × 4"

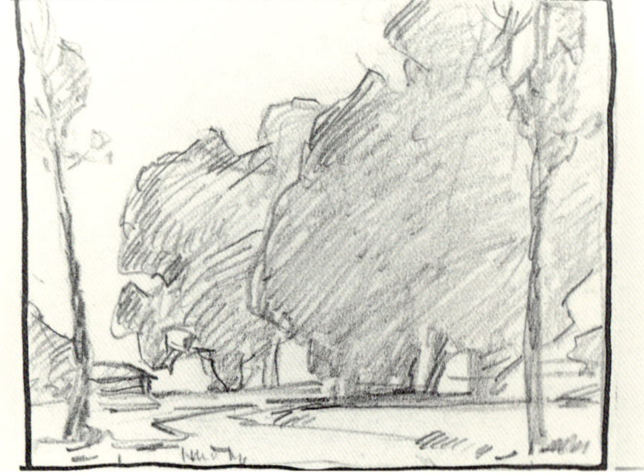

(UN-4) Trees with Building, Another Variation of UN-6 3" × 4"

He must have been thinking not only about the way he would use these compositions in studio paintings, but of all the basic principles that he considered important. This led to his book, *The Composition of Outdoor Painting*, which is still in print.

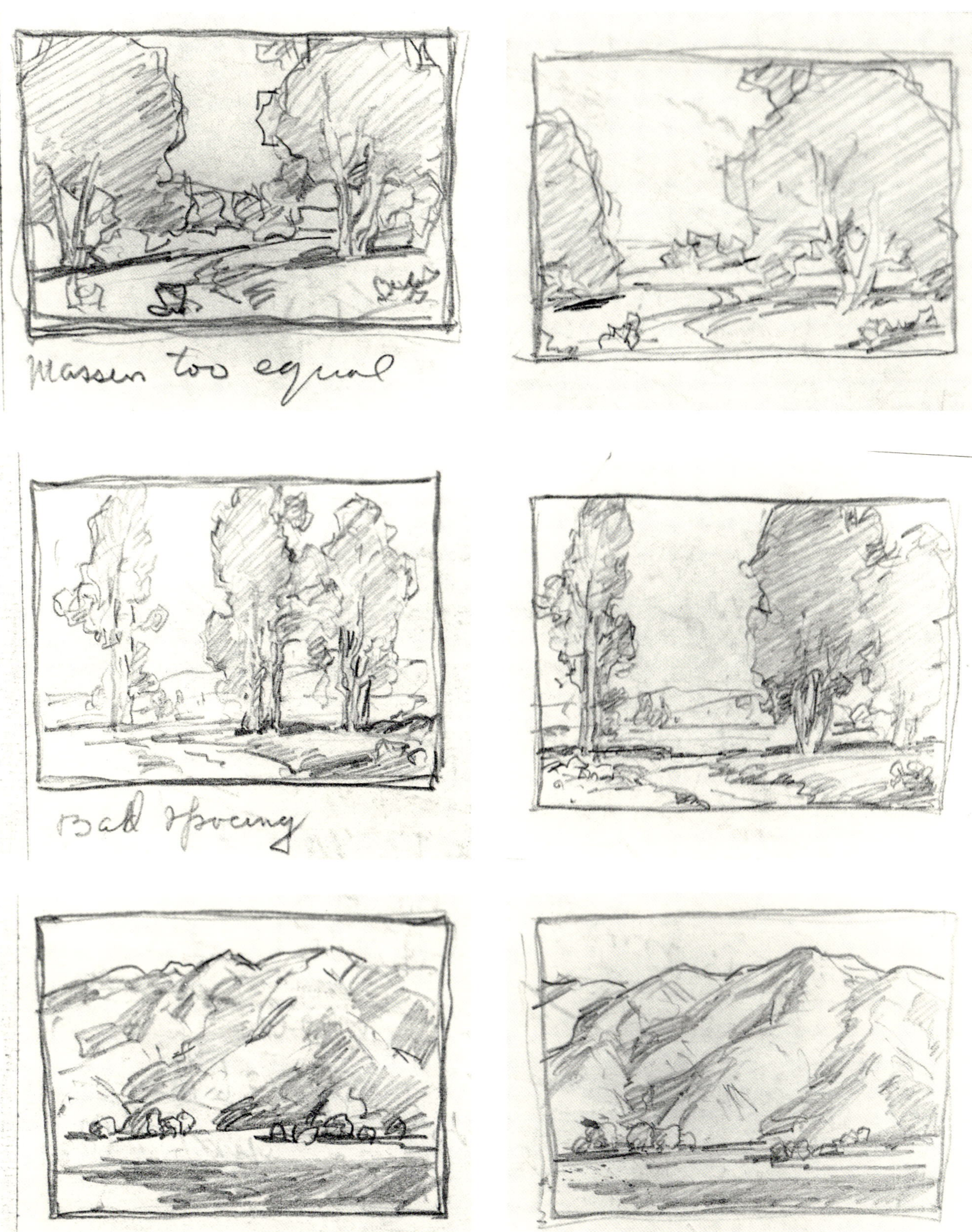

(X-120-27) Comparison of Compositions 10" × 7"

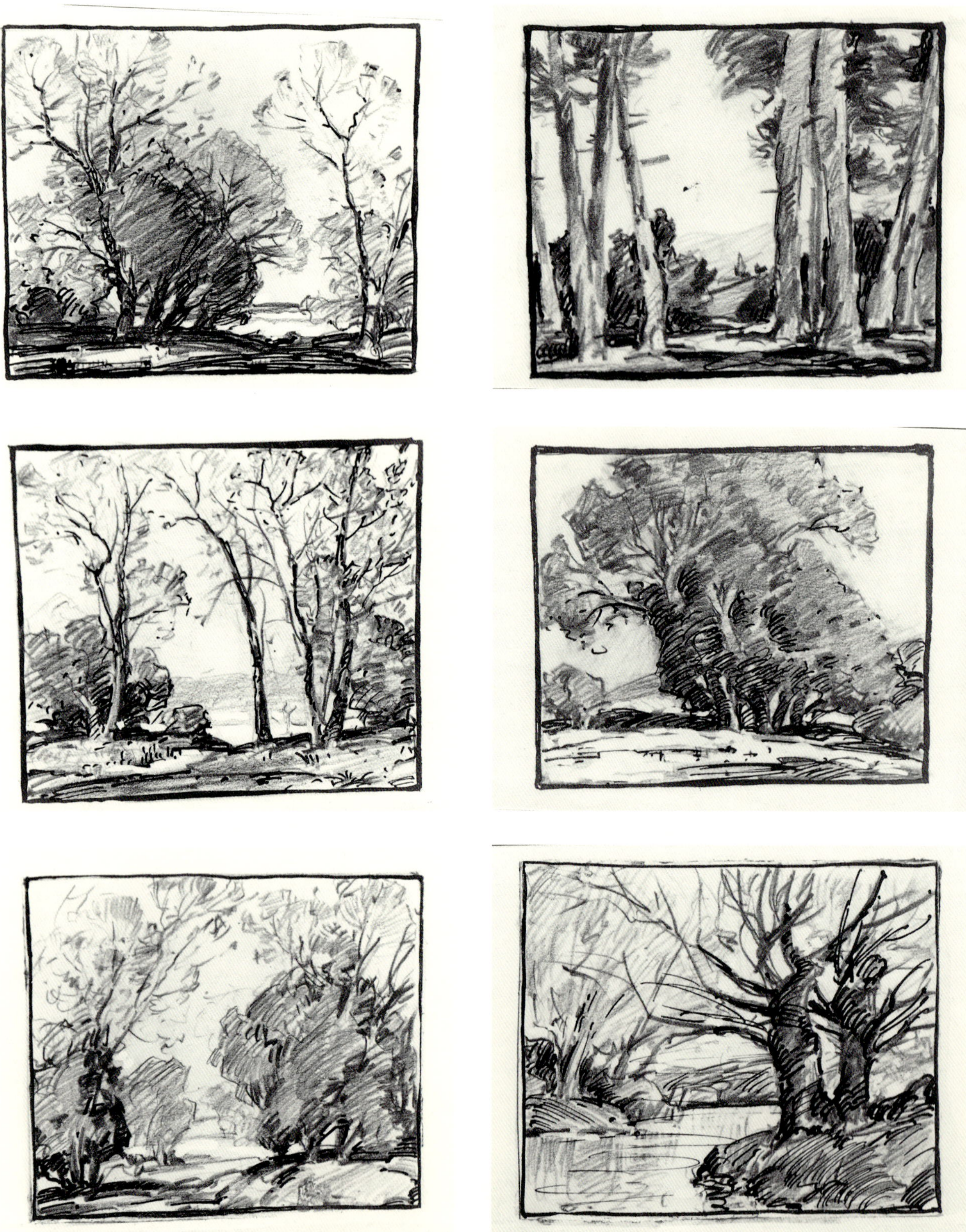

(X-120-29) Tree Motifs 11" × 8"

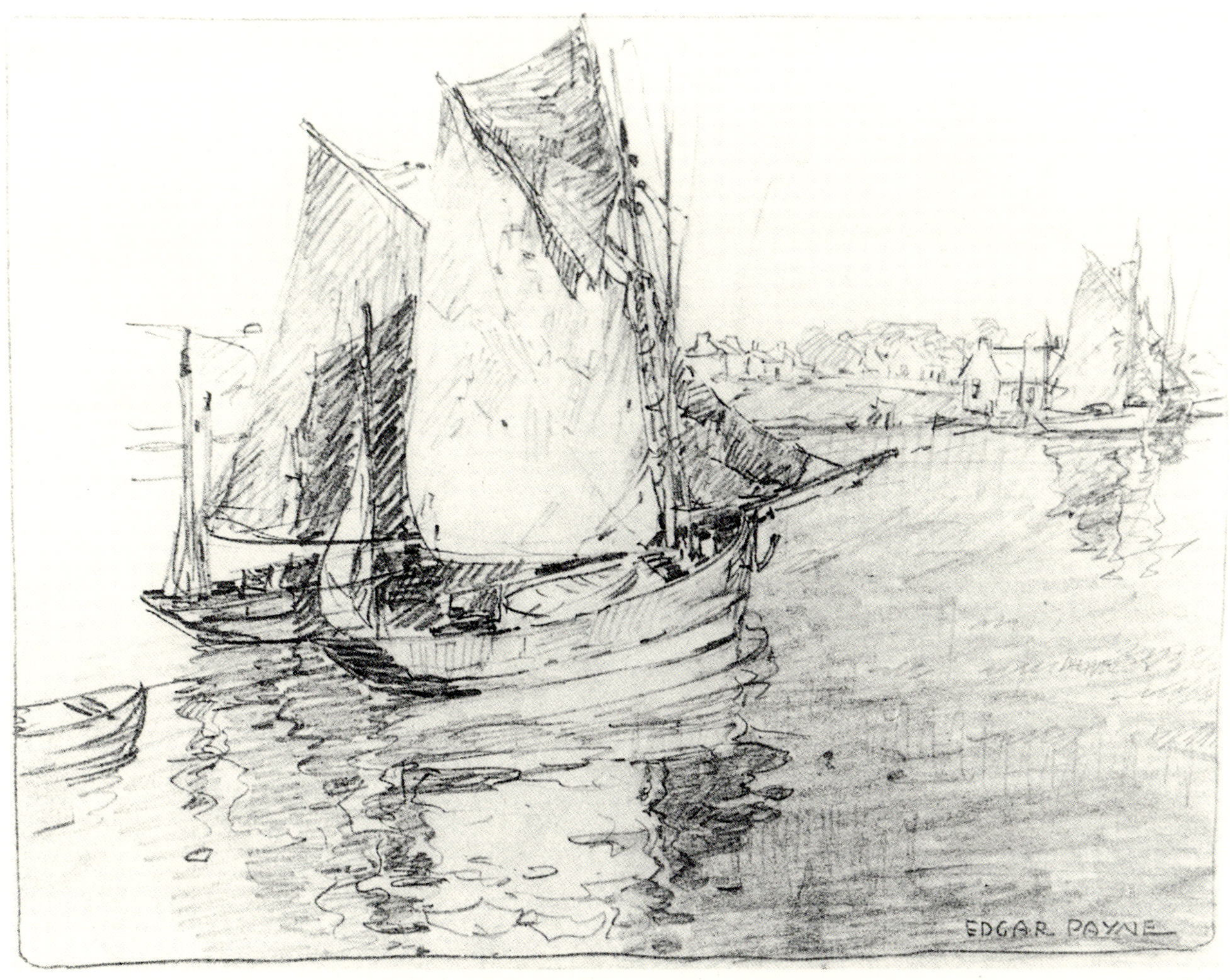

Au Revoir, a Postcard

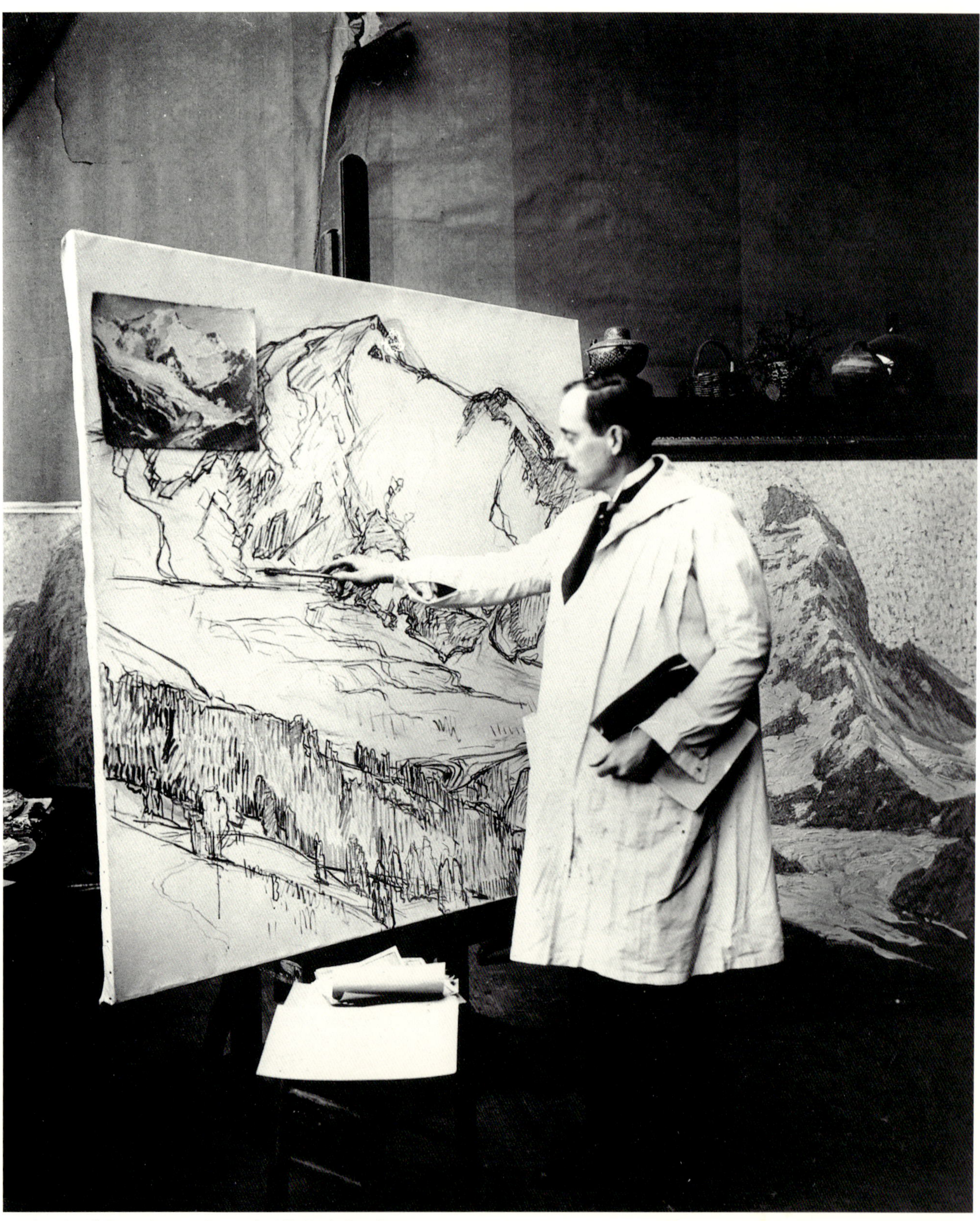

Putting It All Together — Payne in His Paris Studio

Appendix

List of Titles

Chapter I
Studies of California Landscapes and Trees

Page

1 (S-11) Sycamores 8" × 10"
2 (X-120-5) Devil's Gate Dam, Pasadena 8" × 10¼"
2 (M-13) California Tree Study 8" × 10"
3 (X-120-15) Sketch of Leaves on Twigs 8" × 10½"
4 (X-120-11) White Oak Leaves 10½" × 8"
4 (X-120-10) Leaf Study 10½" × 8"
4 (X-120-12) Oak Leaves at Different Angles 10" × 8"
4 (X-120-17) Oak Leaf Sketches 11" × 8"
5 (X-120-14) Tree Study 11" × 8"
6 (X-120-9) Leaf Studies 10½" × 8"
7 (X-120-8) Tree Sketch 8" × 11"
7 (X-120-6) Tree Study 8" × 10½"
8 (M-36b) Back of M-36a Trees 8" × 10½"
9 (X-120-21) Sketch of Trees 5½" × 7"
9 (M-36a) Restudy of X-120-21
10 (M-34) Tree with House 3¼" × 4½"
10 (M-29) Tree Study 5½" × 7"
11 (T-37) Tree Forms 9" × 11"
12 (S-46) Light and Shade Study, Trees 8" × 10½"
13 (S-10) Hills in California 8" × 10"
14 (S-42) California Hills 8" × 10½"

Chapter II
Pencil and Paper Sketches Made in Italy

15 Sketch Maps of Locations (EPH)
16 Simplified Sketches of Sail Types (EPH)
17 (SL-5) Study of a Chioggia Boat Hull 10" × 8"
18 (SL-3) Adriatic Boats, Showing Prows and Sterns 10" × 8"
18 (S-28) Outbound Adriatic Boats 9" × 8½"
19 (SL-6) Details of Lateen Rigging on Adriatic Boat 10" × 8"
20 (SL-9) Detail of Prow, Chioggia 10" × 8"
20 (Z-11) Study of Boat Details, Chioggia 10" × 8"
20 (SL-9b) Detail of Prow from Deck 10" × 8"
20 (SL-4) Details of Deck and Rigging 10" × 8"
21 (SL-8a) Sail 10" × 8"
21 (Z-2) Lateen Sails 10" × 8"
21 (SL-8b) Details of Rigging 10" × 8"
21 (SL-7) Color Notes for a Chioggia Boat 10" × 8"
22 (SL-8) Chioggia Boat Showing Proportions 8" × 10"
22 (SL-10) Measurements of Boat Deck 8" × 10"
23 (M-10) Chioggia Boats with Figures 8" × 8"
23 (S-43) Sails: Study in Light and Shade 8½" × 8½"
23 (U-6) Boats in Chioggia Harbor (Charcoal) 13" × 13"
23 (U-7) Harbor Scene (Charcoal) 13" × 13"
24 (U-10) Fore and Aft Composition (Charcoal) 15" × 12"
25 (M-9) Fishing Boats at Rest 8" × 10"
25 (T-27) Chioggia Boats at Home 10" × 12"
26 (T-28) Parked in the Canal, Chioggia 9" × 12"

Chapter III
France

Page

27 (M-16) Alpine Sketch 4" × 5"
27 (U-8) Alpine Mountain 13" × 13"
28 (T-43) Chateau on the Way to Brittany 10" × 10"
29 (Z-4) Three Boats, One with Dinghy
29 (Z-5) Varieties of Mediterannean Sailing Craft 3" × 4"
30 (Z-12) Boat Studies 3" × 4"
30 (Z-13) Boats — Small Sketchbook 3" × 4"
30 (Z-14) Goëlette, Ancestor of Schooner 3" × 4"
30 (Z-15) Lugger for Use in Shallower Water 3" × 4"
31 (U-3) Breton Street Scene (Canvas Board) 13" × 15"
32 (SS-6a) Breton Sloops at High and Low Tides 6" × 5"
32 (Z-3) Tuna Yawl
33 (S-17) Boats in Harbor, Douarnenez 8" × 11"
33 (M-7) Sardine Sloops, Brittany 8" × 11"
34 (M-8) Breton Boats, Composition 8" × 11"
35 (SS-2a) Color Notes on Breton Boats 6" × 5"
35 (SS-2) More Color Notes 6" × 5"
36 (M-30) Breton Tuna Boats, Showing Prows 4½" × 3½"
37 (M-23a) Tuna Yawls and Sardine Boats
38 (Z-6) Sloop 3" × 2"
38 (T-38) Sailing In 12" × 12"
38 (M-31) In the Harbor 5" × 4"
38 (SS-1) Tuna Boat Showing Sails, Brittany 6" × 5"
39 (SS-4a) Breton Boats with Figures 6" × 5"
39 (S-26) Drying Nets, Brittany 7" × 9"
40 (Z-7a, Z-7b, Z-7c, Z-7d) Notes from a Small Sketchbook all 3" × 4"
41 (SS-3) Tuna Yawls Outbound 6" × 5"
41 (M-35) Leaving Port 3" × 3"
41 (SS-9) Sardine Boats 6" × 5"
41 (W-3) Note on Sail Drape 3" × 4"
42 (SS-6) Hull 6" × 5"
42 (SS-5a) Douarnenez Harbor Area 5" × 6"
43 (SS-7a) Study of Hulls 6" × 5"
43 (SS-5) In Harbor 6" × 5"
43 (SS-7) Sardine Boats in Harbor 6" × 5"
43 (M-23) Sloops in Quiet Water 6" × 5"
44 (UN-2) Back of M-30 Outbound 4" × 3"
44 (S-19) Breton Boats, Shadow and Reflection Study 8" × 8"
45 (S-43b) Back of S-43a Quick Sketch of Prow 8" × 8"
45 (T-20) Breton Tuna Boats 12" × 14"
46 (T-26) Concarneau Harbor 10" × 12"
47 Photograph of Payne's Model of Breton Tuna Boat
48 (SS-4) Breton Women and Fishermen 6" × 5"
48 (SS-9a) Breton Sailors in Sabots 6" × 5"
49 (SL-1) Sketches of Figures 10" × 8"
50 (T-12) Breton Fishermen Studies 10" × 8"
51 (SS-8a) Sketches of Breton Women 6" × 5"